FROM CHINA TO PERU

Withdrawn

From China to Peru

Russell Fraser

A MEMOIR OF TRAVEL

The University of South Carolina Press

© 2009 University of South Carolina

Published by the University of South Carolina Press
Columbia, South Carolina 29208

www.sc.edu/uscpress

Manufactured in the United States of America

18 17 16 15 14 13 12 11 10 09   10 9 8 7 6 5 4 3 2 1

Library of Congress Cataloging-in-Publication Data

Fraser, Russell A.
    From China to Peru : a memoir of travel / Russell Fraser.
      p. cm.
    ISBN 978-1-57003-825-9 (cloth : alk. paper)
    1. Voyages and travels. 2. Fraser, Russell A.—Travel. 3. Travelers'
  writings, American. 4. Scholars—United States—Biography. I. Title.
    G226.F73A3 2009
    910.4092—dc22

                                                                2009004276

This book was printed on Glatfelter Natures, a recycled paper with 30 percent
postconsumer waste content.

Let observation, with extensive view,
Survey mankind from China to Peru.

Samuel Johnson, *The Vanity of
Human Wishes*

CONTENTS

PREFACE

This book is personal memoir as well as an account of travel. Each chapter opens with a bit of autobiography, segueing into the travel piece that follows. What I say of myself isn't freestanding but ties one chapter to another, and the essays on travel have more than the unity of what comes next. Taken as a whole, they offer a reading of what we are like, gathered from observation of the world we live in.

In each chapter time moves between present and past. I begin in the present but return to the past, creating a multilayered account of place and history. As in my earlier book *The Three Romes,* I am writing nonfiction stories. Though they don't have a moral, they have an intention, describing the psychology that moves us. All the fact is true, reflecting firsthand experience, but the experience is filtered through characters, including the speaker. I watch what happens when the characters meet the experience and draw conclusions from the way they react.

The quotation I lead off with, from Dr. Johnson, suggests that observation, as wide-ranging as possible, comes first. But I haven't gone around the world "to count the cats in Zanzibar," and I aim to throw a little light on the places I've traveled to, including their mysterious soul. Seeing the world up close isn't guaranteed to make the heart beat faster. So much humdrum goes with traveling that I've wondered more than once why I ever left home. To remind me where I've been, I take notes and keep a record of my itinerary. But a skeptical voice whispers in my ear, wanting to know if the jottings in my notebook and the lines on my map add up to a meaningful pattern. When I sit down to write, this question is before me.

Travel writers for the Sunday paper find a pattern in their daily routine: for example, "I breakfasted this morning on the Boul' Mich, wrote a few postcards, and took the Metro to the Luxembourg Gardens." I have a garden in my own backyard, and to justify the expense of spirit that goes into traveling, not to mention the out-of-pocket expenses, I want a pattern with more to it than that. But even the daily round has a shape beneath the surface, though detecting it isn't easy. While the frothy stuff on the surface bobs along the stream of time, things of worth sink to the bottom. Thereabouts I take up my position.

I was a lot younger when I began to travel. Things I did then are beyond me today. I no longer aspire to ski the Mont Blanc, and I use a jigger to measure my drinks. I thought it important to see the Antarctic—and don't mind that it's safely in the past tense. But though the face I show the world is craggier than it was, the places I write about are preserved in memory, where neither moth nor rust can get at them. In this respect the written word beats the life every time.

Many friends and acquaintance bore a part in making this book. I single out George Core, without whom nothing would have got done, and the late Staige Blackford, a model editor, always helpful, never obtrusive. Most of the pieces brought together here appeared first in the *Virginia Quarterly Review* under his editorship. Annie Dillard included one in her *Best American Essays 1988,* one comes from the *Michigan Quarterly,* another from the *Iowa Review.* My thanks to the editors of these publications. All the pieces I reprint have been revised, but I haven't sought to update them. Khomeini and the cold war were still going strong when I went to the Gulf, and in my time in Peru the Shining Path terrorists were threatening to take over the country. The Saudi Arabia today's papers are full of is and isn't the one I describe. Al-Qaida hadn't yet been heard from, but the enmity between Jew and Arab was already an old story, like their enduring sameness. Instead of keeping abreast of current events, my book aims at detecting what was true yesterday and is likely to remain true tomorrow.

Though it seems to tell of a man traveling alone, in fact I had company, my wife. She was the director on top of the flies who got me going in the morning and saw to it that I was home before dark. When the two of us lived in Rome, we spent a lot of time in Piazza del Popolo, admiring the paintings in its great church. Just outside the piazza an enterprising vendor sold a line of cotton dresses, cheap but stylish, and I bought a dress for Mary, colorful with the onion domes of Moscow's Red Square. That dress wore out ages ago, and I wish I could replace it with a brand-new one. Failing that, this book is for her.

Wadi-Bashing in Arabia Deserta

Straight out of graduate school and glad to have it behind me, I did what Horace Greeley told us to. I went west. But the flowers in California, though the biggest I'd seen and gorgeous to look at, didn't smell. My teaching job at UCLA had strings attached. I'd been at it only a few months when I was asked to sign a loyalty oath. *Asked* puts it politely, and before Christmas I found myself out of a job.

My colleagues were my friends, nice people you could count on. They cared about the environment, supported our schools, and belonged to the liberal wing of the Democratic Party. All signed the oath, except one rancorous conservative who was damned if he'd do what they told him. Most of my students came from Central Casting, blond young women with ponytails and golden skin, young men who smiled easily and had sunbleached eyes and a great backhand. In some, what you saw was what you got. The best-looking coed in the class turned out to be the smartest, though, also a friend. When I got fired she went to her accountant uncle, who worked for the ILWU, the longshoremen. Jobs on the waterfront aren't easy to come by, but he wangled me a ticket, entitling me to "shape up."

Every day at dawn I drove my ancient Dodge from my apartment in Venice around the coast to San Pedro, one of LA's three seaports. Standing on a chair in the hiring hall, the dispatch—accent on the first syllable—shaped us up. Men with seniority got the day's first assignments, posted to work warehouses "alongshore." Those with know-how were dispatched to load and unload cargo in the holds of oceangoing ships. For men with a strong back, there seemed nothing to it. Appearances deceive, though, and unless cargo is stowed properly it will shift in rough seas, sometimes battering its way through the hull. At the bottom of the totem pole, I waited for my name to be called. If it wasn't I got back in the car and drove home.

Longshoremen come from every stratum of society, and generalizing about them is next to impossible. One thing I can say for sure, though, they weren't always what they looked like. Some were big-bellied brutes who drank too much and cheated on their wives. Some were disbarred lawyers and ex-doctors, and one I knew had a pianist's long tapering fingers. Some of the big bellies were nature's noblemen. I was glad to call them my friends.

But I didn't like California—"it's cold and it's damp." "Go east, young man," I said to myself when spring came round again and the flowers didn't smell. *East* meant East of Suez, however. The cold war was going strong then, and it boosted me into a job. My new employer, the U.S. Information Service, promoted America to the rest of the world. I was to serve as a conduit. In a world that made sense, they would never have hired me. But the government, then as now, couldn't tell its right hand from its left.

The locale they sent me to, one of date palms and desert, was different from any I'd known. Especially the people, not like my next-door neighbors in West Wood. Some, squint-eyed and scrofulous from malnutrition or a disease I'd never heard of, looked like rascals; others, movie-star heroic, would steal the last crust from their mother. My USIS host, a romantic expat, made no distinction among them. People the world over had in common their natural goodness, he said, and were much the same under the skin. Arabs were "our brothers," cleansed by their alfresco life in the desert. Over the years I've thought about this man, wondering if he got out in one piece.

For successful wadi-bashing, you need four-wheel drive and a good head of steam. Land Rovers and Cherokee jeeps are preferred. Pulling out the throttle, you race along the wadis, making a run at the dunes. Some dunes, enormous, dwarf a three-story house. Lying between them are the wadis, old water courses dry most of the year. In the rainy time they flood, and men and animals parched for water have drowned in the desert. The bashing isn't when you hit the wadis but when you top the dunes, a bone-jarring experience. I learned this in Dubai on the coast of Arabia.

A wink of prosperity under the desert sun, Dubai is squeezed between water, sand, and a high place. The water is the Persian Gulf. Below the Strait of Hormuz, a spiny headland called the Ru'us al-Jibal cuts the gulf in two. The Emirates, all but one, huddle together on the Ru'us al-Jibal. Besides Dubai, they are Abu Dhabi, 'Ajman, Ash Shariqah, Umm al Qaywayn, Ra's al Khaymah, and al Fujayrah. Abu Dhabi, the capital, lies along the mainland coast. Behind the coast are lumpy mountains, like tufts of carded wool, says the sura, a verse from the Koran. The Tropic of Cancer bisects the lower reaches of this Trucial Coast. South and west of the imaginary line is the desert. Occupying a 1.25 million square miles, it peters out in salt plains this side of Mecca, not far from the Red Sea. Between the foothills of Oman and the Yemeni border nine hundred miles away, the land is empty. Here is a dead land, said Doughty, an English traveler in the Arabian Desert. He said men returning from it brought home nothing but weariness in their bones.

On the other side of the Strait of Hormuz, the Gulf of Oman runs south and east into the Arabian Sea. Across the water is Iran, a medieval country where the mullahs, Islamic priests, are fighting a holy war against the present. Soldiers in this war don't give or expect quarter, death on the battlefield counting for them as a blessing. One of their hadiths, a collection of sayings ascribed to the Prophet, tells them that Paradise lies beneath the shadow of swords. Oil, vital to the present, supplies the sinews of the war and is brought from the ground by modern technology. Each day, nine million barrels pass through the Strait of Hormuz.

My host, reciting this statistic, has oil on the brain. He is USIS, a fidgety Californian with a turn for metaphor. Oil is "our vital lifeline," and the enemy wants to cut it. He divides the world into enemies and friends. Arabs, all of them, are "friendlies," Russia, an enemy, is "the bear that walks like a man." Though he held fast to his belief in natural goodness, he made an exception for the Soviet Union. Knives were being sharpened a generation ago, and being prudent, he looked to his defenses. Down the road he saw a shootout between them and us. But he banked on the presence, close by in Oman, of our Rapid Deployment Force. Like a Roman centurion on Hadrian's Wall, the RDF kept on the lookout, alert for signs of trouble. Surveillance planes, the AWACS, were its eyes and ears. Airborne every day, they used the fields at Seeb and Thumrait, thanks to the Sultan of Oman, a friendly.

Stuck over with art deco, Arabian style, the hall he puts me into is a pocket version of Radio City Music Hall, where I used to see the Rockettes. A chrome-scuppered pool, Olympic-size but strictly for show, separates this ornate building from the new mosque, austere as the desert. The pool is lined with jacaranda trees, and four minarets rise at the corners of the mosque. In the distance are refineries, black against a cloudless sky. Before I go onstage I get my briefing, a list of no-no's including Khomeini, Israel, and OPEC. This isn't the Chatauqua circuit, and if America has shortcomings I needn't tell the world. A careful young man, my host takes me back to old days in the Navy. Over coffee in the wardroom, officers' country, they let you talk baseball, but politics and women were out.

The American flag and the colors of the Emirates stand in sockets behind the lectern. For props I have a slide projector, a pitcher of water, and a mike that doesn't work. It didn't work in Jerusalem either when I gave my lecture there, but I stayed mum on this coincidence. Seeing no evil, Arabs pretend that Israel doesn't exist. They like you to go along with their fiction. An American banker I know, having been to Israel, neglected to tell them in Tel Aviv not to stamp his visa. When he came to Dubai, they looked at this visa and put him on the next plane back to London.

Fiddling with the microphone, I count the house—thirty bodies, all male, and all but one of them Arab. Splendid in their dishdashas, loose-fitting robes, they look like Semitic patriarchs from the Old Testament. Semitic is what they are, Arabs and Jews sharing the same inheritance. Both include Abraham in their family tree. Jewish *Aaron* is Arab *Harun,* as in Harun al-Rashid, and the standard-bearer of the Prophet was Eyup, or Job. Courteous but impassive, the men in the audience keep their illusionless eyes on my face. What goes on in their heads they keep under their hats.

My subject is the arts, American and modern, with attention to poetry. I tell them how the artist sharpens our awareness but doesn't take sides. Richard Wilbur, for instance. A modern poet, he has this poem, "The Giaour and the Pasha," based on the Delacroix painting. At a signal from me, my assistant, an Arab boy, pops a colored slide in the projector. A giaour is an infidel or "uncircumcised dog," but Arabs don't have to be told. At the rear of the stage, USIS, fidgeting uneasily on his leather camp-stool, wonders where I am going to take this.

"As for the infidels," God says to Mohammed, "strike off their heads, maim their fingers." This infidel, however, has got the upper hand. He sits on horseback, but the Pasha, at his mercy, is down. Looking at the painting, you feel that death is imminent. But the poem has a happy ending, and the Pasha gets off scot-free. People who believe that poetry is lies will say that this ending defines it. If the Pasha is lucky, though, the giaour is blessed. Poised to kill, he holds his hand, so gets beyond himself like a work of art. He freezes in air, staring without purpose, and lets the pistol fall beside his knee.

The head of a victim, said the Prophet, an angry man, was better than the choicest camel in Arabia. He said this after his first battle, when they gave him a head. Their eyes crinkling skeptically, these Arabs, his descendants, consider a resolution where nothing gets resolved. Falconry is a favorite diversion of theirs. The falcon, having the prey in sight, doesn't balance pros and cons but falls like a plummet. However, I am *ahl al-kitab,* "People of the Book." Oddly, this works out to unknowing. Secure in what they know, they applaud me politely. They are *ahl al-bait,* "People of the House of the Prophet."

Shouldering his way up to the platform, Nate Yelverton sticks out a hand. He has a shrewd idea that poetry is for the birds, and unlike the Arabs he is willing to say what he thinks. "More truth than poetry" is one of his sayings. Journeying around the world to tell the wogs about poetry seems labor lost to him. He doesn't like wogs, "shiftless fellaheen," and lumps them all together. Also he doesn't like Jews. Islam and Judaism, brothers under the skin, are both secret conspiracies, he tells me. But where Arabs have their Jihad or holy war, Jews let money do the talking. Have I read the *Protocols of the Elders of Zion?*

In Dubai on loan from Bechtel Co., Yelverton has taken up the white man's burden. Constructing a new desalinization plant, he is helping the Arabs augment their supply of potable water. He calls this working for IBM, Inshallah Bukra Mumkin. I will hear these words often in the Emirates, he says. They mean "God willing tomorrow maybe." A good engineer, Yelverton marches with the army of progress. Bechtel, his employer, is building an industrial city in the desert, on the shores of the Persian Gulf. The railroad, coming up from Dammam, will link it to the capital, once served by camel caravans. Jubail, the new city, is almost in place. When it is finished, Yelverton says, a third of a million people will live there.

The first time we met, he was bellied up to the bar at the Mena House in Cairo. Calling for Wild Turkey, he didn't bat an eye when he got what he called for. Yelverton expects this. Getting things done is his business, a fight against odds. When he walks, he weaves and lurches. Mohammed, said Arab chroniclers, had this strange, lurching walk, "as if he were ascending a steep and invisible hill." In his cups Yelverton is apt to turn maudlin, sometimes breaking into song. Surprising in a big man, he has a melodious tenor, reminiscent of John McCormack. He exercises this on sentimental ballads that call the Irish home to Erin and old tunes from the hymnal where they wrestle and fight and pray. His business card, fished from a plastic sleeve in his wallet, has kabbalistic signs like Greek sigmas and gammas. Bold horizontal lines connect open loops and little corkscrews like pigs' tails. Above and under the lines, clusters of dots inflect this mysterious writing. The other face of the card gives his name in English, N. B. F. Yelverton, and beneath this the name of his firm. The initials, he says, stand for Nathan Bedford Forrest, a Confederate general who got there fustest with the mostest. Putting down his drink, he pencils in a phone number with a Dubai exchange. "If you're ever in the U.A.E."

Day, coming all at once, dawns in the U.A.E. like noontide. The air is thin, and the mountains stick up like erector sets. Detail, qualifying what you see, gets swallowed in immensity. Sun beats on the dead land, conferring the clarity that goes with moribund things. Not blurred by half-lights and shadows, contours are sharp, and good and evil look like themselves. This makes life simpler. Humbled in the dust, Arabs say how Allah, impalpable unlike the God of the Christians, inherits the earth, letting nothing escape. Ibn Khaldun, the Arab historian, has a hundred litanies like this one. A Berber from North Africa, he lived on the fringes of the Sahara. This waste of scorching sands, mountains, and stony uplands is bigger than the continental United States. Men are minerals, Mohammed says: some, his fellow Muslims, are precious like gold, while all others are drossy. Possibly banal, this saying takes on a harder meaning in the desert. Men, uncounted like grains of sand, undifferentiated too, have their brief incandescence, then lapse back in matter.

Mohammed, like Yelverton a man for clear-cut distinctions, began his new cult of Islam in the desert. He did this when he fled from Mecca to

Medina, a ten days' journey across empty sands. In his native place, enemies waited to kill him. There was the wife of Abu Lahab who strewed
thorns in the sand where he walked. He cursed this man and wife in one
of his suras. "Cursed be the hands of Abu Lahab: he shall perish! . . . Fag-
gots shall be heaped on his wife."

The Hegira showed Mohammed how this wish might father the deed.
Coming out of the desert, he called the sword the key of heaven and hell.
"The Lord destroy the Jews and Christians," said the Prophet, all of them
in Arabia who didn't worship the God of Islam. Arab soldiers weren't
troubled by doubts and hesitations, and except for the Covenanters,
Scotch Calvinists strong in the possession of truth, no better fighting men
ever lived. Each day of Ramadan, the month of fasting for Arabs, begins
when they can distinguish a white thread from a black one. You can do this
any day in the unfiltered light of the desert. Arabs call it Rub al Khali, or
Empty Quarter.

Modern hotels stand tall in the desert, and businessmen around the
world have made them a home away from home. Some wear Norman
Hilton suits and Ferragamo shoes, but the briefcases they carry are plastic. Air-conditioning whirs faintly inside the hotels, where the climate,
neither hot nor cold, never varies. Outside, the Arabs meet the climate
halfway. Square wind tunnels sit on top of their houses. The burning air,
passing through these tunnels, is cooled by water or dampened cloths.
This gives some relief to the people in the houses. However, they still know
where they are.

Muzak, soft but perky, fills the lobby of the Holiday Inn. This is in Ash
Shariqah, just up the road from Dubai. It being early December, the music
suits the season, and they are playing "Rudolph the Red-Nosed Reindeer."
My Avis rent-a-car, picked up at the airport, has air-conditioning, a radio,
and a tape deck. Upholstered in velour, the interior is red with black
stripes. Arabs, reserved in last things, like their surfaces bedizened. One
of their caliphs, when he went on his travels, slept beneath a black satin
tent. The poles were silver, the rings were gold, and the ropes made of
wool or shot silk. But their first caliph left only a camel, a single slave, and
a mantle. Before he died, he spurned this mantle with his foot. "I have
given back all that," he said, "and I am well and happy." When I start the
car, the radio, left on, plays Kris Kristofferson and "Bobby McGee."

Money, a great leveler, has homogenized the Emirates. Like tourist
islands in the Caribbean, emptied of culture, they have nothing personal

to show. Everything you need comes in from the outside, oil being the single exception. In the souk, or market, not far from the brackish creek that links Dubai to the sea, you can purchase Del Monte pineapples imported from Hawaii, Earl Grey breakfast tea, artichoke hearts, plastic yo-yos, throwaway pens, and many of Heinz's 57 varieties. The vegetable man, Bagghal, offers apples that might be McIntosh apples. Sometimes he sings, "Apples, apples, rosy as a young girl's cheek." This market doesn't stun your senses like the Bab el Louk in Cairo, where the heads of butchered animals are mounted over the doors of the shops. They have live chickens in wicker arks, though, and if you want a chicken for dinner they will slaughter it for you on the spot.

Men, idle and magnificent, kill time in the souk, fingering the merchandise and kibitzing with friends. They wear the familiar headdress, "a napkin with a fan belt," Yelverton says. The women wear the black veil or burka, and some of these veils are trimmed with gold thread. The nose and lips of the women are covered, but their hooded eyes are visible, like a fencer's behind his mask. A peripatetic Arab merchant, an everyday presence in the bazaar, hawks a cluster of gorgeous tropical snakes. That is what they look like until he holds them up for inspection. Steering wheel covers, they shimmer in the sun. Ibn Khaldun compared the world to a market like this one. Set out for display, the wares were sects and customs, institutions, forgotten lore. Mutable, not constant, they didn't persist in the same form, however, but changed with the passing of days. This was a sore affliction, the historian said.

Leading to the world outside, the creek, an arm of the sea, brings the world to Dubai. Some Arabs, strong for the old ways, say this is how the rot gets in. Platonists in their bones, they despise the world and the flesh. This goes with their notorious carnality, a source of pleasure but no more than that, the principle being that what's up front doesn't count. In his *Laws,* Plato put the good state far inland. Merchants and such never came there, and this provincial place kept its virtue intact. Provincialism, said Ibn Khaldun, was the key to Arab greatness. He thought that Arabs in the desert, savage, not sociable, were more disposed to courage than sedentary people, also closer to being good. They didn't obey the law, being ignorant of laws, and didn't go to school, but stood to the rest of men like beasts of prey or dumb animals. Jealous of the stranger, Arabs cocked an ear for every faint barking. This xenophobia preserved their *'asibiyah.* Rosenthal, translating Ibn Khaldun, renders the Arab word as *group-feeling.*

But the tale, baffling the teller, has an unexpected ending. Leaving the desert, Arabs, bent on conquest, took to the sea. This sullied their lineage. They meddled with strangers, and the closely knit group was a thing of the past. After the conquest, said Ibn Khaldun, Arabs acquired "the stigma of meekness." Our English language still remembers their sea terms. "What is our 'admiral' but the Al-mir-al-bahr of the Arabian Sea," Holdich asks in his *Gates of India,* "or our 'barge' but a barija or warship?" Careened in the mud by the bankside, trading vessels, caulked and painted, await the next voyage. The thrusting stems of these dhows are like giant toggle switches for opening or closing an electric circuit.

Bouncing off the water, the unrefracted light explodes in fragments, creating a movie set. The movie is a Western, *Duel in the Sun,* and the hero and villain, outlined against the sky, are stalking each other. The people in the street stand up like gnomons, uncompromisingly themselves. Poor or pretentious, the buildings can't evade what they are. Nuance, Arabs think, is for effeminate people, and their art, like their politics, is mostly inno-cent of chiaroscuro.

Palestinian Jews, sun-spattered like Arabs, share their yen for broad strokes and primary colors. Hallucinating in the sun, I go back in mind to Palestine. In Tel Aviv, the capital, an old movie is playing, white settlers vs. Redskins. The hero, clean shaven, rides a white horse. You can tell the vil-lain by the pricking of your thumbs. Out in the country, still biblical coun-try where shepherds tend their flocks, military checkpoints, bisecting the roads, are manned by soldiers toting automatic rifles. Dressed in combat fatigues, the soldiers, men and women, are sexless. In Israel, everybody goes to war.

Barbed wire, running with the roads, separates the beleaguered state from the Jordan River. The wire, a secondary line of defense, also func-tions as metaphor, dividing sheep from goats. Stockades topped with wire surround the kibbutzim, lonely outposts in the desert. Outside are the hostiles. Arab merchants in the city, paying out treasure, keep these guer-rilla fighters in pocket. Self-appointed vigilantes keep tabs on the mer-chants. But the other side is vigilant too. "Buy Blue and White, Not Arab," read wall placards in Jerusalem, posted by the Jewish Defense League. Blue and white are the colors of the Israeli flag.

A free port on the gulf, Dubai has its own dry dock, a modern harbor nearby at Port Rashid, also a trade center, state of the art. Along the curv-ing drive that sweeps up to the entrance, fan palms, pomegranates, and

dusty pink oleander do what they can to mollify its abstract design. Little
flame-colored blossoms surround the fruit of the pomegranate. Wood and
wire screens protect these growing things, otherwise the desert, always
on the prowl, would destroy them. Arabs understand this, a hard lesson
learned. Centuries ago, when they conquered North Africa, they found an
enormous thicket covering the wide littoral between Tangier and Tripoli.
Under the shade were hamlets where men and women fostered life in
society. They cultivated the land, sunk wells, and had their arts and crafts.
These little enclaves on the edge of the desert, artificial, not natural,
needed tending. Today the land is treeless, and nine-tenths of the people
who lived there are gone. The ruins of Roman oil mills break the surface
of the plain.

Jews in Tel Aviv are like Arabs in Dubai. Admonished by the desert,
they don't take their land for granted. As you fly into Ben Gurion Airport,
the land below you, flushed with green, looks like a garden. Aaron, a great
magician, has touched the rock with his wand. The garden that used to be
desert bears plums and apricots, barley, wheat, and banana trees. Hangers
of bananas are thick on the trees, and the shiny bracts of poinsettia, con-
trasting with the yellow flowers, show as blood red. The blue and white El
Al carrier serves kosher food. Handed round by the steward, the daily
paper is printed in Hebrew. Some letters in this Hebrew alphabet undulate whimsically, like the Arabic on Yelverton's calling card, and are
marked with dots, signifying vowels. The Israeli steward, fair-haired and
muscular, makes me think of those Anzac soldiers, prodigious sons of
scrawny fathers, who came back from the Antipodes to startle the world
at Gallipoli.

Outside the Dubai Hilton, my home away from home, rose of Sharon
in concrete tubs splashes bright color against the facade. Water from the
local desalinization plant, courtesy of Yelverton, cascades in a rococo
fountain. More precious than oil in these parts, it isn't hoarded on the
Trucial Coast, Arabs having found money to burn. Getting rid of indigenous things, the Emirates have got rid of poverty too. Before the gushers
came in, Arab poor lived on crumbs from the tables of the rich. For Eid
al-Adha, the Feast of Sacrifice honoring their prophet Ibrahim, well-to-do
Arabs sacrificed a sheep and gave the meat to the poor. Now the dole, a
state subsidy, feeds both rich and poor. In Dubai, unlike the Caribbean,
nobody goes hungry.

In the up-to-date hospital, care is free. Dark-skinned nurses are all starch and no nonsense, and their peremptory voices sound like Mary Poppins. Most of the doctors are Indian or Pakistani, but some have degrees from London or Trinity College, Dublin. On the phone their accents are Harley Street, plummy or clipped. Even on the hottest days, the chief resident wears a business suit, his pouter-pigeon belly covered by a decent waistcoat. A gold fob with a seal, attached to a pocket watch, hangs over his belly. Like a Harley Street doctor, he doesn't answer to *Doctor* but *Mister*.

The Trucial Coast was English once, and if you are English once this is as good as forever. Re-creating life back home, transplanted English from Sussex and Kent persuade themselves and others that England is really like that, a demiparadise or other Eden. Back home their drizzly climate is ripe like old cheese. They ignore this, however. Indifferent to the heat of the desert, they go out in the noonday sun. English make their own weather. I marvel at the knack they have of warping the world to suit their perception or making it over in their image and likeness. It tells how Britannia, a dot on the map, ruled the rest of the world for so long.

Soccer thrives in the Emirates, Dubai having the best eleven, and between Dubai and Ash Shariqah rivalry is keen. The manager of Barclay's Bank keeps a string of polo ponies. Weekends on the playing field outside Deira, linked by tunnel to Dubai, local residents, correctly dressed, meet to play polo. Long before the English, Arabs did this too, but cricket is a Johnny-come-lately. Though a recent import, it has taken hold, and some of the grander houses, laying down sod, have added a miniature cricket pitch out in back.

Britannia today, a magnet for colored people, is no longer a tight little island. Some English resent this. The man who had the flat below me when I lived in London said he didn't know what the world was coming to. This was after the war, and the "Gypos" in Cairo had just burned down Shepheard's Hotel. The world he remembered looked like a map in an old atlas, circa 1900. Red was for British, blue was for French, and these colonial powers divided up the world between them. A few scraps and orts were left over for the Dutch, Portuguese, etc. In this man's lifetime, however, the primary colors had begun to leach out or run into each other. He detected a yellow tide seeping from the East. Gandhi in particular upset him. This Middle Temple fakir parlayed on equal terms with the representative of the king-emperor. My neighbor imagined him striding half naked up the steps of the viceregal palace.

The colonial governor has long departed from Dubai, but their Arab ruler is still dreaming a form on the world. A compulsive builder, he is H.H. the Sheikh. "As in Shake 'n' Bake," Yelverton says, correcting my pronunciation. His voice, high-pitched and feminine, sounds like the Delta country south of Memphis, Tennessee. A homogenous country, this is where Yelverton lives in his mind. When he was a boy growing up in the Delta, people knew who they were and where they were going. The fat soil, well watered, produced bumper crops. Rice and cotton were the staples, but if you put a dry stick in the ground it put out suckers.

Living in the East for a long time, this expatriate wants to go home. To my surprise, he has a patriotic poem, committed to memory, that says this. "So it's home again, and home again, America for me! My heart is turning home again, and there I long to be." But he won't go home and knows it. The home his heart is turning to no longer exists, and if I want particulars, all I have to do is read the papers. Like a Trojan fleeing the doomed city, he has brought away his lares and penates, however. Wherever he goes, they go with him, a chip on his shoulder.

Arabs in Riyadh, the capital city of the Saudis, have Yelverton's friends to thank for their new international airport. Named for King Khaled, this sprawl of glass and concrete is anchored to the plateau on the edge of the city. Riyadh in the old days was a sleepy oasis on the pilgrim road to Mecca, but modern office buildings are replacing the mud-brick houses, and they have an oil refinery, a cement-making plant, and a university, the first in Arabia. The fortress wall that surrounded the city is gone. Riyadh, no longer itself, is a hodgepodge where East jostles West. Foreign workers, crowding in, give trouble to the Najdi population. These Najders would like to keep themselves to themselves, Yelverton says, but can't do this.

A traveled man who knows Arabia like his own backyard, Yelverton had to see it before he knew it. I knew it before I saw it, thanks to C. M. Doughty and his *Travels in Arabia Deserta.* The unabridged edition of 1888 shared the bookcase in our living room with Palgrave's *Golden Treasury,* Creasy's *Fifteen Decisive Battles,* and a broken set of Charles Dickens, bound in green cloth and lettered in gold on the spine. TV was for the future, and movies, expensive, were rationed to one a week. Grateful, I read these

volumes cover to cover. In those Depression years, we made our own entertainment.

Still a borough of homes and churches, Brooklyn before the war was
god-fearing, white, and mostly middle class but shaky. Near poverty, lev-
eling distinctions, bound us together. Nobody we knew owned an automobile, excepting Mr. Klauberg on the corner. The subway cost a nickel,
and my father rode it twice a day, coming and going from his office in midtown Manhattan. This changed with the war. The economy boomed, putting money in our pockets, and the automobile, a centrifugal force, came
into its own. Superhighways, an escape route, went up around the city. At
this time, southern blacks, coming to the city, changed the face of New
York. They had their different mores and spoke a different tongue. Getting into his newly acquired car, my father drove out to Long Island and
stayed there.

When we left the house on East Twenty-sixth Street, a lot of things we
owned went to the secondhand dealer. With them went my dog-eared
copy of *Arabia Deserta,* a loss I regret. Doughty is sometimes hard going,
and Garnett's one-volume abridgement does a service. But this writer is
most himself when taken in large doses. An uncommon Victorian, he
harks back to stately writers of an earlier time, and the sleep of the desert
refreshes his book. Like Aaron with his rod, redeeming the dead land, he
drew life from wasted sand-rock, spires, needles, and battled mountains.
It took me years to get over this gorgeous prose that reads like poetry.

"How couldst thou take such journeys into the fanatic Arabia?" they
asked him. But the desert is where you find it, and Doughty knew the
heart's desert better than most. He dreaded "unknown mankind" more
than wild beasts. Turks in Constantinople would murder you, he said, but
let a hound live. Abyssinian blacks, settled in the desert, saw an enemy
behind every bush. Arabs, unused to the sight of a stranger, hated what
they didn't know. Irately they asked each other, "Dost thou take me for
a Nasrany! that I should do such an iniquitous thing." A Nasrany is a
Nazarene or Christian.

But the Bedouin bade the stranger sit and eat. Doughty said he was
"full of the godly humanity of the wilderness." He never said where the
godly thing came from, but you feel it was earned, not handed to this
Bedu on a platter. Versed in "the desert comity," he offered the stranger
welcome, the offer setting him apart. "Were the enemies upon you, would
you forsake me who am your wayfellow?" Doughty asks him. "'I would,'

he said, 'take thee up back-rider on my thelul (riding camel), and we will run one fortune together.'"

A cable from Washington, handed in at the Hilton, gives me new marching orders. They have scratched Beirut, where Druse, Maronites, and Shiites are killing each other, and my next speech, three days from now, is set for Chulalongkorn. This Thai university is situated in Bangkok, halfway across the world but only an overnight hop on KLM. I have time on my hands, and Yelverton proposes that we make the most of this. Next door in Ash Shariqah, the Tourist Center runs safaris into the Empty Quarter. "Wadi-bashing, the Brits call it." Domesticating the desert, he makes this sound like Sunday at the beach.

At first light, when the Land Rover collects us at the hotel, the sky, still empty of sun, is only a smudge, and the desert along the highway rolls like pale water. But there isn't sky or desert, and the highway is a fiction spun by civil engineers. Contours, blurring, melt into each other. In Arabia and elsewhere this is unsettling, and until the sun comes up we don't know where we are. Sufi mystics in Arabia, making little of distinctions, lived in this half-light. "I am become the wine-drinker, the wine, and the cup-bearer," one of them said. He was Bayazid, who lived a thousand years ago.

But the sun is only biding its time. Particles of mica, embedded in the highway, gather the fierce light and hurl it back at our windshield. We sit in front with the driver, a local tribesman from Ra's al Khaymah up the coast. The Queen of Sheba had her palace there, Yelverton says. The driver wears the dishdasha complete with burnoose, but, rubbing elbows with Westerners, he has sloughed the old ways. A new kind of man, only just veneered with modernity and a smattering of English, this Abeyd-al-Malik is eager to please. "You American?" he says. "Is good. I like Americans. No like Russians."

The door of the Land Rover, painted red, has yellow letters in English: Sharjah Safari Co. Behind the enclosed cab, the flat bed, open to the air, is fenced with wooden slats. When Abeyd-al-Malik goes on safari into the hidden villages of the Hajer Mountains, he carries pots and pans lashed to the chassis, also cheap cotton goods, the rough cloaks they call *jubbah,* canvas tents and tent poles, and panniers of charcoal. In exchange he brings back goat's hair dyed red with kirmiz, ropes made of palm fiber, oil of citron, fresh dates, and date baskets. The baskets, on sale in the market, are *zanabil.* Arab men, fastidious, use the oil of citron, a lemony perfume.

Mohammed, not all sturm and drang, says in one of his suras how he had loved three things in the world, perfumes, women, and refreshment in prayer. At any rate, says Yelverton, he had his heart's desire of the first two.

Billboards streak past us, one advertizing "Pepsi!" in Arabic and English. On either side of the road, the desert is littered with the offscouring of modern life, polystyrene packing blocks, rusted hubcaps, exploded tires, plastic junk that lives forever. Fifty yards farther in, though, the desert is empty. Materializing out of the sands, a market complex, spanking new, rises like a mirage. Mixing different styles, Moorish, Turkish, and Beverly Hills, it isn't accommodating, only eclectic. Some of its buildings are Turkish and look like nomad tents in stone, others like Brighton Pavilion. The desert, lapping this market, waits to take it back again.

Outside Dubai the road turns east, then south, following the old Buraimi Trail. Camel caravans, crossing into Abu Dhabi, took this trail through the Empty Quarter to the kingdom of Arabia. They carried their provisions with them, skins of water and messes of barley and rice. Nothing lives in the desert, only yellow lizards and hyenas that feed on decay. Pinnacled rocks and broken kellas, old redoubts, define the horizon. The kellas guarded cisterns, dry ages ago. Camel droppings in the sand are a welcome sign of life.

The oasis at Al Buraimi blossoms behind its mud walls. Carved out of the sands by men, not dropped from Nature's hand, it is the product of thought and painstaking. *Ghosb* is their Arab word, meaning created "by effort." The walls, layers of earth stiffened with bricks, make a palisade against the sand. Taller than the walls, the castor-oil trees have large, star-shaped leaves and fuzzy red flowers, and their skinny boles, reddish-brown, are girdled like shoots of bamboo. From the branches of the frywood trees, yellow pods hang like tongues depressed for inspection. Woman's tongue, Arabs call the frywood. Date gardens, lush green, glorify the oasis. A gala in the desert, the gardens are flecked with colored lights. The orange lights are mangoes, also bougainvillea. Like charity, it covers the walls of the houses, bleached out or scabrous. Chinese shoe flowers, rosy red, grow in plots before the houses. The ovate green leaves, edged with teeth, are sharp enough to draw blood. Yellow flowers like puffballs hide the dark brown bark of the gum trees, our common acacia. Camels, not choosy, eat the leaves of this tree, prickly with spines, and their drovers use the wood for cooking fires.

But the desert, a state of mind, has left its mark on Al Buraimi. It comes up to the walls like Moors coming up from Spain, hellbent for Tours. Then, without warning, it stops. This is where Charles Martel, a great hero, has raised his baton. In 732 Moors got their comeuppance at Tours, Creasy said. So far and no farther. Startled, I can see where a line has been drawn, first the white sand, drained of color by the sun, then the alfalfa, a lushness of dark flowers. Forage for goats and camels, it unrolls beneath the date palms as if Arabs had rolled out a carpet. This is a mystery, the stuff melodrama is made of.

Black and white, in my experience never quite themselves, shade into each other, and nothing I know is black or white altogether. Day, gaining on night, and night, becoming itself, do this little by little. Some melodramatic fictions argue to the contrary—for instance, the *Christmas Carol* tale of two characters. First we have Scrooge the monster, and a monster is all he is, then nice old Scrooge, his opposite. The oasis at Al Buraimi resembles this improbable fiction. A green thought, it confronts the desert like the difference between either/or.

Cursing fluently in Arabic, Abeyd-al-Malik brakes to a stop. A drove of camels, in no hurry, lurches across the road. Their hairy feet, unshod, are squishy blobs like jelly fish, and as they move they envelop the ground. The lead camel, evil looking, has a mind of its own, narrow but determined. Coming to a halt, it collapses slowly like a jackknife being folded. The front legs go down first, then the hind quarters. When a camel sits, unless you are used to this, it is hard to avoid pitching over its withers. Indignant but perfunctory, the drover jabs at the camel with his pointed crop, a piece of almond wood. He does this until it struggles back to its feet. British on the Trucial Coast complain that hard-hearted Arabs mistreat their beasts of burden. The plight of dumb animals distresses these British, and letters to *The Times* reflect their concern. A hundred years ago, they founded the SPCA. But camels, like the old Adam, aren't tractable by nature. If you want them to obey you, whipping doesn't come amiss.

Getting down to stretch our legs, we head for lunch and a cup of coffee. Abeyd-al-Malik, fearing for the Land Rover, chooses to stay where he is. He says that Al Buraimi people will steal the coins from a dead man's eyes. From the *shurfa* of the mosque comes the summons to prayer, violating the desert silence, sympathizing with it too. Both blessing and malediction, this is the Sura of Praise. Arabs, says Yelverton, recite it five times a day. "Guide us in the right path, not in the path of those Thou art angered with." An uninflected crying, the muezzin's chant is tuneless, and Yelverton, grimacing, puts his fingers in his ears. "The old-time hymns had a tune you could carry." Surprising the locals, he illustrates with Charles Wesley's "Soldiers of Christ, Arise."

Blocking our path, mangy yellow dogs sun themselves in the street in front of the restaurant. Not bred or nurtured, these dogs are all dog. Growling, they want to bite us, but they haven't spirit to do this. Above the door the signboard, scalloped with neon tubing, is lettered in Arabic. Yelverton, cackling, makes this out as "Al Hambra's Place." A common room like a living room with the kitchen in back, the restaurant has a divan, taking one wall, also a TV set. The divan, says Yelverton, is for their nightly gatherings, *diwaniyas*. Late into the night, Arab men sit on this divan, drinking bitter coffee and canvassing the state of the world. The women, having their chores, stay home with the children.

Seated at deal tables veneered with Formica, old men pick at their food. Some, like Yasir Arafat, wear the red-checked *ghetra* wound with *agal,* a length of black rope. Wrinkling his nose, Yelverton advises the mutton, home grown. The fish, oily mackerel, is trucked in, he says, from Umm al Qaywayn on the Gulf. A sharp tang on the air, oil of citron cuts the smell. Their eyes glued to a soap opera, the old men ignore us. The black-and-white figures on the flickering screen speak an unfamiliar tongue, but their antics are familiar, and subtitles aren't needed to tell the hero from the villain. According to Yelverton, this Arab version of *As the World Turns* is beamed to Dubai from Kuwait.

Beyond Al Buraimi, a rickrack of metal girders signals the end of the highway. Where there was concrete, now there is sand. The map, dispensing with lines, is all stipples and bears the legend "No defined boundary." Stopping the Land Rover, Abeyd-al-Malik unscrews the caps from the tires, letting out air, then turns the car into the desert. Shy of the intruder, a flock of camels retreats before us, but the black goats, cropping the tribulus plants, stand their ground. "Bedu country," our driver says. Rimming the desert, eroded humps are crumpled like sodden asbestos. "Hajer Mountains." From the crest of a dune, a solitary camel watches our approach. Evidently what he sees from his distance alarms him, and, turning, he heads down the other side.

White from a distance, the sand, seen close up, is grainy brown, textured with pebbles. Later this changes, and the sand turns golden amber, the color of sterility. Even the waste soil of the desert, said Doughty, whose eye was keen, is full of variety. Old rainfall, a damp memory in pockets underground, still supports a little life. The fissured bark of the *ghaf* tree, evergreen, is covered with gray hairs and needle-sharp twiglets. A Scots poet, Hugh MacDiarmid, says his songs are like this, tenacious shrubs that grow in the wasteland. Fending off erosion, they put "a withy round sand." Pale green fruit like heads of cabbage hugs the branches of the *ghaf* tree. "Food for camel," says Abeyd-al-Malik.

Noisily the Land Rover moves through silence, unbroken except for the soughing of wind. Teasing the sand, the wind plays tricks. It makes ridges and artistic patterns, as if some cunning artificer had happened this way. Always "as if." In a history of the dervishes, I find this about an Arab nomad who wandered in the Empty Quarter. He said he knew there was a God "by the same by which I know from the traces in the sand that a man or an animal has crossed it." Yelverton says, however, that what he saw was the work of the wind. In midwinter and early summer it blows from the north, driving the sand before it. Then the desert turns into a dust bowl.

Color of amber, massifs of sand float in the afternoon haze. "*Qaid*, the Bedu call them." Scoured by wind and water, the gravel flats between the dunes are dotted with outcrops of ashy white gypsum. Salt bushes, vivid green or gray-green, grow on the perimeter. Piling on speed, Abeyd-al-Malik hurls the car at the dunes, downshifting when he hits them. The front wheels, chewing sand, want to go through, not up. However, our momentum, gained on the wadis, brings us up and over. Force, accumulating, has to go somewhere. Running the obstacle course in the Navy, you hit the wall full tilt, grabbing for the top with your fingers. If you did this in one motion, without breaking stride, simple physics did the rest. Only it wasn't much fun.

A boat in rough water, the Land Rover labors up the dunes to the crest. For a moment we hang suspended, then, holding our breath, go down. On the other side the sand, scooped out by wind, is a trough in the wave. Treacherous, it gives no hint of this until we meet it head on. The Land Rover, shuddering, threatens to capsize. It rights itself, however, and the up-and-down begins again.

Abeyd-al-Malik means to keep going as long as there are wadis and dunes. Sound and fury is the element he lives in. We want him to stop, but "this bugger," says Yelverton, doesn't understand English. Understanding well enough, Abeyd-al-Malik has a mind of his own. Under the hood, however, the radiator begins to bubble, and the temperature needle swings over to the right where the gauge is colored red. It stays there. Climbing out of the car, Abeyd-al-Malik wads up a corner of his dishdasha, making a pot holder. Gingerly, he unscrews the radiator cap. The last of the water, vaporized, jets into the air like breath on a frosty morning.

Yelverton, furious, yanks down the water can, attaching a length of flex cable to the spout. He upends the can, taking care not to splash any water on the block. In the heat we drive slowly, and the needle on the gauge turns back to the left. Yelverton, making the worst of a bad business, calls down seven plagues on Abeyd-al-Malik. This driver, all innocence, doesn't understand English.

Deep in the desert, the massifs make a ring like old dolmens at Stonehenge. Inside the ring Bedu shacks, protected from the *shamal* (wind), hunker down on the sand. The shacks, a single building, are stitched together with burlap, scraps of weathered wood, and corrugated metal like the rusting doors of old boxcars. A stovepipe pokes up from the roof, and the entrance, a dark pit, is partly hidden by a swag of canvas, looped to one side of the frame. "Water!" says Abeyd-al-Malik, wanting to make amends. He gives the wheel of the car a half turn, and we head for the Bedu encampment.

In front of the building a racing camel, hobbled, grazes the salt bush. Do I know why the camel is called the ship of the desert? Yelverton asks me. "Because it's full of Arab semen." The camel, wary, lifts its head, assessing the stranger. Moist and swollen, a wad of bubble gum balloons from its mouth. Cooling itself, the camel holds this pink sac to the air, then sucks it back again. The bubble, collapsing, makes a noise like bathwater when you pull the stopper from the tub.

A man, a woman, and a boy emerge from the tumbledown building. Impudent, not abashed, this nomad boy has his hand out. He is dressed in rags, and his avid eyes, exploring us, glitter with opportunity. What he sees is baksheesh, dollar bills mounted on three pairs of legs. Spread the wealth, he is saying, and won't take no for an answer. *Malesh!* says our driver. "Thanks just the same!" The boy persisting, Abeyd-al-Malik gives an edge to his tongue. *Malesh!* he says again. But this time he means "Forget it!"

Most Arabs, dark-skinned, are burned by the sun, but the Bedu is dark in the grain. He has kinky hair, walleyes like a pike's, and isn't bidding the stranger sit and eat. "One of the children of Ham." Arabs will tell

you, Yelverton says, that Noah cursed this errant child with blackness.
Unlovely to them, black is the color of evil. Ibn Khaldun says this. He
thought the damned were black, like the devil in our old Christian paint-
ings. Kinky hair, a badge of servitude, goes with being black. "Great God!"
Doughty has them saying. "Can those wooly polls be of the children of
Adam?"

The Bedu wears the long robe but, hurrying out to defend the wagon
train, has left off his burnoose. His hair, mostly gray, is patchy with yellow
like an adolescent girl's bleached with hydrogen peroxide. Around
his waist the rough cincture, knotted palm fibers, holds a dirk and a seamless *girby.* This homemade canteen, goatskin or sheepskin, glistens with
droplets of water. Bedu men, says Yelverton, wash their hair in camel
urine. City Arabs don't like them, and Abeyd-al-Malik keeps downwind
of this one. Bedu flaunt their apartness, a reproach to men in cities. Indifferent to creature comforts, they live on camel milk and dates from the
oases. Some tint the whites of their eyes with blue dye. Bedu don't make
good neighbors. The tribe gets their allegiance, but their hand is raised
against the outsider. Skirmishing like kites and crows, they have their
blood feuds, passed on from father to son. Shedding blood doesn't distress
them, and they don't wear the stigma of meekness.

"Hey you! Ali-ben-Shifty!" Yelverton says, seeing a dark face and a bed-
sheet. Cupping his hands, he holds them up to his mouth.

Reluctant, the Bedu, one man to our three, hands over the *girby.* Tilt-
ing it, Yelverton squeezes out water. As he drinks, he takes stock of the
woman. She wears the black *bukhnaq,* a calico scarf edged with bright
thread, also a loose-fitting gown. Her skin, unlike the man's, isn't swarthy
but pale. Splotches of henna paste, rosy red like an apple, keep the sun
from her forehead. The black hair, parted severely, makes a widow's peak
in the middle of the forehead and falls in loose braids to her shoulders.
Work and childbearing take their toll of Arab women, most being shapeless at thirty. This Bedu wife still has her young woman's body, apparent
to Yelverton beneath the cheap cotton *kandura.* Deliberately, he strips off
this gown with his eyes.

The Bedu doesn't need telling to understand that a line has been
drawn in the sand. Not getting outside himself, Yelverton misses the
anger. Arabs are Arabs, and it never occurs to him how this nomad Arab
might differ from others. Eyes rolling, the Bedu thinks about crossing the
line. His fingers feel for the dirk at his belt. Chattel, like goats and camels,

this woman belongs to him. Pushing the boy before her, she unhooks the canvas flap and disappears into the hovel. Abeyd-al-Malik, smelling a fracas, heads back for the car.

Two cocks on a dunghill, Yelverton and the Bedu circle each other. I am their witness, impartial, and getting it down. To close the circle, all that lacks is the violence there is no going back from. A little late in the day, Yelverton thinks twice. Sweat, beading his forehead, makes dark blotches under his arms. Undecided, he holds up his hands, a placatory gesture. The Bedu ignores this. One of the people of King Ibn-Saud, a cattle lifter and cutthroat, he likes a resolution where something gets resolved.

But the duel in the sun breaks off unfinished. At the sticking point, the Bedu backs down. His heart, crowded with blood, is empty of pity, the last thing in the world you would find there. But even in the desert, witnesses tell tales. Knowing this, he has his second thoughts, not the same as Yelverton's. Having raised his arm in anger, the Bedu lets it fall and turns away.

Fictions, compared to this encounter as it really was, have it all over the truth. "More truth than poetry," Yelverton likes to say, but misses the point. True-to-life shows a muddle, the poet showing the truth as it might be. The writer, seeing how the ending is only the tip of the iceberg, fills in the part underneath it. His privilege doesn't extend to sleight-of-hand, though, where they want you to think that what ought to be might be. E.g. the Bedu, dirk in hand, has Yelverton down. But as he lifts his hand to strike, he looks into his heart, finding pity. This happy ending is filched from the green and gold volumes of Dickens in the bookcase on East Twenty-sixth Street.

Yelverton thinks that all fictions are like this: taking the wish for the deed. Not born yesterday, he knows that under the warm skin of the world is great cold. I agree he has a point. The duel in the sun, mere sound and fury, still needs its conclusion. Being a writer, I undertake to supply it.

First, though, I have to deal with things past. I need a beginning, also a middle where important things get done. As my scenario begins, the Bedu, not made up yet, is like and unlike the nomad boy he has sired. An unwilling scholar, he needs time for study. This Bedu is lucky, and time is what they have given him. From early days they let him see how the world he lives in, various like the waste soil of the desert, isn't made in his image and likeness. On Eid days, celebrations that mark the end of Ramadan, the abstinent time, or the sacrifice of Ibrahim the Prophet, they dressed him in the black *bisht* edged with gold braid. They marched him off, complaining, from house to house in his neighborhood, where he bid "Eid Mubarak" to the neighbors. "Blessed be your celebration." Later, in his sitting room—never mind that this *majlis* is the floor of a hovel—he practiced fuming the incense. He polished the *mabkhar*, fragrant with perfume, until the brass nails were gleaming and he could see his face in the mirrors. From the *marashsh* chased with arabesques, he spilled the rose water over the cupped hands of his guest. Entertaining this guest, a stranger, he was all ears. His tongue, impertinent, he kept in his heart.

Doing this for a long time, the Bedu, schooled, becomes the hero, "full of the godly humanity of the wilderness." He has acquired the stigma of meekness. Something given, it falls like a bolt from the blue. But he doesn't take to it naturally, the way a duck takes to water. This stigma that makes the difference, separating sheep from goats, is also something he has earned.

Where my scenario ends, the Bedu gets beyond himself. Astride his victim, he swings an arm, preparing to kill. But the blow is intermitted, a broken parabola. Letting his arm fall, he doesn't do this from fear or prudence, and his gesture is a meditated thing.

When we regain the highway, Abeyd-al-Malik lays on the whip. He wants us home again before the desert settles down for the night. Yelverton, dejected, hugs himself against the door of the cab. Gnawed by the worm of conscience, this ill-tempered giaour doesn't like the sorry figure he has cut. But that is only what I think, taking the wish for the deed. Earnestly he says, "I'd rather sleep with her naked than him with all his clothes on." Coming up on Al Buraimi, we slacken speed but don't stop. The sun, a glowing clinker, is low in the sky, and the yellow dogs that look like jackals have disappeared from the street in front of "Al Hambra's Place." But a group of Arab men, getting in each other's faces, are talking up "Jihad!" while they wait for the restaurant to open.

2

Inca Dinka Doo

A stint in the navy hadn't satisfied my wanderlust, much less made me eager to join the world of nine to five. I wanted the life of a wayfaring stranger. "See America First," said my patriotic elders, and when I got discharged I looped a ditty bag over my wrist and took off. I meant to set foot in every county in America, of which there are 3,140. At the rate of one a day, it would have taken me almost ten years. A few months, it turned out, was enough. But hitchhiking taught me things, some with me still.

For starters I learned to serve under two flags. One was the body, the other the spirit validating its existence. To serve the body didn't mean letting it all hang out, as some I knew did in the sixties. It meant taking a pattern from that fabulous creature, the centaur. Half man, half horse, the centaur stands for the plenary life. Neither flesh nor spirit, it amalgamates both. Hedonists and ascetics cleave to one or the other. This makes life less complicated, but the result is an abbreviated man.

On my ascetic side I warm to general statement, and early on I wrote a book chock-full of it. I could easily have joined the abstracting tribe—my name for them is the intellectualizers—in whose company I've spent most of my life. I discovered that intellectual activity has little to do with intellectualizing, however. A popular mistake merges the two, but where the intellectual life turns toward the world, intellectualizing flees its embraces. It thinks that what's up front—dress and manners, le mot juste, a discriminating palate—doesn't count. Many in the groves of academe are intellectualizers. They favor flannel shirts and corduroys, and of course their chins are "valanced." Well, they didn't catch me!

Going out on the roads was partly an expedient, a way to realize the plenary life. First the living, then the reflecting on it "in tranquility." I wasn't lonely; on the contrary, traveling offered an escape from the self. Acting and singing do that, and once, at a time when I had been living too much in my head, I took to singing arias from opera. Some famous travelers crave being alone, making solitude a virtue. Ernest Shackleton was meditating a circuit of the Antarctic continent, no more desolate place on earth, when he died on South Georgia. My idea was that by canvassing the world, I might fill my inner larder with impressions, food for thought in future years. I had in mind the old fable of the spider and the bee, one spinning a web out of its own vitals, the other foraging abroad. My model was the latter.

Having little in my wallet, I scraped on food and stayed in flops and fleabags. The down-at-heels life was intentional too, bruising body to pleasure soul, and for a while I thought it romantic. West of Missoula, Montana, a sign in the common dormitory read "Don't spit in the sink." Near Albuquerque, New Mexico, I looked into an Indian's black-as-basalt eyes, unreadable except for their hatred. Ever since, I've avoided living close to ground level, and resist the temptation to glamorize people who do. Some haven't any option, a reason to pity, not praise them.

My day brightened outside Flagstaff when two young women in a late model coupe saw my thumb in the air and pulled over. Both were nice to look at, and I could tell they were asking themselves about me. "Climb aboard!" said the redhead, holding open the door. But they were going to the Grand Canyon, whereas my route led southeast to El Paso. "I'm sorry," I told them. "Suit yourself," they said, heading away out of my life. El Paso when I got there wasn't all that much, and to this day I've never seen the Grand Canyon.

Lima, Peru, reminds me of Detroit, nice residential quarters on the city's outskirts, big hotels in the center, in between a vacuum. Abandoning their city, well-to-do Limeños live in modern high-rises above the Pacific or in the suburbs of Miraflores and San Isidro. Enclosed gardens, they are like Dublin's Pale when the English ruled Ireland. Outside lived the Irish, "rough rugheaded kerns."

Everything you want has its price in the suburbs, and computer shops and record shops, even a version of Rizzoli's, aim to please. Movie houses, some of them palaces like the old Paramount in midtown Manhattan, feature the latest-run movies. You can buy a suit off the peg, or gentleman's tailors will make you one to measure. They do a good imitation of London's Savile Row except that the suits, Latin style, are too tight in the shoulders. Sidewalk cafes offer Johnny Walker Red, and for clients in a hurry automated banking machines supply money. Businessmen and professionals can't live by bread alone, though, and churches, one on every other corner, cater to the needs of the spirit.

My friend Rickey lives downtown in a one-room studio off Plaza San Martin, but would like to live in Miraflores. His dream house, a Spanish-type colonial landscaped with oleander, hibiscus, and potentilla, comes complete with its gardener and watchdog. Thick-walled to keep out the heat, houses in Miraflores are set back from wide boulevards lined with royal palms and poinsettia trees. Around the houses the whitewashed palisades are topped with shards of glass embedded in concrete. Bougainvillea, a loosely thrown carpet, half covers them.

Rickey wears three hats, pilot, bookkeeper, and sales rep or pitchman for Aero-Tours of Peru, but all three together won't get him past the front door. Anglicizing *Ricardo,* a concession to tourists, he is Rickey Mendez-Hoffmann, Spanish and German, and like a third of his countrymen a mestizo, part Indian too. Raised in the Amazonas, he fled the country for the city a long time ago, but the straight black hair, high cheekbones, and black eyes tilted up at the corners tell of a remote Indian past. This mestizo turns his back on the past, preferring to live in the present. Better still is the future, luring him on. Modern Indians, called Quechua, the first syllable pronounced as in *catsup,* know what the future holds, and unlike Rickey aren't often disappointed.

It almost never rains in Lima, so the houses don't need gutters or eaves troughs. But coastal fog, the *garua,* shrouds the city from April to December. Things come up from the ground without tending, mold included. In the Parque FDR the ancient olive grove, surrounded by Norfolk pine and lush stands of bamboo, still bears after four hundred years. Saturated with the drizzle that threatens but doesn't fall, the mild air is clammy, and returning from a shop or promenade you have to peel the shirt from your back. Herman Melville, en route to *Moby-Dick,* sailed into Lima but left in a hurry, finding it "strange and sad."

Air-conditioning, mandatory in office buildings and the better hotels, irons out much of the strangeness, however. When you close the door on your sanitized hotel room you might be anywhere or nowhere. The Lima Sheraton, where I put up, looks like the Waldorf, minus its bird cage. A huge mural, imitation Orozco, dominates the lobby, but the angry peasants in the mural are pretending. In alcoves off the lobby, tourists sip pisco sours, and a string quartet plays Strauss and Lehár at teatime.

Detroit keeps tight on its secrets, locked in an inner city, but in Lima the seams have burst and "young towns" or slums flourish on the periphery. A third of Lima's six million live in these *pueblos jovenes.* Santa Rosa is one, rising from the sand dunes east of Chavez Airport. This international terminal, named for Peru's first airman, hopes to capture tourist dollars, and planes leaving for abroad and coming back run on time. If you fly internally, all bets are off.

Campesinos in Santa Rosa, fleeing the countryside for a better life in the city, crowd the straw-sided shanties, roofed with cardboard or corrugated tin. Neruda, the Chilean poet who wrote about Peru's Incas and their fortress city, Machu Picchu, had harsh words for cities like Santa Rosa. He said that each day a little death overtook the people who lived there. Power lines don't run out their way, and they do without water, electric light, and plumbing. To cook, they use kerosene. This fuel is hard to come by, much of it siphoned off to the Huallaga Valley, where coca is turned into paste. From the bitter, green coca leaves, refined with kerosene, sulphuric acid, and acetone, farmers in the valley make cocaine. Highly valued in Peru and elsewhere, it keeps the cold off the soul. Yankees take most of it, but Indians are great users, Incas were too, and Spanish clergy in Cuzco depended on the coca crop for their tithes.

Running inland from the beach, the expressway brings you downtown to the Plaza de Armas, one in every city, like Main Street USA. The Civic Center, at thirty-three stories Lima's tallest building, flanks the plaza on one side, and the Palace of Justice on the other. Cynics speak knowingly of the "Palace of Injustice." Its writ runs in the city, not always a blessing, but out in the countryside Sendero Luminoso, "Shining Path" guerrillas, live by their own law. Wanting to tear the country down and start over, they kill rich and poor impartially. Túpac Amaru rebels, named for an Inca leader killed by the Spanish, kill Senderistas. Peru's exasperated army pots away at both, often bagging the innocent, unlucky ones who get in the way.

Peruvians don't love the army, and soldiers on guard duty outside the pale wear black masks like ski masks. Only the eyes are visible, and their

own mothers wouldn't know them. The soldier guarding the justice building stands at ease, however, and you can stroll at your ease in the city. You
will want to look sharp for pickpockets, though. I wear a body pouch,
strapped around the thigh.

Houses in Lima, using what lies to hand, favor bamboo and adobe.
Some householders, keeping up with the Joneses, paint their facades
shocking pink; others, making the worst of it, settle for grime and decay.
Most buildings keep a low profile, mindful of earthquake. The last one
shook the city in 1974. Limeños, living on the bubble, wait for the next
one. They don't wait in fear and trembling but take disasters in stride, part
of each day's business. When I'm down in rats' alley where the dead men
lost their bones, I try to be like them, singing a song of sixpence, my version. "There's still a lot of wine and pretty girls in this best of all possible
worlds."

New and old rub elbows in the modern city, sometimes leaving sores.
Where the pavement ends, dirt streets begin. Cactus grows in the streets,
and I note a vulture in the market. This week in Lima the garbage collec-
tors have walked off the job, nothing new, but the vulture raises eyebrows.
Public transport is by minibus, crammed to the gunnels. Buses move
slowly in the clotted traffic, and a seat is a good point of vantage. Young
men with time on their hands roam the sidewalk, keeping pace with the
bus. Street vendors called *informales* run beneath the windows, holding
up their wares, pocket lighters, "Inca" souvenirs, ballpoint pens, and
keepsakes, mainly religious. Billboards, like stage curtains hiding the life
behind them, advertise orange "croosh" and sweet soft drinks, *gaseosas.*
Inca Cola, colored gold, is the favorite. Some billboards, promoting
movies, depilatories, and underwear, show fanciful images of woman
south of the border. One, her hand on her hip, wears a come-hither smile
and looks like Dolores del Rio.

My hotel phone, flashing yellow when I get back to the room, con-
firms a lunch date with Rickey. Leaving early tomorrow for Nazca and the
southern desert, we need to coordinate plans. The trip to the desert, a
trial run for Aero-Tours, is Rickey's idea, and going with him, I have a free
ride. We meet at La Rosa Nautica on the boardwalk beside the sea.

Cheaper restaurants, *picanterias,* serve spicy foods like *recoto relleno,*
hot stuffed peppers, but at La Rosa, a tourist haunt, they set a blander
table, tempering the wind to the lamb before they shear him. This week's
specialty is "Foods of the Inca," a recent craze in Los Angeles but not often

seen in Peru. Upscale delis in Los Angeles, appealing to a jaded palate, do a lot of business in Inca vegetables and fruits, and I am told that Japanese pay $18/lb. for *pepinos.* Yellow and purple, the *pepino* tastes like honeydew melon.

Our menu suggests that we try the *ulluco,* a candy-striped root, also *oca,* like potatoes with the butter and sour cream taste built in. Inca farmers cultivated a wide range of crops, more than Heinz's fifty-seven varieties, but the Spanish banned all of them, excepting lima beans and potatoes. "Dark, dirty, and highly sinister," they called the potato, using it to feed the slaves in their silver mines and sailors below decks in their galleys.

Reserving the Inca specialties for another time, we lunch on *qui chaj-tado,* seared guinea pig, with a bottle of Chilean wine. Rickey, raising his glass, drinks to happy days. Visions of El Dorado dance in his head, better than today's humdrum. His job with Aero-Tours—"fetch and carry," he says ruefully—is only step one on the road to fame and fortune. Long before the Incas, people in Nazca were growing cotton, a cash crop, and a man who put his mind to it could make his fortune in the desert. But money is only the second most important thing, and Rickey wonders if a farmer's coveralls would suit him.

Cleared for departure from Jorge Chavez at 9 A.M., we wait for two hours on the runway. But we are over the desert by noon. If you stand on the desert floor the shallow indentations don't seem worth noting, perhaps the work of a predator or the wind that rises late in the day. But from five hundred feet up, they widen our eyes.

The breaching whale is an orca and bigger than the soccer field at their Estadio Nacional. It lives in the Pacific, lapping the salt flats west of Nazca. Some figures are geometric, rectangles and triangles, one of them trapezoidal. Preserved by the drought that bakes this sterile plateau, straight lines that might be railroad tracks run toward the horizon. Five valleys of the Rio Nazca cut the plateau, but the riverbed has no water for much of the year, sometimes for years on end. An American archaeologist, using carbon-14 tests, has dated a sighting stump found in the sand to 500 A.D. Opinion differs, however, and others insist that the Nazca lines originated centuries before this. No one knows who made them or why.

At the controls of the single-engine Piper, Rickey gestures with a black-gloved hand at the window and down, flashing his neon-bright grin. It isn't cold in the cockpit, only noisy when he slides the window back, and the leather gloves, like the leather helmet with earflaps and goggles, are stage props. Always on stage, he finds the images he lives by in old Hollywood movies, tales of the Bengal Lancers, Graustark, or the French Foreign Legion. Which came first, his pilot's license or the accessories, vintage "Dawn Patrol," is a question. Banking sharply, our propeller plane fights the wind, then, gaining headway, noses closer to earth. The figures in the sand, coming clearer each millisecond, rush up to meet us, my stomach lifting with them.

The odd menagerie includes a hummingbird (good luck if it favors your house), a beaky parrot, a condor with fluted vans, at one o'clock the dog-fox. Man's best friend, he followed the mountain gods, and I remember that the man in the moon kept a dog. Like the spider and lizard, the monkey, living in the tropics, promised rain. This one has a scrolled-up tail and a giant penis. Desert dwellers in the old days hoped to carry on the race, or perhaps they had sex on the brain.

Spiraling lines, more monkey business but nonrepresentational, suggest a motif, and on the littoral the whorled seashells repeat it. In a landscape destitute of form, someone was making connections. Poets and scientists do this all the time, finding order in chaos. Prescott, our famous American historian who took Latin lands for his special preserve, looked at them with a rationalist's eye. I read his *Conquest of Mexico* and *Conquest of Peru* in the old Modern Library edition, boyhood reading whose lessons sank deep. It has taken me half a lifetime to unlearn them. The world according to Prescott wasn't a clutter of fact but a moral fable with beginning, middle, and end. Providence insured that the ending would be happy. But not for everyone. Incas, Prescott thought, might have equaled the glories of Baghdad or Damascus. "But other and gloomier destinies were in reserve for the Indian races."

Sun, glancing off the waste gravel, throws some patches in relief, leaving others in shadow. Etched in the stony soil, a flower and tree vie for attention with a pair of splayed hands. The tree is the *huarango,* and Rickey says that the hands, being short a finger, are sacred. Deformed children, born of thunder and lightning, rejoiced in their deformity, he tells me. Other than the geoglyphs, only a scattering of crescent-shaped dunes, *medanos,* break the "lone and level sands." From the air they resemble ancient tumuli or grave mounds, but no one is buried at Nazca.

Sixteenth-century Spaniards found tombs on the highlands only miles away, though. They said how the skulls, still malleable in infants, were pinched and squeezed to look like volcanoes. This conical shape honored the mountain gods or turned away wrath. Not far to the north, mummified bundles, laid up in dark galleries hollowed out of the desert, have come to light in our time, and some Indian pottery, fired with straw and llama dung, survives after two thousand years. You can see what is left of it in Lima's National Museum. Mostly, however, *huaqueros,* grave robbers, have picked the country clean.

Incas were chauvinist before the word was coined. Swallowing the Nazca culture, they did this deliberately, wanting history to conform to their version, not somebody else's. They said history began when the sun god, creating the first Inca, instructed this founding father to lord it over the earth's four quarters. He was Manco Capac, and he and his descendants draped themselves in the mantle of godhead. The mantle, at least, was real, made of bats' skins or the silky wool of the vicuna, a sawed-off member of the llama family.

Incas, tracing their family tree to the sun and his sister, a moon goddess, cast their images in gold and silver. Making sense of the world, they called gold the sun's sweat and silver the tears of the moon. On my kitchen wall a bas-relief likeness, shiny black plastic, shows these twin divinities, the female nestling close to the male. Fantasizing Europeans said the Inca race descended from Kublai Khan or the twelve tribes of Israel. Sir Walter Ralegh in Shakespeare's time heard that the founder was a certain Ingasman or Englishman, his name a corruption of Incas plus Manco. Words mean what people want them to, and I have an Irish friend who thinks that Shakespeare the spear shaker was an Irish soldier.

The Peruvians are a mixed race, at least a third of them mestizo. They mingle Indian blood with Spanish, German, and Italian, even Chinese. Many deny the Indian part of them, thinking Indians inferior and wanting to be racially pure. Garcilaso de la Vega, the original mestizo, born of a Spanish knight to an Inca princess, told the story of the Incas in *Royal Commentaries,* collected the year Shakespeare died. Prescott dubbed him counsel for his unfortunate countrymen, and said he pleaded "the cause of that degraded race before the tribunal of posterity." A Catholic and "therefore" accustomed to large drafts on his credulity, Garcilaso addressed himself more to imagination than "sober reason." But his work possessed some merit, "clothed with the beautiful form and garb of humanity."

Prescott's mischievous idea is that "style is the dress of thought," where the loaded word is *dress,* meaning cosmetics. His style is an index of his habit of mind, which hangs a curtain of abstract words between the reader and the natural world. Evoking a scene, he summons up a "magnificent prospect." It mingles rocks, woods, and waterfalls with "the rich verdure of the valley" and the shining city in the foreground, "all blended in sweet harmony under the deep azure of a tropical sky." Sometimes the harmony shatters, but the same teleological impulse guides the pen. Rivers, "rushing in fury" down the mountain slopes, "throw themselves" into the yawning abyss, and hideous reptiles hide in trees or slimy pools, waiting to seize the unwary. This gives them their reason for being. Prescott's savage world reverses nineteenth-century images of the peaceable kingdom, but whether savage or benevolent it has its drapery of purposes and forms.

The difference between him and Garcilaso as historians is more than stylistic, however. Prescott draws on a psychology, worth elucidating. Call it Whiggish in the eighteenth-century sense, liberal in our sense. He and his once-famous peers, J. L. Motley, Macaulay, James Anthony Froude, Henry Charles Lea, Henry Hallam, Herbert Spencer, see what they want to see, taking the wish for the deed. Motley, whose version of the past seemed to define it when I read him as a young man, speaks for them all. In his *Rise of the Dutch Republic* he describes the conflicting "forces" at the center of history. "Now backward, now upward, yet, upon the whole, onward," they move the "new" society "along its predestined orbit."

Garcilaso doesn't believe in a new society or New World or in anything new beneath the sun. Though he enlivens his work with "mythical trappings," a plus in Prescott's view, he insists that "there is only one world," and his tale of atrocities and much else bears him out. The Spanish, burning the royal Inca, compel his followers to carry the wood for the flames, but the followers don't need instruction. "We'll drink chicha from your skull," Inca warriors sang, exulting over their enemies. "From your teeth we'll make a necklace, flutes from your bones."

Much of Garcilaso seems deliberately pointless, and I am tempted to suppose him a wit who is imitating history. A Spaniard asks an Indian what name the land goes by. The Indian, misunderstanding, thinks he is asking: What is your name? "Beru," he answers, adding "pelu": *I was in the river.* So the Spanish put the two words together, and that is how Peru got its name.

As for other details of Peru's prehistory, there are none. The Spaniards, taking over, saw to it that the annals of the Inca died with them. Nothing remains of their precious metalwork, melted down into ingots for the royal mints at Toledo and Seville. Only the despoilers record what it looked like: "many vessels of gold, lobsters of the sort that grow in the sea, birds and serpents, spiders, lizards, and llamas, also figures of women, natural size, all of fine gold and as beautiful as if they were alive." Incas lacked a written language, trusting to their *quipus* to interpret the past for the future. The knotted strings, coiled and stored in jars, yielded their secrets to the *amauta*, skilled in reading the different colors and lengths. But the Spanish killed off these professional "rememberers," and the history of the Inca is lost.

An object lesson in history, the Moche Valley in the desert's northern reaches once housed a "sacred place," Huaca del Sol. Scientists, scanning with their computers, estimate that 130 million sun-dried adobe bricks went to build this temple to the sun god. Like Burgundian Cluny, medieval Christendom's grandest holy place, it dazzled pious pilgrims until a new dispensation swept away the old. Broken bricks and a rubble of potsherds litter the coastal plain.

Some monuments in Peru still resist time's tooth and man's thieving, Machu Picchu, the lost city in the Andes, coming first to mind. Hiram Bingham, the American explorer, was looking for something else when he stumbled on it in 1911. This Yale man carried a flagpole, seven feet long, on his travels to Peru and, reaching the top of Mount Carapina, shook out the university's flag. Rickey, like New Yorkers who have never been to the top of the Empire State Building, has yet to see Machu Picchu. But he has seen *Lost Horizon*, so can tell you what this real-life Shangri-La must look like. Climbing up the mountain, he plays the part Ronald Colman played in the movie and, getting to the summit, stares at the city between peaks.

Machu is the old peak, Huayna the new one, surrounded by boiling waters, the Urubamba. Glinting through giant ferns at the foot of the mountain, the river makes a horseshoe turn past fruit orchards and terraced fields, greening with sugar cane. The terraces are *temporales,* this Spanish word defining itself, and the river takes its name from a Quechua word, *uru,* a caterpillar or grub. Urubamba is the flat land where grubs devour everything that grows. Scorpions infest the orchards, and the yellow viper, or fer-de-lance, lives on the mountainside. The *mato palo,* a parasitic fig tree, grows in the jungle that borders the cultivated ground. It has its "tropism" and, sending out tentacles, attaches itself to the fruit trees. Up top on the saddle, a government guesthouse accommodates travelers if any want to stay the night.

Cuzco, sixty-seven miles away, isn't much of a journey, but *pongos,* chasms like wounds, open on the soundless tumult of the river. The ferrocarril, switchbacking on the steeper grades, takes its time. Cactus, broom, and saw-toothed brumelia grow beside the roadbed, and silvery eucalyptus trees, native to Australia, grow in the temperate air of the valleys. I can't find how they got to Peru. Alpaca and llama ewes herd their lambs in the upland pastures, the llamas supercilious, the frizzy-haired alpacas without a clue. Curs—"yaller dogs," omnipresent in the countryside—wander on and off the tracks, watched by impassive Indians from their circular sod huts. Indians, like llamas, adapt without fuss to the thin air of the *altiplano,* fifteen thousand feet up. Used to the lowlands, I suffer from altitude sickness, a headache like a hangover, nausea too. Muleteers deal with this *soroche* by punching holes in the ears of their mules.

Thousands of stone steps, chiseled by Inca masons, climb up to Machu Picchu. Its streets and plazas, terraced like rice fields, are lined with temples, humble clan houses, gabled houses for nobility, and barracks for soldiers. Ashlar stone dresses some of the houses, but all are open to the sky, the *ichu* grass that once thatched them having rotted ages ago. Rough nubbins or bosses break the ashlar facing. Perhaps they helped the builders shift stones with their crowbars or had another meaning, unguessed at.

A causeway above the river gorge joined the city to others like it, hanging between sky and earth. Mist, eddying up from the gorge, mingles with cloud, sometimes forming shapes—a whale, a dragon, a helmeted head. Names are not always the consequents of things, and this is only what they look like. The volcanic peaks, though shocking in their immensity, are hospitable to life, unlike picture-postcard mountains in New England. They discharged "basic" lava, not acidic, and so enriched what they might have destroyed. On slopes above the empty city, Indians grow wheat and barley in narrow plots, or *andenes,* cut by Incas from the rock. They didn't lack for land, ruling more than a quarter of the continent, Prescott says, and accounting for their sky-built city teases thought.

Neruda, in his poem *The Heights of Macchu Picchu,* asked himself what it all added up to. Blood of peasants cemented the buildings, lifted "stone above stone on a groundwork of rags." Priests and ideologues, justifying the blood, think it watered the tree of liberty or helped expiate our sins. Rickey, though no ideologue and not into religion, shares this hopeful view. But Neruda, like an old *amauta* interpreting the *quipus,* can't find the

evidence that might support it. Invoking the dead builders, weavers, reti-
cent shepherds, tillers of fields, and masons high up on their treacherous
scaffolds, he sees that their blood made a furrow, however. Devoid of
meaning except in itself, it seemed worth recalling, and he spoke for dead
mouths, meaning them to speak through his own.

Motley, speaking for the progressive school, goes farther. Noble-born
protagonists in his history of the Dutch Republic, though they sit on top
of events, don't shape them. Just as Tolstoy told us, these makers and shak-
ers are only pawns on the board. But what happens to them, and step by
step to us, is "directed and controlled, under Providence," by our Heavenly Father. This purposive view of life inspirited FDR, whom I admire
just this side of idolatry. He said, "The course of history is ineluctably
upward." One needn't be a cynic to find that history doesn't always support him.

This doesn't say that history lacks meaning. Some poets I admire have
their sense of history as coherence, only more qualified than Motley's.
The Italian poet Montale, leading off his dark and personally painful
"Ballad Written in a Clinic," uses Neruda's word *furrow* (Ital. *solco,* Sp.
surco): a thing plowed and prospectively bearing. Out of the "furrow of
emergency" or bloody furrow of history comes a yield worth having. But
you can't condense it to an epigram, and its meaning is circumscribed by
itself.

Incas, choosing Cuzco for their capital, glorified it with the sweat of the
sun, a mistake. "I have come to take their gold away from them," said
Pizarro. He and his conquistadores, mostly adventurers down on their
luck, hoped it would turn up in the New World. Glorifying their own
god, they needed stones for their temples and took them where they
found them. Around Cuzco's Catholic church of Santo Domingo runs the
outer wall of the Incas' Coricancha, "golden enclosure" of their Temple of
the Sun, and Santa Catalina's nunnery wall once guarded their House of
the Virgins. Who conquered whom is worth asking. In Cuzco's cathedral
the Madonna on the choir stalls has an Indian face, and the crucified God
above the altar is black.

On a rise overlooking the city, a statue of Christ confronts the Inca
fortress Sacsahuaman. Marching fifteen hundred feet on the north side,
the pile of gray-blue limestone dwarfs the walls of Agrigentum, Greek
Sicily's holy of holies. Three gigantic tiers, each supporting its terrace,

ascend to parapets, enfiladed on three sides by mountains. Twenty-ton boulders, rough-hewn and polygonal, face the lowest tier, but elsewhere the stones are squared and marble-smooth. Joined as if they grew that way, they look almost seamless, and you can't insert a matchstick between the chamfered edges.

Thirty-thousand Indians labored seventy years to build Sacsahuaman. Incas did without the wheel and draft animals to pull it, but some of Sac-sahuaman's building blocks, lifted from quarries many miles distant, measure eighteen feet by six feet. What hand hewed these stones, then brought them to this height, remains a mystery. Six hundred years later the stone megaliths look down on the tiled roofs of Cuzco. Thousands of feet below, descendants of the Incas still cultivate quinoa, their sacred "mother-grain," threshing the grain with wooden clubs.

A jeep rolls out of the hangar when we land, and we get a ground-level tour of the dusty town and environs, a few imposing buildings, official-looking and built of *sillar,* the white, porous volcanic stone they use in southern Peru. Some are plastered over and painted in pastels, one or two faced with Spanish tiles, *azulejos.* Potatoes and carrots grow in plots beside the highway. Tethered goats run out their tether, and cattle, udders straining, crop the stunted grass. Coffee is stirred with condensed milk from a can, and I wonder what happens to the milk from the milch cows.

Morose behind the wheel, the Indian driver does his job, nothing extra. The cat has got his tongue, and if he has a name we don't know it. I have a name for him, "Coolidge." Ancestors of this Indian governed Peru, but Indians are to Incas as modern Greeks to the builders of the Par-thenon. "Madly ungay," Isherwood called the Indians.

Coolidge wears a knitted cap, close fitting and tasseled on top. Ignoring the heat, he has pulled down the flaps of his headgear. A college boy's cast-off T-shirt, covering his chest, is emblazoned with the motto of Dart-mouth College: *Vox clamantis in deserto,* "A voice crying in the wilderness." He has a broad chest, outsize shoulders, and arms ropey with veins like a twist of tobacco. Coarse trousers, llama and alpaca wool, cover his legs. In scorpion country, no one goes without sandals. Dutch-boy clunkers, his are made of llama skin, fastened with metal brads to a slab of galvanized rubber. I bought a pair in the market at Pi'sac, but the uncured skin stank and the rubber, old tire scraps, never conformed to the foot.

The llama, a dwarfish cousin of the camel, supplies the Indians with clothing, woolen blankets, cargo sacks, and fuel—dried dung or *taquia,* also sun-dried *charqui,* our English word *jerky.* Standing no more than three feet tall at the shoulder, the llama seems inoffensive, almost a house pet. Beneath the clown's nose, a black button, the mouth curves up in a sickle-shaped grin. When provoked, however, llamas take dead aim, spitting bitter saliva. If it gets in your eye, you know it. Fully grown, they weigh as much as four hundred pounds and can carry half their weight for six to twelve miles a day, longer if you push them. Indians do better, carrying the country's weight on their shoulders.

Built close to the ground, they scrape a living from it, pieced out with cottage industries, fruit of the loom. Inca women used the backstrap loom, often found in grave sites, and Quechua women use it today. You see them sitting cross-legged beside their heaped-up rugs and sweaters at Sunday markets in the countryside. The sweaters, colored like Joseph's coat, are meant for the tourist trade, and most women wear shapeless black dresses. One size fits all. Their hair is coiled in ringlets, the head crowned by a black derby or black felt fedora. Some favor a white Panama hat, and some of the hats look like stovepipes. An important market, Pi'sac squats on its mountain bluff above the Urubamba, northeast of Cuzco. The Hotel Ollanta, close to downtown Cuzco, will take you out by van, a corkscrew journey over streams and jagged hills, the road corkscrewing higher as it seeks the plateau. Crosses beside the road remember loved ones who went over when the brakes went out or the driver fell asleep at the wheel. Some drivers, hedging their bets, pin a St. Christopher's medal to the visor above the windshield.

Bodies, pressing close together in Pi'sac's Plaza de Armas, fill the open-air stalls and the shops on either side of the street. Down the middle of the street runs an evil-smelling gutter. Some shops employ sign language, helpful to those who can't read. A plastic bag hanging outside the shop means a telephone, the only one in town. Tourists, seizing their chance for a colorful photo, want the women in the plaza to hold it. Like Russian women bundled in sweaters one on top of the other, they wear layers of underskirts, poking out from under. Instamatics record this costume, but some women, fiercely modest, turn away before the shutter clicks. They think the camera has the power to suck the soul from the body.

Homemade umbrellas, cotton sheeting stretched over bamboo frames, protect them from the sun on the cobbles. They sell popped corn, high-laced boots, and statuettes of St. Rose of Lima, also musical instruments—some the size of a bassoon, others clusters of little tubes like panpipes. Indians in Pi'sac, like most in the countryside, would rather you called them *campesinos* or country folk, *Indian* being a term of reproach. Many chew coca leaves, a wad the size of a brazil nut. Some begin the day with a tipple of *chicha,* fermented corn. Gray in color, this intoxicant smells like stale beer. Prescott, always hopeful, called it "sparkling *chicha.*"

Spanish-speaking when they have to be, Indians speak Quechua by choice. Almost half in Peru still use the old tongue but don't make themselves heard in the din that rises from the parliament in Lima. "Lima se desinteresa para nosotros," runs the standard complaint. "In Lima they care nothing for us." The capital city is a world unto itself, but beyond it are other worlds, intensely themselves. "When you no longer see trees you are there," said Ruiz, the early navigator, meaning the desert. Two thousand miles long, it ends in stupefying mountains, twenty to fifty miles inland. In the valleys of these cordilleras mighty rivers, the Huallaga and Ucayali, begin, both entering the Amazon, mightiest of all. The confluence of waters creates a third Peru, the jungle.

Iquitos, its capital, spreads itself beside a tributary of the great river. Lean-tos line the river, trees take root in the mud, and in this Jack-and-the-beanstalk country, plants shoot up thirty inches in a day. Heat, almost embodied, guarantees rain, not the gentle rain that drops from heaven but a deluge. Through the heat comes the shrilling of insects. North of Iquitos, the Amazon begins its four-thousand-mile journey to the sea.

Belen, a popular tourist draw on the river, is known to locals as "the Amazonian Venice." Rickey, raised nearby, parrots this phrase, seeing his country through a gauzy curtain between the world and the mind. Natives in Belen live on rafts in the river. Afloat most of the year, in the dry months the rafts sit on mud. Each has its fishing skiff, woven from bundles of a hollow reed, *totora.* Like traveling salesmen, the boatmen go from "door to door," crying their wares. Money being scarce, Belen's people don't buy but barter, and what goes around comes around.

Naked brown-skinned children, letting down tin cans, bring up the day's drinking water from the river. They omit to boil it, though, and some, their bellies bloated with parasites, look like little old men. Indians, called "bow and arrow boys" by English travel writers, live in the jungle on both sides of the river. Daubing their faces with pulped *achiote* seeds, they wear necklaces strung with boar's teeth and hunt with poisoned arrows and blowguns. The darts are tipped with curare, paralyzing if it gets in the blood. Not long ago Indians over the border in Brazil attacked a party of geologists, killing two and wounding a third.

Selva is the word for the Amazonian jungle, like Dante's *selva oscura* except that the poet's world acknowledged design. Indians, wielding machetes, hack paths through the dark wood, but rain, a hundred inches per annum, quickens new growth and most of the work goes for naught. The river leaks or the earth sweats. Logs, lashed with creepers, furnish crude walkways over the quaking ground. You must walk them gingerly, like foot soldiers looking for land mines. Biting ants hide beneath the shiny leaves of the *palo santo,* or holy tree. When the rains are heaviest, in the first two months of winter, the winged males and females swarm at nightfall. Insectivores know this, and in the morning if you look for an ant you don't see one. A few impregnated females, getting away before the feeding begins, found a new colony elsewhere.

Green and black frogs, heard but not seen, live in the mangrove swamps, food for alligators and snakes. The anaconda, forty-five feet long, is the biggest snake and can swallow an alligator whole. Some snakes, frightening their prey, make it shoot adrenaline into the blood stream. This tenderizes the meat. Vampire bats employ a different technique to similar ends, injecting victims with a serum that prevents the blood from clotting.

Victorian naturalists, crisscrossing Peru's jungle, made little of its high-colored side, and their understated prose denied the need for getting excited. Docketing matter-of-factly in learned treatises with Latin titles, they called the often obstreperous world to order. H. W. Bates, a great collector of specimens, sent home 14,712, most of them insects. He said the blood-sucking vampire, genus Phyllostoma, had an inoffensive character, its grin and glistening black eye notwithstanding. Alligators were "rather troublesome" but essentially timid. Richard Spruce, a "bryologist" (liverworts and mosses), could kill them if he wanted to but didn't care to waste powder and shot.

Spruce had a poet's temperament and, quoting Lord Byron, said he held "converse with nature's charms" in the jungle. Bates is more low-key and makes you feel that he has stepped through the doors of an English drawing room to walk the lawn in back of the great house. Common dung beetles, flying about at evening, evoke the "'shardborne beetle with his drowsy hum,'" a familiar presence in "our English lanes." The sodden ground of the tropics, gray mist veiling dead leaves and rotting vegetation, plus the cool atmosphere soon after sunrise, remind him of autumn mornings in Leicester. Sexual mores were no less pure than "in similar places" at home.

The music of drawing rooms isn't heard in the jungle, but it has its noises too, and I stop my ears against them. Incas did the same. Conquering all in their path, they left off when they got to the *selva*. Notable is the thump-stop-thump of the log drum and the nail-on-blackboard sound of the *caracasha*, a notched bamboo tube played with a fiddle stick. For dreary monotony nothing exceeds the Indian flute or *quena*, however. When I can't sleep, I think of the drone of the *quena*. Made from a reed or an animal's femur, it has a limited range, two to six notes. The notes, uninflected, have no meaning, only duration.

Wind, rising as the day advances, alerts us that it is time to go, and heading out to sea, we take the short route home to Lima. Visible from the air but obscured by the noonday sun, a thin line bisects the shapes in the desert. Indifferent to the images Nazca people lived by, Inca engineers cut their coastal road straight through them, a rude swath twenty-four feet wide. This standard measurement equals five Indian bodies laid end to end. The coastal road, running from present-day Colombia to Chile, spanned upward of three thousand miles, the width of the continental United States. Sun temples and stone-laid palaces stood alongside it, also large complexes called *marcas*. Like our modern highway plazas—filling stations plus restaurants, picnic tables, and hostels—they offered a rest for the weary. Half a millennium later, modern engineers took the same route south, and the Pan-American Highway parallels the old Inca road.

The pope, a whirlwind traveler, has been to Lima in our absence, leaving a trail of confetti. *El Comercio* gives the gist of his homily, delivered to cheering thousands in the Estadio Nacional. A lion is in the streets, according to the pope, "seeking whom he may devour." He gives the lion a name, godless materialism. The papal visit has much improved Lima's streets. The garbage is gone, new paint freshens the traffic lanes along Jiron Union leading to the cathedral, and for the time being pickpockets keep their hands to themselves. Outside the pale, however, distant thunder reverberates. Shining Path guerrillas have blown up power pylons high in the Andes. Nightly blackouts darken half the city, its air-conditioning is down, and the water purification system, fueled by electric power, no longer functions. Bodies on ice pile up in the morgue. (The grave diggers have struck, also the doctors.) In the central post office mail lies undelivered, at latest count five million letters and parcels.

Just when we don't need them, the dog days descend on Lima, and nothing mediates between me and the climate. Prescott, doing Lima, "the fairest gem on the shores of the Pacific," took note of the climate, its dryness corrected by a vaporous cloud. Sheltering grateful inhabitants from the tropical sun, it hung like a curtain over the city, "imperceptibly distilling a refreshing moisture." If not everyone was grateful, Prescott didn't know this. Chance, blundering into his student's life at Harvard, cost him an eye, poked out by a crust of hard bread. Later the other eye failed, and for most of his adult years he lived in a darkened room, devoting himself to research. A tireless researcher but too frail to travel much, he never got to Peru.

I say goodbye to Rickey at an Italian coffee bar around the corner from Parque Kennedy. Italians since Garibaldi's time have flocked to South America, hoping for a fresh start in the New World. Rickey, alert to this, thinks about setting up a tutorial service to smooth the passage from Old World to New. But he needs a big dictionary, Spanish-Italian, and even Rizzoli's has failed him. Perhaps, when I get back to the States, I will find one.

Air Peru, indifferent to seat belts and tables and seat backs "in their upright position," runs an easygoing ship but returns me to Miami in one piece. As we settle into our final approach, I look through the port window at the modern El Dorado, its orders imposed on sand. Condos crowd the water's edge, behind them row on row of tract houses, each with its fenced-in backyard. Once Seminole Indians lived where the houses are. Scotch-Irish came later, mostly dirt farmers, some plantation owners, in their wake Negro slaves. Rich Anglos, out of love with Newport, Rhode Island, followed, then Jews deserting New York, last a great influx of Cubans. They hoped for life after Castro.

Surfaces sparkle in Miami International Airport, though traffic at high season approaches Chicago's O'Hare. Buses, a magic carpet, sort out foreign travelers from domestic, digital screens predict arrival and departure times, and most carriers follow the script. Signs in the terminal are lettered in Spanish, and the voice on the intercom speaks Spanish with an English translation. I gather from the papers that a Hispanic tide is rising in American cities, like prices in Peru. Waiting on a connecting flight, I call my son in New York but get a recorded message in Spanish. Later I learn that he has a Bolivian roommate. I inquire about this. "You don't like Hispanics?" he asks me.

Waldenbooks in the arrivals lounge stocks a few dictionaries, Spanish and English. But Spanish-Italian is too much to hope for, and I am home a month before I locate this ticket to fame and fortune. It goes off direct to Lima from the publisher in Englewood Cliffs, N.J. Rickey hasn't ever responded, however, and perhaps in Lima's central post office a package with his name on it awaits delivery with the rest of the mail.

3

Little Red Schoolhouse in Italy

When I was a graduate student at Harvard, you couldn't buy a condom in the state of Massachusetts. Standing up for my rights, I went from door to door calling for repeal of the law. I targeted Charleston, a section of Boston largely blue-collar, Irish, and Catholic. Though I gathered few signatures on my petition, I came close to getting punched in the nose.

What made me bother the man of the house, interrupting his Sunday dinner? I must have been into self-flagellation, like many lefties I've known. But partly, I think, the end I aimed at did me credit. I wanted to make the world better. Nothing wrong with that, and young people who don't share this impulse are soul-dead. The trouble, as I see it now, was that the end and my means were remote.

As I saw it then, America needed a complete overhaul. The rich were lining their pockets, the poor pined away, and the ship of state drove on the rocks. Lecturing the scribes and pharisees, I told them what had to be done. Change the laws and you change the man, I said, with all youth's assurance. What I really wanted was to get rid of history.

Literary history was my business and pleasure. Less bloody than the battles-and-leaders kind, it had its casualties too. If you were a target of Dr. Samuel Johnson's, a great shooter down of pretension in the age before our own, you seldom or never recovered. A night owl, Johnson sat up late with friends in London taverns like the Cheshire Cheese on Fleet Street. Enthroned in his own corner, he vanquished all comers with the power of his wit. These combats delighted us both.

But the prodigy of intellect thought that intellect alone could do little, and that shocked me. He wasn't a frivolous man for whom the intellect is only an instrument on which one plays. To the contrary, he was serious, he was moral, and exercising his wit, he hoped to arrive at the truth. The imperious man was deeply skeptical, however, and believed that God's grace made the difference for success or failure. "There but for the grace of God go I."

Unlike me in my youthful time, Dr. Johnson didn't believe in progress. The kind of change you could legislate put money in our pockets or took it away but didn't affect our salvation. Like me but with a difference, he wanted to escape from history, a record of "all the ills that human hearts endure." But the ills were native to us, he said, and laws and kings alike had no power to cause or cure them.

That might have bred despair, and a man I know, seeing to the bottom of politics, squatted in the fireplace and heaped ashes on his head. This is a figure of speech, but you get the idea. Dr. Johnson, seeing farther than most men, didn't despair, though irrational terrors beset him and he was melancholy to the point where suicide became an option. But he so loved the world and its sweetness that he wouldn't willingly leave it. In London for the first time, I did my best to be like him. "Come, sir," I said to my then-wife, a stand-in for Boswell, "let us dine at the Cheese." Its pudding was famous, a savory mess of kidneys, oysters, larks, mushrooms, and beefsteak, and you could smell it as far away as St. Paul's.

They turn up for lunch at the Villa Serbelloni, Bellagio, real-life functionaries of the Italian Communist Party. Not in my wildest had I dreamed of breaking bread with the likes of them. They ought to be rabble-rousing in the village below us, but they are sipping *aperitivos* on the graveled walk beneath the monkey tree. I reflect that these are *grossi pezzi*, however, "big shots" from Rome, not blue collar. The Left has its hierarchies too.

Giuseppe Boffa, foreign affairs editor of the Communist daily *l'Unità*, lives remote from the noise and stink of the city, high on the Gianicolo almost next door to the American Academy. A powerfully muscled man in his forties or fifties and bald except for a neatly trimmed fringe above the ears, he looks like a Renaissance cardinal. Mantegna might have painted him. His companion, Sergio Segre, the CPI's chief spokesman in foreign policy, belongs to the Party's Central Committee. "Senza dubbio," he is saying, "no doubt about it," proclaiming his or "their" willingness to go along with NATO and keep Italy independent of foreign control. We don't speak of Russia, but that is what he means.

This was a long time ago, and since then a lot of water has flowed under the bridge. Russia is still with us but no longer the evil empire, and Communism has died everywhere except in the universities, where its decayed condition gives it a certain cachet. (The corpus of literature is a corpse in the universities, said Allen Tate, all the more appealing to professors.) The cold war is yesterday's news; NATO, once a Western bulwark, has become a supranational club. But the bad old days live in my memory, and I return to them often, for the same reason I take a prophylactic. I want to be sure they don't happen again.

The Villa Serbelloni flies the American flag and is owned and run by the Rockefeller Foundation. A conference center for international gatherings, it offers a haven to writers, composers, and scholars in residence, most of them American. Acres of poppies and oleander segue into topiary gardens, the boxwood cut in the likeness of squirrels and rabbits. Skittering across the paths, lizards dart in and out of the boxwood, and the north Italian air, though warm, never scorches. Below the villa Lake Como winks in the sun, a few sails like doves, on the verge the mountains rising. Secured against their flank and high above the water, the monastery church of San Martino leans over Catenabbia. Wayside shrines like the Stations of the Cross march with the rutted road that goes up from the village. The shrines, lettered with Latin sayings from the Old or New Testament, remember the Passion of Jesus.

Down the lake is Dongo, where Mussolini went into hiding after he fell from power. Communist partisans, finding his hiding place, brought him to Milan and hung him upside down on a meat hook. This seems less retribution than an image of history. In Stendhal's *Charterhouse of Parma,* Fabbrizio, called "of Dongo," walks back to his native village all the way from the famous battle of Waterloo, but as the novel describes it, confused. Stendhal called this view one of the two most beautiful in the world. I don't quarrel with the description. No quarreling with anything here, a civilized version of Eden's Garden before the Fall. To make the Garden complete there is the Serpent, presented by the two Communists, insinuating guests.

But the visit is successful, everybody on his best behavior. Surprising me, Signor Segre, who tells the Party what to think about foreign affairs, hits it off with my American friend from the Council on Foreign Relations. Caleb Calloway is the friend, known to me as Cal. Born in Hankow, China, before it became Wuhan, he remembers how ocean liners anchored in the Yangtze, close to his father's church on the edge of the British Concession. Calloway Sr., a Methodist preacher from Pawtucket, Rhode Island, must have expected his firstborn to follow in the path of the righteous. Disappointed, he did what he could to lay a guilt trip on his son. On my pop psychology side, I think that Cal's career in public service is a secular version of the missionary life he rejected.

Our guests are well-mannered, careful not to overstay their welcome. "Abbastanza," says Boffa the Renaissance cardinal, setting down his Cinzano. "Enough is a feast." As the two of them get up to leave, they pump our hands like car salesmen, with special attention to Cal. Would the "egregio Signore" care to spend the next day at a Communist Party training school, south of Bellagio? I am interested and wangle an invitation. I think they think I am CIA, the man in the trench coat on the periphery.

In the morning a young chauffeur at the wheel of a new Citroën picks us up at the villa for the drive to Faggeto Lario, a third of the way to Milan. It rains often in the mountains, and driving is scary on the narrow road that runs beside the lake. Little Italian cars take our life in their hands. Sitting on our tail, they flick up the high beam, and though we want to let them pass we can't do this. Venerating the motorcar, Italians have precedent. Nine hundred years ago a Milanese bishop invented the *carroccio*. This "sacred car," like an old Duesenberg crossed with a love seat, became the emblem of the Commune. When Italians in the city-states went into battle, they brought along their *carroccio*, parading it before the enemy the way Orthodox Greeks and Russians paraded their icons. The ultimate disgrace was to lose your *carroccio*. The more things change, the more they remain the same.

Milan, throbbing, as in headaches, with industry and commerce, advances year by year on the country around it. The men behind the wheels of their Fiats are its banner bearers. You can see far out across the Lombardy plain, target of their development schemes, from the viewing platform on top of the cathedral. "A ziggurat for the Tower of Babel," Cal calls it, not much liking this huge Gothic pile. But the big church gets an entry in his index of architectural firsts, being one of a kind. When Cal took his degree in Italian history at Boston University, he spent hours

across town at MIT's Kresge Auditorium, looking from different angles at
Saarinen's warped roof and undulating brick walls. Stand him in front of
an old Italian church and he will show you how Romanesque turns into
Gothic and Gothic turns into Baroque. I am a "moldy fig" at home in the
past, and his eye for bygone things is congenial. It might have pleased his
father the minister too, except that all the old churches are papist.

Milan's cathedral meets you like a blow to the stomach. The glorifying
of man was all the rage when they finished it four centuries ago. Acid rain
has done a number on some of the exterior statues and threatens the trac-
ery over the vaults. Water drops, heavy on the air, make an evil mix with
the airborne pollution from the factories of the great city to the south.
This creates an eye-smarting haze. Last night an orange moon rose above
the lake, improbable as a picture postcard. Its beauty, my Italian friends
tell me, comes from the industrial smog that gets a little worse every year.

Spanish majordomos used to run this part of Italy, and I remember
how Manzoni gives their likeness in his novel *The Betrothed*. Afterward the
Austrians made the north an imperial redoubt. Then came the Germans.
In the Second World War they held it for Hitler against the Allies. Look
around the placid countryside, however, and you see little evidence of its
turbulent history. The scars of old battles have greened over long since, a
caution to the hatreds that fueled them.

In the early sixteenth century the Holy Roman Emperor sent his
armies from the north to chastise the pope in Rome. Not holy or Roman
but bad enough to be an emperor, he was Charles V of Spain, once the
world's biggest landlord. Pope Clement, a target of Cal's anecdotal scorn,
watched from Castel Sant'Angelo while an old woman came through the
lines, bringing him a gift of lettuce. Soldiers strangled her in view of the
watchers on the walls. Cal has a proverb inspired by the Sack of Rome:
"On the soil which the Spaniard has trodden, no grass will grow." Across
the Tiber on the Janiculum Hill, however, the grass is lush on Monte
Mario. Before they sacked the city, imperial troops lived in tents on the
mountain, home today to the Cavalieri Hilton. A city within the city, it has
its own putting greens, also closed-circuit TV.

Lake Como lies below us to our right, and through the haze we make
out the greasy oil slick that slops against the rocks and the stone embankment beside the highway. Fifty meters wide and gaining, it seems to go
on forever. Early in the morning some *burino* in a powerboat had flushed
out his tanks—in our mind's eye we see him doing it, a furtive little man

looking over his shoulder—before beginning the run back to Como city. If he is caught (but being long gone, he isn't catchable now), he will expect to be fined for polluting. It would cost him twice as much to get the same dirty job done in dry dock. Everyone is outraged, also resigned. The wife of the manager at the Villa Serbelloni makes the appropriate comment: "I'll call the Commune and listen to the lies they will tell me." We agree there isn't much the Commune can do.

The rain has stopped and the sun has burned off the haze as we pull up to the cadre school, just in time for lunch. Lumping together three large buildings, the school sits against a landscaped hillside, at its foot a private beach, or *spiagetto*. Sallow-skinned boys and girls are tossing a beach ball back and forth in the water. Hydrangeas, blue and pink, flower along the skirts of the drive, and the vegetable plot is enclosed by a lavender hedge. An old man in a floppy hat and a carpenter's apron hiked up at his belt is staking tomato plants and pricking out heads of lettuce. Where is the dark satanic mill I am expecting?

Roughly two dozen Communists, male and female and most in their early twenties, are living at the cadre school, scholars-in-residence. For three or four weeks they will listen to lectures in political and economic theory. CPI locals in the area around Milan foot the bill for their tuition and living expenses. Hereabouts, the party, not a despot, is a hope. To make room for more students, workmen are running up additional housing, and in Faggeto Lario the future looks like a going concern. Adjacent to the training center stands a Catholic church. We learn that some students attend daily Mass. No one sees an incongruity. In Italy they live and let live.

Everyone knows how Italians accommodate, a virtue or vice, depending on your point of view. One of their popes, a great hunter, ordained a deacon in his stable. A great drinker too, he drank to the devil, hedging his bets. Eight hundred years ago Italians chose a Jew for pope. This wealthy offshoot of the Pierleoni thought Rome was worth a Mass. Not all approve the accommodating habit. Cal, taking a sour view, calls it "Laodicean," too tolerant by half. Fighting a holy war, he divides the world between good and bad, like Plato's god when he divided the apple.

The meal we sit down to begins with prosciutto, cantaloupe, and figs. Then comes the pasta course (gnocchi), then octopus, clams, and snails. We think we have had enough, but pheasant appears, and for each of us a substantial fish, fresh from the lake, then mercifully—sign of the beginning of the end—*insalata verde*. The wine flows like water and tastes a lot better. Viva l'Italia! Maybe, under the forbidding surface, these Communists are like everybody else.

Table talk is conducted in French and Italian. I throw in as I can and find myself picking up quickly, almost holding my own. Playing tennis, I play better against a superior opponent. My opposite number, Signor Corghi, the Communist MP from Como, is talking animatedly, making headway as he talks with the almond-eyed young woman who faces us over the table. Her name is Fausta, and her familiar features, modern plus ancient, look out of Giotto paintings. She considers Signor Corghi with an estimating eye, the same eye that considers the fruit and cheese. He might be fresh from Terre Haute, Indiana, a swarthier version of the old-fashioned American populist Gene Debs. Coexistence is in, free enterprise too, and his key word is *diverso*. "Unlike the Holy Ghost," his party doesn't come down from on high. It isn't a monolith, either, i.e., like the USSR. The new society is going to make room for each of us and our different ideas. "Pluralistic," he calls it.

However, this society has limits. "Antisocial elements," like the Vatican and its power brokers, won't get a hearing. An amiable man who plays chess with the local padre—losing, he says ruefully, three times out of four—Signor Corghi aims to "liberate" Vatican City. Princes of the Church are the "caryatid of thrones still reeking with the scent of human burnt offerings." How can this be, I wonder. Thrones in Italy disappeared at the end of the war when their new republic got rid of the House of Savoy. Signor Corghi sees my eyebrows twitch. "Garibaldi said that," he tells me.

Also this republican hero, being in a hurry, said that "the Papacy is only a form." Acclaimed around the world, he made a great hit in England, where forms hang like barnacles on the ship of state. Entering Trafalgar Square, he bowed to the multitude, Christ on Palm Sunday. He toured the Crystal Palace, shape of things to come, and laid a wreath on Ugo Foscolo's grave. A romantic poet who died in exile, Foscolo called the past to the aid of the present. "Proteggete i miei padri," he wrote. "Protect my ancestors." Garibaldi, turning his back on the past, had something else in mind.

In the bad old days, according to Signor Corghi, Vatican power brokers set up three popes in Rome, one in the Lateran, one in St. Peter's, a third in Santa Maria Maggiore. The Lateran pope, twelve years old when they chose him, sold the papacy to the highest bidder. In the Vatican they are still buying and selling but do it under the counter. The "keys of the kingdom" open a cash box. This is what they mean by their power to loose and bind. Judging the past in the name of the present, Signor Corghi makes a sweeping condemnation. "Dall'alto in basso!" *Down with all that!*

I don't love popes and thrones but have a reservation, keeping this to myself out of politeness. When I lived in Rome, my favorite dropping-in place was St. Sebastian's on the Palatine Hill. This corner of the Palatine is fenced off from the ruins, and to get to the church you have to climb up by the country lane of St. Bonaventura. On the concave shield above the door, bees are emblazoned, the emblem of the Barberini pope, Urban VIII. In the seventeenth century he restored St. Sebastian's. (With the other hand he locked up Galileo.)

But the fresco behind the altar escaped his restoration, and bits and pieces of a double frieze mottle the wall above the apse. A sketch in the Vatican, made a long time ago, shows you what this frieze used to look like. The brawny old men who have hoisted up haloed figures on their shoulders are the Old Testament prophets. Each carries an apostle. In the weird procession on the Palatine Hill, the present rests on the shoulders of the past.

Thumbed to the walls around the refectory, the colorful posters are lettered in Cyrillic. They show Soviet workers and heroes of the Red Army. The workers and heroes, larger than life, brandish rifles and hold aloft the hammers of industry. Behind them the sun, rising, is red. I am reminded of the statues and bas-reliefs, carved from Brescia marble, in the Foro Italico, Rome. Mussolini chose this site for the Olympic Games of 1940. The games never came off and Mussolini lost his war, but today in the Foro young fascists, fixing bayonets and lobbing hand grenades, are still advancing on the future. Ardor covers them like whitewash.

Though Cal is at home in Italy, speaking its language almost as well as his own, he has a skeptical view of Italians. Their taste is for the grandiose, he says, passed down from the days of the Caesars. Renaissance popes cultivated this taste, and tour guides in the Vatican point with pride to the huge bronze pinecone—"like a mastodon's jaw"—that stood in front of old St. Peter's. In the sixteenth century the popes knocked down the old church, wanting something bigger. They admired the pinecone, though, and brought it into their house. "A dust collector on the grand scale," Cal calls it.

But it seems to me that size is only part of the story. No one wants a smaller pyramid. Perhaps the real culprit is the muscle-flexing style, growing on the world for some centuries now. When you go to the Vatican, the end-all and be-all is a visit to the Sistine Chapel. Moving with the crowd on your way to the chapel, you pass a cavernous *sala* hung with seventeenth-century paintings. Heroic figures in the paintings, out of the Michelangelo factory, go by in a blaze of undifferentiated color. Though Michelangelo is always himself, his imitators, except for getting coarser, look the same. Some artists, composers too, promote a style that buoys up lesser talents. Not this one.

Talk over coffee has veered around to the fascist ascendancy and its modern representative, the Movimento Sociale Italiano. You see the red, white, and green flame, symbol of the past that wants to be the future, stenciled on the walls of buildings and railroad embankments, more noticeable as you go south. Cal, who touched gloves with fascists in the Second World War, thinks the MSI is a force to reckon with. "Fascism is only biding its time." Enlisting the day after Pearl Harbor, a Sunday, he foot-soldiered from Anzio all the way to Florence. Though others at the table shrug in disbelief, he fears we have "scotched" the serpent, not killed it.

But Signor Corghi and friends assure us that the past is *finito*. This sounds to my skeptical ear like Macbeth before his his past began to rise against the present. "What's done is done." However, these Communists aren't thinking of continuity but closure. They have an authority, Berlinguer, the party chief. "A new phase in world history is opening," he says, reporting to their last National Congress. Custodian of the new phase, the Party, taking power, will shut the door on the past. Once installed, it won't let power go. Parting company with Cal, I agree that the MSI— they pronounce it *meesee*—doesn't seem much of a threat.

We play ping-pong after lunch, "communist against capitalist," somebody says, making a joke. Am I in fact a capitalist? In my bad Italian I dispute this, trying to say what I am. Not a capitalist exactly, maybe a democrat, lower-case *d*. This is a different kettle of fish, but how to spell out the difference leaves me groping for words. My hosts, nodding agreeably, aren't listening hard. In the context of the cadre school and the future it looks forward to, who cares about nice distinctions?

English grammar, a fetish of mine, turns on these distinctions. Mostly, nobody hears them. So grammar, like art and music, isn't first of all efficient but self-delighting. Good to get it right, though. There is more to say than this, and taking pleasure in nuance makes a political statement. Attention to little things is how the future gets built, the big things taking care of themselves.

Italians in the older time understood that, a reason I like to go back to their old churches. Santa Maria Maggiore, near the terminal in Rome, is one of these churches. "Improved" in modern times, the outside resembles a French *hôtel de ville*. Inside, though, things look up. Pope Sixtus III built this church named for Mary fifteen hundred years ago. On the arch above the altar, she wears the robes and crown of a Byzantine princess. But the regal woman is humble and does the meanest chores. In the act of spinning, she heaps a basket with purple wool. *Lanam fecit:* "She made wool." These words on gravestones remembered Roman matrons.

Though the pope's mosaics are clear to the naked eye, the ones on the side walls, only bits of color, are placed so high you need binoculars to see them. With the help of the binoculars, pharaoh's soldiers come into focus. Those in the foreground, drowning in the Red Sea, look frightened to death. One has wavy hair, almost marcelled. The man who made the mosaic took pains to get the hair right, though from down in the nave nobody would know the difference.

To my surprise, I have an attentive listener. This young Communist— he wears a tweed jacket patched with leather at the elbows and sucks on a big briar pipe he hasn't earned—prides himself on a logical mind. The earth is round or else flat. I can't have it both ways, and no third possibility exists. Quoting Lenin, he tells me: "You're either for us or against us." Signor Corghi, indignant at this breach of good manners, wags a finger in front of his nose. "Punto e basta!" *Enough of that!*

But I am grateful to Leather Patches, and the third possibility, not beholden to the world of either/or, intrigues me. My mind, searching out examples, goes back to Piazza del Popolo and the great Roman church that opens on the square. A *palcoscenico* or stage, the piazza is also a picture gallery or *pinacoteca*. Painters in the gallery are mostly High Renaissance. At the twilight hour, their subjects descend from the walls. They come in all shapes and sizes, the pedant, the miserly shopkeeper, the swag-bellied priest, the soldier full of strange oaths, the pert soubrette, a lady's maid, the uxorious husband, the old pantaloon. Announcing their type, they transcend it, however, and aren't symbols, only themselves. This one's face, a romantic poet's, is like "an alabaster vase lit from within." Some Italian faces bear out the comparison, beauty that shocks you and crudest calculation making an unlikely mix. Sentimentalize these people and you will lose your pocketbook or worse.

The church in the piazza has seen a lot of coming and going. Martin Luther worshiped there before he broke with Rome. A chrysalis and butterfly, depicted on a pair of medallions, take your eye to the right of the door as you enter. Symbols, they make their meaning clear. Where life was inert, it promises to quicken, and the grub in the cocoon spreads its wings. Luther, remembering, compared the soul to a butterfly, radiant after life's fever. Life, he was telling us, was bad down here on earth, but it would be good later, up in heaven. Truth in Rome and elsewhere is mostly trickier, though. Bernini, who has a naked Truth in the Borghese Gallery not far away, isn't really proposing that truth is most itself when naked. A lighthearted allegory, his voluptuous statue is more carnal than true. Faithful to the Roman psychology, it shows you nakedness with her clothes on. For single-minded men, this works out to confusion.

Santa Maria del Popolo is catholic, meaning all-encompassing, and doesn't burn candles to the naked truth. Statues and paintings dignify the church, but the frescoes, Pinturicchio's, are its glory. Celebrating the Virgin and attendant saints, they accommodate the pagan Sibyls, doing this without fuss or disjunction. Antisocial elements who were there before the coming of the new dispensation, the Sibyls affront the single-minded man. He is the Calvinist in a red shirt, à la mode in our time, big on political correctness. If he had his way he would send them to Hell *presto subito.*

Sibyls and saints, immiscible like oil and water, shouldn't swap back and forth, the Calvinist tells us. In this Roman church, however, they make an emulsion where nothing precipitates out. The oil slick, polluting Lake Como, is different. An alien presence, it rides on top of the water, forever itself.

A photograph of Mazzini, the voice of revolution, dominates the room to which we adjourn for questions and answers. A type of the schoolmaster learned in unambiguous things, he spent his life in the wilderness, drawing up blueprints for the new Italy. Mazzini is looking straight ahead. If he were looking sideways, he would see on one side the framed features of Palmiro Togliatti, leader of the Communist Party, on the other Antonio Gramsci, the martyr to Fascism. Murdered by Mussolini, this author of *Open Marxism* had much to say about his fellow Communists' coarsening of language, the first rung on a ladder that led to the coarsening of conduct.

The director's wife—her English is excellent, her special interest the emergence of the novel beginning with the bourgeois fabricator Daniel Defoe—is introducing "our distinguished American guest." I am forking up the last of my salad when she calls out my name. Appalled, I get to my feet, clear my throat, and say the first thing that comes into my head. Though I am a skeptic, I believe in doing the world's work and making the best of bad bargains. One thing leading to another, this brings me to the papacy, "the one great thing left to Italy." The room falls dead silent, but I plow ahead. In a fallen world, and never mind that the papacy is much falling itself, it preserves the best of the past. This guarantees the future. Two cheers for the papacy. Sitting down, I keep my eyes on the floor.

I am only the undercard at the fights, and Cal is the main event. He looks around the room, making eye contact. Not a man you can easily ignore, he has prematurely white hair butch-cut like a youngster's in boot camp, and his blue eyes, unusually pale, bore through you to discover how little is there. Also he has an edge to him, left over, says my pop psychology text, from the fire and brimstone he breathed in as a boy. Without mincing words, he lets the students know what is wrong with their view of the world. I think he is picking a quarrel, and I say so later and in private. He answers that straight talk—saying how the U.S. government, in Chile or Vietnam, has made a bad business worse—would be taken by this audience as a confession of weakness. "Sorry, son," he says, when I try to set the record straight. "You're either for us or against us."

After the heavy lunch and the ping-pong, I feel like a snooze. But the students snap me out of it. Though Cal's finger-wagging puts them off, they kindle, and this makes them attractive. A few do their best to reply, and what they say suggests conviction, reasoned out, not delivered by rote. Growing up in a country that gives them the back of its hand, they speak from experience, "hard knocks." In their experience it isn't the poverty that rankles. Not lumpen-poor, an unleavened lump, they are the yeast in the dough. Not opera buffa either, they haven't much humor, care being the element they live in. They will likely wait for years, after leaving their universities, to find a skilled job that can use them. Some won't ever find it.

The Q & A session is mostly low-key. Anxious to play the host, the students are super polite, except for my tweed-jacketed friend. Lighting and relighting his Peterson pipe, he gets a lot of mileage from the first-person pronoun. Friends hiss him with affection until he sits down again.

But I want them to tell us why they chose the Communist Party. They answer that it gives them a chance to realize themselves, offering a less selfish alternative to the old hierarchy, church and Christian Democrats. These young Communists, whether anticlerical or practicing Catholics, agree that the church renders to Caesar. What it takes from one pocket it puts in the other. "Pray for separation of church and state," says Leather Patches, an unexpected flash of humor.

He has a case, and even Cal, a little grimly, allows it. The Party, a new broom, has cleaned up Bologna, exhibit A in its Red Belt. Mussolini drained the marshes, a good thing to do, and some say he made the trains run on time. The solution from above has something in its favor, being cruel in order to be kind. Jingoes have another solution, saying that Italy must banish the alien and recover the indigenous thing. According to them, a new liberal philosophy has sapped the old virtues. "Italy for the Italians."

When I used to walk on the Palatine Hill, my route took me past a deep well or *mundus*. Two thousand years ago it marked the center of Rome. Evil spirits, not dead but present possibility, came out of this well to warm themselves at the fires of the living. A physical place, the well on the Palatine is also a metaphor. It says that the past waits to come 'round again, and the dark spirits, like the alien, are part of ourselves.

Envying Cal his conviction, I wish I could take comfort from my own less than rose-colored truths. But I find myself more depressed than sardonic. On September 20, 1870, the armies of united Italy, entering Rome, put an end to alien rule. Their Risorgimento meant a new beginning, starting out from scratch. But the new society dragged the past along with it, not the vitalizing past, the spirits from the *mundus*.

Cal is a pessimist, halfway to cynic, and his Italy as it was and is in the present is an Italy that "ever shall be." "They've got their nation-state, and what good has it done?" Do I know how many millions of them can't find employment? That's not because the Italian is *pigro*, a lazy bones. If they couldn't use him in Italy, other countries could. Who built the Forth Bridge in Scotland, those tunnels under the Alps, the railroads in America, the

Suez Canal? Even today, poor Italians in the south are still clearing out. The Risorgimento, leaving their poverty alone, calls them "Arabs." Wearily, Cal says, "Let's go home."

Making my *addios,* I feel a hand on my shoulder. I turn and there is Leather Patches, still scoring points. He thinks my friend from the Council on Foreign Relations has a "hard-hearted" view of his fellows. Perhaps, I say, it's the optimists who are heartless. This stumps him. Doggedly, he says, "Here at the school we believe in the future. We sit at the feet of Mazzini."

Suddenly, I get steamed. Mazzini, is it, that false prophet of the Risorgimento! Laying his hands on young lives, he talked about the common good and "the sacrifice of the individual to society." Rome, he told the *gioventù,* "shall be the holy Ark of your redemption." He said they owed it to the future "to proffer our *morituri te salutant*" from Rome. *Our* is a good one, and you didn't find him in the trenches. Young Italians, soul of the revolution, died on cue. Partly they were used, worse than dying. *Grossi pezzi* made out better.

Leather Patches looks at me the way some juniors look at seniors, and what I say goes right by him. "That's just the point!" he says. He rubs the bowl of his pipe against the side of his nose. "It's the capitalists we have to get rid of."

Walking back to the car, I remember the wall plaque beside the main staircase in Harvard's Widener Library. Writing from his cushy villa in Tivoli, the poet Horace is saying how sweet and decorous it is to die for your country. The words sound better in Latin.

Years ago in Prague before the fall of Dubcek, I saw a production of *Romeo and Juliet,* Shakespeare for modern times. Played as a parable, it pitted youngsters against oldsters, Stalin and his sclerotic cronies. "The time and my intents are savage wild," one absolutely opposed to the other, the hero says as the first curtain rises. He wants to be himself but the "time"— elders, state and party—destroys him. In this schoolhouse in Faggeto Lario, the roles are reversed, and the party means youth and progress. Perhaps these young Communists, lifting it to power, will renew the world's great age.

Near the door, at the corner of the head table that crosses the *T* of the classroom, a middle-aged man with wire granny glasses low on his nose has been reading the paper, not *l'Unità* but *Corriere della Sera.* He knows where the news is. A Communist theoretician, he ignores the talk, having heard it before. Passionate talk is for idealists, and arguments pro and con no longer hold meaning. This man remembers Gramsci, his awed students tell me. Later in the afternoon, he will lecture to the students. Like the young Bolsheviks in Madame Mandelstam's memoir, they hang on his words, taking the wish for the deed.

Outside Faggeto Lario an accident has snarled the traffic, and little cars like bumper cars face each other, blocking the highway. To get back to Villa Serbelloni, we must take a different road. Near journey's end it brings us to Varenna—Romanesque churches in the piazza, a ruined castle perched over the town, Bellagio like the prow of a ship across the water. Cal notices the bell tower of the older church, narrowing like an inverted *V* as it rises. "You don't often find this," he says to me and himself, and fishing out a note card makes an entry for his architectural index.

From the top of the campanile, the view will be splendid. Wanting to see it, we get down from the car. *Spingere,* says the sign beneath the buzzer by the door. I push this buzzer repeatedly but nobody answers.

Worth a detour, some churches in the countryside surprise you, for example Gravedona's a few kilometers away. The crucifix over the altar is more than eight hundred years old. Shut out of the campanile, we try its neighbor, hoping for a surprise. Restoration is in progress, and workmen, digging up the floor, have gone away for siesta. Sambuca bottles lie beside the empty graves. But the ancient *ambone,* a double pulpit, redeems the day. Ascending this high place, the deacon didn't mean to impose, like modern judges on their dais, but delivered glad tidings to Zion. Most old pulpits have two flights of stairs, says Cal, our cicerone, but in this church only one stairway remains.

Outside the church crudely lettered *scarabocchi* scrawled on the walls propose the identification *USA = Democrazia Cristiana = Assassini.* In the church porch a solitary vendor is selling cheap reproductions of profane and sacred art, also coffee trays painted with the faces of Pope John and Palmiro Togliatti. In the park at water's edge, other vendors peddle beer and Coca-Cola. A Communist Party *festa* is in progress, and a jazz combo competes with the loudspeakers that blare at the crowd. *Bimbi,* running wild, catch it from their parents. *Ascolti!* that red knit suit cost a fortune. Draped around the bandstand and over the railing that encircles the park, the swags of bunting, red and yellow, are stitched with the hammer and sickle.

Bales of straw have been broken and scattered across the lake surface, and the oil spill has begun to stick to the straw. After all, the Commune has been minding its business. Tomorrow the gluey substance will be gone from the lake. In this country a better tomorrow, shot with brightness like the famous silks of Como, is always on the horizon. Emperors, popes, and Mussolini have come and gone, and the world still turns on its axis. Today is another matter, though, and in the afternoon sunlight, the fish, already dying, float belly up in the water.

4

France's Two Cities

It never ceased to amaze me that I got paid for teaching poetry, like sitting in a rocking chair on the front porch. Of course no job is harder, but that is another story and will keep. My principal poet was Shakespeare, whose grace notes promote the sense of air about the plays. Like the old masters in Auden's poem, he pays attention to a world outside the spotlight. Dogs go on "with their doggy life," oblivious of the catastrophe, but what happens on center stage isn't credible without them. Gratuities are of the play's essence, and you could say that Shakespeare gives us more than money's worth. This agrees with my Scottish sense of fitness.

Nothing is meaningful for him without "respect," as his Portia tells us in *The Merchant of Venice*. In Shakespeare's lexicon, the word *respect* means context, and it must environ the subject, whether physical or immaterial; otherwise there isn't a subject. Philosophers like to speak of the *ding an sich,* or thing in itself, but that is a fiction, and a thing has existence only as it relates to some other thing. Necessarily, general statements ring false, unless attached to a how, when, and where clause. Shakespeare doesn't venture them, not ever, despite *Bartlett's Familiar Quotations.*

If asked whether you would willingly tell a lie or lay down your life for your country, you had better answer, as he does, "It depends." Some, thinking this wishy-washy, prefer their truth unqualified, as when Iago tells us, "'Tis in ourselves that we are thus or thus." The plot of the play, a way of describing the larger context that envelops all the characters in it, comments on their psychology, and commenting on Iago's, reproves him. The insistence on context spoils the game of the old women who like to work Shakespeare's sayings into samplers and hang them over the mantel.

(The old women are often men, not all of them old.) When Hamlet says, "Frailty, thy name is woman," Shakespeare's character is doing the talking, not Shakespeare. People who want the facts, ma'am, don't see the point of this circumscribed kind of writing, and Shakespeare is more honored in the breach than the observance.

Interest in him began to wane toward the end of my teaching career. It didn't happen all at once but sneaked up on me, like age. Though colleagues still pointed students in Shakespeare's direction, that was as a halfway house en route to something else. His characters turned into types illustrating a thesis, while the plays turned into social or political tracts. Sometimes the author didn't know what he was doing, and the critic elucidated his intention. Sometimes, it appeared, there wasn't an author at all.

Looking back, I can see that I got out of the university just in time, departing from one end of town as the posse was coming in from the other. A hatred of the Word Made Flesh swept through the groves of academe, leaving only blackened tree trunks, like a forest denuded by fire. Displaced by ideas, palpable things you could take hold of went to the trash can. In my years as department chair at Michigan, I used to compare a well-formed department to a Bartlett pear tree, taking its crooked shape in response to natural imperatives like sun, rain, and soil. Those who were listening thought that I'd lost it, and since then they have laid the ax to the tree.

If I had to choose a single piece of the planet for saving, I'd choose Burgundian France. Burgundy in its heyday took in much of modern Belgium, stretching south as far as Provence. Since then it has tightened its belt. Sens, further north in the valley of the Yonne, marks its northern boundary, its southern passing through Cluny, once the light of the world, now a ruin. The Loire River is a natural boundary on the west. Chartres lies above the river, of Burgundy though not in it, like some great aquatic creature left behind by the tide. On the east is Dijon and below it the Côte d'Or, named for its golden earth. Noble wines grow in this earth, coveted helplessly by people like me.

More than place names in the atlas, Burgundy is an *état d'esprit* or state of mind. What it means to my mind is a handful of churches, already ancient when America was young. Sens is the first of them built in the new style, Gothic and feeling for heaven. Others, looking back to Rome and its rounded arches, feel for the earth at our feet. Modified by Norman conquerors, this Romanesque style doesn't aspire, though the people that favored it made the world tremble. Towers like traffic cones are part of its profile, but seem moored to the vaulting below. Norman churches take their power from restraint, and vitality in check tautens the guylines.

The English countryside has its own General Issue church, but its profile, like the mindset that produced it, is different. Gray-stuccoed, perpendicular, and looking good from a distance, it looks less convincing up close. *Audace! Toujours audace* is a motto for Gothic, and it must succeed hugely to succeed at all. Burgundy's great churches mix this "French style" with old Romanesque. St. Lazarus in Autun is characteristic, as old as the hills but crowned with a new Gothic belfry.

The new isn't imposed on the old but rises from it, and the mix isn't the same as a hodgepodge. There is the comprehensive spirit, then there is the eclectic or *je m'en fîche* spirit that doesn't give a damn for anything, so draws the line at nothing. Near the middle of Burgundy, Saulieu, an old post town known for good eating, has its mandatory cathedral, St. Andoche. Though it still holds its head up, French revolutionaries and English soldiers in the Hundred Years' War have left it sadly bedraggled. The carved capitals on the pillars widen your eyes—look, for starters, at Balaam and the Ass—but the choir and cupola tell of a later time when taste took a beating, and the word for this church is *eclectic*.

Every big town in Burgundy gets a star in the guidebook for its cathedral, like St. Étienne in Auxerre, looking across the Yonne to cherry orchards and vineyards renowned for Chablis. Pleasure boats ride the Yonne as it flows through Auxerre, at ease on both sides of the river. The train from Paris takes an hour, but when you buy your ticket you must ask for "Aussere." If, however, you are asking for Vix, as in the "Tresor de Vix," an Iron Age survival due east in Burgundy, you don't muffle the x but pronounce it. Though the French are sticklers for correctness, they speak an impure tongue that bends the rules or honors special cases. Otherwise, no one could stand them. Three hundred years ago, alarmed by this generous streak in themselves, they created a French Academy to clean up the language, and purists today carry on the good fight. Being alive, the language fights back.

St. Étienne is St. Stephen, whose name remembers the first Christian martyr, stoned to death in Roman times and often depicted with a stone in his hand. He epitomizes our history of violence, but out of it comes its opposite, and his memorial flowers in peace. Biblical figures on the walls of St. Stephen are truer to life than the people next door, and the stained glass in the ambulatory blazes with blue and red medallions. In the Wars of Religion, Protestants decapitated most of the statues. Exalting the spirit over the flesh, they swept through Burgundy's old churches, leaving their telltale, destruction. Two centuries later, the Revolution took up where these reformers left off. Making a deity of reason, it prayed to liberty, equality, and fraternity, like the Trinity but abstracted. For a long time at Sens Old Testament prophets above the south doorway seemed to utter jeremiads in stone. Not any more, and the revolutionaries, abhorring the Word Made Flesh, shortened them all by a head.

Time's ill wind doesn't always blow ill. In Auxerre the abbey church of St. Germain, falling to pieces after a thousand years, has uncovered an older church beneath it. Tombs and underground chapels mix Gothic, Romanesque, and Carolingian styles, and some of the columns reuse Gallo-Roman work from Arles. Stout pillars support the ceiling, between them trompe l'oeil pillars painted in fresco. In the subterranean church the natural world and the world of spirit run together, convincing the eye. Wall paintings, some of France's oldest, show St. Stephen dragged before his accusers. Already the stones are flying, but he doesn't duck and, leaning forward eagerly, prepares to enter an open doorway. Above his head a helping hand descends from the clouds. Up there is the City of God.

The saint's eagerness wasn't everyone's, many taking their time, often their own sweet time, on the way to the Heavenly City. The men who painted the frescoes knew that life was a pilgrimage but honored it while it was passing. They weren't deep-dyed sinners, only laggards in the City of Man. Though many lived contentedly in the here and now, they didn't turn a blind eye on salvation. Others, hastening on to the City of God, stole a backward glance at the world. "Lord, I have loved the beauty of Thy house," said St. Odo of Cluny on his deathbed.

Love for the world pairs with its opposite, a hatred of *terra damnata*, and France then and now accommodates both. In the Year of Revolutions, 1848, its chief of state imagined "two true and natural governments," each vying for a place in the sun. One looks to the past, the other hangs out at the Café du Progrès. One, death on the big picture, opts for little things, while the other pulps them like forcemeat. Challenging this other, too much with me on my travels, I have invented a twelfth-century Frenchman, Amadeus de Bourg-Dieu, "God Lover of the City of God." His heavenly city is earthbound, however, and his God is born of a woman.

Jean Thorez, a tour guide I know, spells out the difference between the two cities, one sacred, the other profane. History in France is the tale of "two nations," he tells his charges, one the "notables" or uppercrust, the other those it sits on. Most of France's down times you can trace to the notables, embodied in the ancien régime. History's new broom has swept it into the dustbin, however. Though he deplores violence, he has to acknowledge that you can't have change without it. The guillotine was an instrument of justice, and the Terror "an emanation of virtue." He is quoting Robespierre, he says, giving credit where credit is due.

Both of us have been working the same time-honored sites, me for the fun of it, he for his tour guide's stipend, and it isn't surprising that our paths continue to cross. But I take a deep breath when I see him again in Auxerre, holding up a placard with his name and title, "M. Jean Thorez, Licentiate of the Sorbonne." Dignity is part of his stage-Frenchman's kit, like the waistcoat on his paunch and the wax on his moustache. The tourists he is shepherding, mostly American, aren't easily cowed, though. Skipping the "mister," many address him as "Gene."

His minilecture, trimmed to sound bytes, mixes history and anecdotal detail. Gene says he wants "un oeuf à peler ensemble"—an egg to peel together—that is, he wants to set the record straight. If, for example, 4,400 villages in France are named after saints, it's no wonder that progress has faltered. St. Martin, the patron saint of private charities, tops the list. Cutting his coat in half, he gave half to a poor man, leaving the giver worse off than he was and the receiver no better. Gene's version of history runs upward. It has color to spare, like the jacket of a popular novel. In the "dark ages," feudal landlords with a gleam in their eye wouldn't take no for an answer. Serving maids in low-cut dresses did what they could to keep virtue intact, but were no match for the *droit de seigneur*.

Farsighted for a dandy, Gene misses the world under his nose. Though he takes to ideas like a duck to water, all but the boldest shapes, textures, and colors elude him. Religious he isn't, but he puts me in mind of a great religious man, St. Bernard, one of Burgundy's finest. When engineers of genius were building the cathedrals, this saint exalted faith above works.

Beauty he "deemed as dung," and the monasteries he founded, like Fontenay near Dijon, barred the door to art. Once, walking for a day on the shores of Lake Geneva, he asked in the evening where the lake was.

French peasants around Dijon, the ancient capital of Burgundy, come at the world from a different perspective. Indifferent to the forest, they lock in on the trees. History and its up and down doesn't impress them, but they remember their local saint, special like the *vin du pays*. He was Benignus, most of whose big church went to placate revolutionary zeal. But as the tour books say, Dijon is still worth a detour. Claus Sluter, Holland's gift to Burgundy, escaped the new broom, and his sculpted head of Christ is still on display in the old refectory beside the cathedral. The bust of Rameau, high cheekbones and a superior smile, still fills its niche in the local museum. He drew ravishing music from catgut.

Still environing the ducal palace, the eighteenth-century townhouses are *hôtels particuliers*. I like the delimiting word. Triangular patterns, rusty, dark red, and bright yellow, zigzag across their tiled Mansart roofs. The triangles look like fish scales before the iridescence goes, and aren't perfect but serried, crowding together as they ascend. Though St. Bernard lived close by, Sluter the artist gives the city its savor. He stands in the courtyard of the Musée des Beaux Arts, a short, powerful, blocky man dressed in his artisan's smock. On his head he wears a soft-cornered cap like those velvet crushed caps scholars wear in academic processions. His learning isn't theirs, though, and his hand holds a stonecutter's mallet.

Stands of poplar fence the fields beside the road to Fontenay. Emptied of people, the land can't have changed much in eight hundred years. Conical Norman towers, black, without ornament, give it a skyline. The road skirts a little lake where men in skiffs are casting lazily, sun glinting on their artificial lures. French make the best lures, curved like the scallop shell pilgrims wore on their way to the shrine of St. James. In the hamlet beyond the lake every red-tiled roof has a TV antenna. This is change.

The abbey greets you without fanfare, but its cloisters are special. Norman arches undulate like waves in the ocean, and the chaste double columns are purged of mortality. Together they come close to vindicating pure form. Up a flight of stairs off the south transept, the dormitory is vaulted with a chestnut ceiling, hooped like the inside of a barrel. Along either wall of the long, narrow building, the lancet windows are mullioned. Glass panes between the lead dividers dispense with color, however, and

hard-packed dirt serves for the dormitory floor. A warming room near
the scriptorium warmed frozen fingers, but otherwise the monastery did
without heat. Dominating the forge, the fireplace means business, like the
anvil and whetstone. Windows pierce the walls, and a swallow, flying
through one of them, crosses the room and flies out another. "Sic transit
vita," I say to myself, St. Bernard getting into my head.

Left of the entrance, the dovecote is Norman, a miniature donjon. The
privet hedge smells uriniferous, like *rognons de veau*. Butterflies skim the
hedge top, though the flowers it encloses, white, spiky, pale lavender and
pale shades of green, are bleached of all but the suggestion of color. Set in
closely cropped grass, tapering arborvitae frame the four corners. Not a
pure ideologue, St. Bernard cared for nature, whatever he thought of
men. "One can learn more from things in the woods than in books," reads
a saying of is on the wall in the anteroom. "The trees and the rocks teach
you of things that otherwise you would never understand."

Once they had him to Cluny, Christendom's greatest abbey. Comfort-
able in a valley between rich grazing lands and the wooded slopes of
Macon, it boasted the largest church in the world. Four centuries later,
new St. Peter's, Rome, was about on a par with Cluny. Inspecting its
cloisters, St. Bernard didn't like what he saw. On the sculpted capitals
monkeys, lions, and centaurs cavorted, and he wondered what these creatures, half-beast, half-human, were doing in the house of God. Though he
poured scorn on their "mis-shapen shapeliness and shapely mis-shape-
ness," the mind of his time runs much on the unlikely pairing. In Burgundy's heartland the basilica at Vézelay is named for Mary Magdalene,
once a prostitute, canonized later. Unlike some moderns, she wasn't born
again but mended.

St. Bernard had his mighty opposite, Abbot Suger of St. Denis, the
"royal abbey." Giants in their time, they divide the twelfth century between them. France's kings and queens were buried at St. Denis, until the
Revolution broke open the tombs. Named for a martyred saint who
walked out of Paris with his head in his hands, it remembered the spot
where he ran out of steam and fell dead. On the foundation of the old
church, Suger built the first Gothic cathedral, a *Biblia pauperum* in stone.
The common people, holy "plebs" of God, couldn't read or write but
learned what they had to from this illustrated Bible. St. Bernard called it
"the workshop of Vulcan," artificer of the pagan gods. Suger said, however: "The dull mind rises to truth through that which is material."

Gene, my bad-penny friend, has a nearer way to truth and, looking through the world, sees the bare bones beneath it. Gallic people get credit for this super-rational talent, like the detective Hercule Poirot, ransacking his little gray cells. But old Gaul is divided in two parts, at least, some of its people descending from Proust. Stupefied by a piece of sponge cake, he wondered endlessly how it tasted and smelled. Gene has read Proust— what hasn't he read?—but about the famous madeleine he has nothing to say. Like the armchair detective, he does best when he deals with pure logic.

Logicians in Suger's time, previewing our modern horror of things "Eurocentric," were bullish on the present but filled with contempt for the past. Suger turns this around. We were dwarfs who stood on the shoulders of giants, and the artisans he instructed, fanning out from St. Denis, limned his psychology in pictures. A rose window at Chartres shows the Old Testament supporting the New, and the Evangelists carried by prophets. His great image, the Jesse Tree, has Christ rising from the root of the prophet. Intellectualizers found the image provincial and the ancestors boring. But "the recollection of the past is the promise of the future," a saying of Suger's. Life wasn't orderly nor society a theorem, and the tree that figured both grew up crooked.

A man of God at home in the world of the senses, he lived long and died happy, said his monkish biographer, "because he had enjoyed to live." Meanwhile he wrote poetry, told stories with gusto, and spoke his delight "in the beauty of God's house." He liked to eat and covered his bed "with pretty fabrics in daytime." Out of his atelier came the art of stained glass. When the king went off on the Second Crusade, he served his country as regent. But the cell where he slept on a pallet of straw measured ten feet by fifteen.

Discovering everything in everything else, the old-fashioned intelligence makes my scientific friends smile. Under its scrutiny our world that seems only particles in flux takes on a crazy coherence. Kubrick the moviemaker, throwing up a bone, turns it into a rocket ship, and the medieval sleight-of-hand man does something like this with his sequence of threes. Where moderns see a prime number, he sees the cement of a place we can live in—the Three Wise Men, versions of the three persons of the Trinity; the three hours that Jesus hung on the cross; and the three parts in which earth is divided. Because the African third of the earth was dark, another story for another time, one of the Wise Men is too. There they are at Autun, asleep on a single pallet, too tired to take off their crowns.

From the church's twin towers, you look west to the Morvan hills, Burgundy's granite spine. On the near side of the hills, the oak forests sheltered Druids. Two millennia ago, the city itself was Roman, but only a pair of gates and the skeleton of a theater recall this. Coming in from the east, you drive through Roman arches split by a Corinthian column. Up the road the Middle Ages awaits you. Between this proximate past and the remoter past, the modern world raises its head.

It does this on Rue l'Arquebus, home of Prix Unique, a multistoried supermarket. Fresh out of provisions, I take the elevator out in back by le parking. It has an instrument panel with color-coded buttons and fruity symbols like a slot machine's. No attendant mans the panel, but an old gent in coveralls gets on when I do. He is all grizzled peasant, I am another type, known as type A, and each of us acts as expected. Decisive like the general who didn't reason why, I press the red button, setting off an explosion of bells.

"*Nous sommes dans la choucroute,*" evidently "in the sauerkraut," the old one informs me, showing the whites of his eyes. His thumb like a hammer thumbs another button, and the *1812 Overture* falls silent. Emerging on the second floor, known as the first floor, *le premier étage,* I am blinded by white light, the kind that goes with apparitions. In its spooky glow packaged vegetables, canned fruit, tins of anchovies, and giant rolls of toilet paper come to life like animated cartoons. The intercom, stereophonic and not to be evaded, is playing music of the Grateful Dead. On the radio this morning, France's minister of culture, deploring the tide of neologisms, has had words for the tide of "cacaphony," too. Seeping in from you know where, it threatens "our national fiber."

Not an American import for nothing, the supermarket has gin on the shelves. Clutching my trophy, I head back to the parking lot, this time via the stairs. Electric power, lighting the fluorescent lights in the stairwell, doesn't disclose its modus operandi—no packets of energy moving from *A* to *B*—but cause and effect have their apparent relation. I don't need to take it on faith. Once I cut a live wire with a pair of wire cutters, and I still have the cutters with a hole in them to prove it. Medieval people missed this experience, and their sense of relations is different.

You can skin the cat in more ways than one, however. Men and women of Autun, rooted in the physical world, weren't aware of a "ghostly paradigm" beneath it, but the way things worked got their attention, and the questions they asked were real posers. Notoriously, they asked how many pins you could stick in an angel's bum, or was it bums on the head of a pin? Connoisseurs of number asked about the four rivers of paradise— still there between the apse and choir—wondering why they had to be four. The answer to this one is easy.

Numbers like 3 and 4, potent like magnetism or an electric current, made nature's insubordinate parts toe the line. Four winds blew about the earth, divided in four quarters like the cardinal virtues and the north-south-east-west of the compass. Four Gospels irrigated the world, and the rivers of paradise did the same for the Garden of Eden. The capital at Autun shows how they did it. Tickling old funny bones, four crowned figures carry jugs on their heads and, upending them, turn the dry earth to water.

St. Lazarus still dominates the old town south of the river, but most of its patrons are tourists. The saint who gave it its name, brought back from death by a miracle, is in his grave for good or looks down from an empty heaven on a dwindling communion. When St. Hugh, Cluny's greatest abbot, died at the beginning of the twelfth century, his monastery's daughter-houses, scattered through France and as far away as Poland, numbered nearly 1,200. As the modern age dawned, a new psychology questioned their merit. "Freed from the heavy Gothic night," said Rabelais, "our eyes are opened to the single torch of the sun." Though prone to jokes, he wasn't joking, and his "Gothic" meant the old days, all that wasn't modern.

Soon after his death, Huguenots pillaged the library at Cluny. Later, the Revolution sent what they spared to a great bonfire, like that on the Unter den Linden. Smashing the statues inside and out, soldiers stripped the lead from the roof. Rain rotted the timbers. A merchant from Macon, having bought the monastery for building materials, laid out a street through the center of the nave and blew up the bell towers and chancel. By 1823 only a transept tower remained.

Until the other day, few have regretted this. "Great God, what ugliness!" said Stendhal at Autun, and Pater allowed Vézelay "little or no sense of beauty." Eighteenth-century canons, cleaning house at Chartres, demolished the ancient rood screen separating nave and choir. Bits and pieces survive in the crypt to let tourists like me know what we're missing. Canons at Autun and Vézelay plastered over the sculpted figures on the tympanum and interior portal. At St. Lazarus they broke off the head of Christ and broke up and took down the *Temptation of Eve* that used to adorn the north lintel. In our eclectic age when one man's taste is no better than another's, the Christ of Vézelay is available again, freed from its

plaster coat. Next to Autun's cathedral, Eve, put back together, reaches
once more for her apple. A nude temptress with full breasts and heavy-
lidded eyes, she has Botticelli hair falling to her shoulders. Gislebertus,
stonemason of Autun, did Eve's likeness. Uncharacteristically, he carved
his name beneath the Last Judgment: "Gislebertus made this."

The mark of his hand doesn't vary. Leaves and palm fronds on his capitals resemble a woman's boa, swept-back wings are for angels, for his
devils pointy ears, buckteeth, and electric hair like an Afro. You can tell his
women from his men. Gene the tour guide has a modish piece in the *Nou-
velle Revue Française* comparing the medieval image of woman—he mentions Gislebertus's Eve—with our deconstructed modern image, familiar
from certain paintings by Picasso. Like thesis and antithesis, if I take his
meaning, with synthesis still over the horizon.

In the same *NRF* piece, this ingenious cicerone plays "What-century-
would-you-choose-to-come-back-in?" He wants to come back a hundred
years in the future, when the *isms* that beset us no longer exist and the
world's great age has begun. Joining in the game, I choose to come back in
the High Middle Ages. Not as a peasant, though—as abbot of Vézelay.

Festooning the little town, swags of wisteria grow on the walls of
houses and on freestanding walls. At right angles to the road climbing up
to the church, the highway ends in lush, champaign country, not flat but
broken with hillocks. Yellow and green crops alternate in the fields, a pattern repeated in the two-toned arches that hold up the church roof. As the
light wanes starlings swoop past the open windows of my hotel, their up-
and-down like a roller coaster's. Reaching the top of the rise, they steady,
then plunge.

I lie awake, looking over the rooftops until the midnight sky makes a
cheap Christmas card, sprinkled with a million stars. Dawn is French and
theatrical, a moment of éclaircissement and on me before I know it. In the
early light the squared-off fields stand out sharply, like geometric figures,
but as it strengthens they lose definition. Contours begin to shimmer, and
a painterly world, "pointillist," takes over from the mathematician's. Cock
crow begins at first light. Chiming in with the rooster, king of his dunghill,
coal-black hens cluck in the garden below.

The "white noise" is from the trucks, downshifting as they climb the
little hills and descend. Like an automated camel train, they are carrying
produce from the country to the city and its markets. Old Les Halles,

where early risers broke their fast on onion soup and pigs' feet, is gone with the snows of yesteryear, and the trucks, rolling through the night, are bound for the modern market at Rungis. Nothing in the past to match the metal-on-metal screech of their gears. Silence, the one intolerable thing to moderns, filled every pore of the medieval village. You could smell it a mile away, though.

Some in the village made a fetish of abstention, heroizing crazy anchorites who bruised the body to pleasure soul. Capitals at Vézelay supply the details. St. Benedict, retired to the desert—and why was its stony soil their ideal landscape?—is tempted by the devil, leading on a woman he knew in his youth. But the saint tears off his clothes and throws himself into a thorn bush. "Misogynist," Gene calls this culture of denial, getting part of it right. *Amor vincit omnia,* they told themselves fearfully, seeing how sexual love had power to blot out the life everlasting. Woman was "Satan's lyre," and on one horrific capital she shrinks away as the devil gropes her naked body. Behind him, a jongleur plays a merry tune on his horn. Whatever this means, it means mischief.

But the same twelfth century that licked its lips at fevered sexual images sponsored the cult of the Virgin. You see her at Vézelay on the south portal, heroine of the Christian epic. Not ethereal, either, she is flesh of our flesh. The devil she spurns comes out of nightmare—dwarfish, macrocephalic, with a simian forehead—and is also a figure of fun. The god born of her body is both the Pantocrator and the Son of man, intimate with all the ills flesh is heir to. Even in their greatest age, the Greeks, radiant with health, strength, and poise, have nothing to show us like this.

Though Vézelay's art is didactic, a dread word to moderns, its teaching needs delighting, the two going together like the yolk and white of one shell. The St. Eugenia capital, seventh pillar on the north side, means to instruct us but doesn't mind a bit of tickle. Quick-marched to the altar by her father, the local bigwig, this unwilling saint detoured to a monastery, hiding out for years in monk's costume. Some of Shakespeare's women dress up like men, triggering the happy ending where you have to suspend disbelief, and Vézelay wasn't above it. Accused of rape by a lustful woman—she hadn't heard that appearances deceive us—Eugenia bares her breasts at the trial. This astounds and persuades the trial judge, who else but her father. You remember his eyes as he looks around, stage left, for the exit. Devotees of last things find the story beside the point, and St. Bernard will have asked them about it.

On Vézelay's northern slope, he preached the Second Crusade and Richard the Lion Hearted mustered his army. Above the plumes and banners, St. Mary Magdalene looked out from the height of heaven. Grapes, a Sargasso Sea of them, flow down from her basilica, behind it the blue Morvan hills. A single tower where symmetry wants a pair of towers rises over the west front, to its rear the long roof, topped by dome and finial. The narthex, a huge vestibule, admits you to the nave. When the doors are open, you sight along an avenue of light, lined by white-and-brown columns. Or the nave is a country road lined by plane trees, and patches of bark have peeled off the trunks of the trees.

The Christian temple is full of surprises, giving entrée to the centaur who tutored Achilles and Ganymede in the claws of the eagle. Each brings the ancient past into the present, and that is lucky, like the Fortunate Fall. But this ecumenical world doesn't cancel distinction. Over the central door of the narthex, earth's citizens show off their difference, some turbaned like Othello's Turk, others with dogs' heads or huge ears like the vans of a windmill. "Vertically challenged," a pigmy needs a ladder to get up on his horse. Modern men and women, agnostics in religion but true believers in their politics, say that all are equal, omitting the qualifier, "in the sight of God." Without it, the saying is foolish, and the stone tableau only a freak show.

Huffing and puffing, I walk up the nave toward the apse and its radiating chapels, dragging my old man's body with me. I am a medieval pilgrim, paying my respects to some "holy blissful martyr," at the same time a modern man en route to my death. This trip to the past had pleasure for its end, though, and I don't mean to be gloomy. Like the bishop-princes of Sens, who indented the dining table to make room for their bellies, the abbot and friends of his ate well at Vézelay: crayfish, frogs, boar and venison, fairy-ring mushrooms, fat snails. Gorging on cheeses, they favored creamy Chaource and powerful-smelling Epoisses, washed down with the wine of the country. Truth to tell, it has its debit side, stimulating venery. In the old days, however, the celibate life was only a goal they strove for. If their reach exceeded their grasp, that wasn't the end of the world.

Keeping flocks and tilling the soil were the two "paps" of France, said the great duke Sully. He was friends with Henry IV, the same who thought Paris worth a Mass, and what he said four hundred years ago seems on target to me, motoring back in time though the country. As Paris and environs disappear in the rearview mirror, the modern world and its veneering burn off like morning dew. South of Évreux, shocks of wheat and cylinders of hay, one to feed the farmer, the other his flocks, stand on end in the yellowing fields. Some are planted in sunflowers, blazing like Van Gogh's. Protected from the motorcar by strands of wire, white cattle, the famous Charolais, are beefing themselves up for the table. Men have worked these fields forever, and they are broken, like all civilized places, to the hand.

Marching with the N-10, pollarded trees cut nature down to size. But no fence or housewall lacks its obligatory creeper. The creepers creep, however, not asserting themselves like trees in California, and nature and man have worked out an entente cordiale. Public spirit hasn't caught on here. Litter blows along the highway, and from the windows of cars, more of it, a jet stream, keeps coming. No "Adopt a Highway" signs on French highways. I don't say that's wholly a good.

My route south carries on to Bordeaux, but I get off at the exit for Chartres. East of town, the roadside cafe, a convenient pit stop, invites travelers to choose among partridge, pheasant, hare, and trout from the River Eure. This takes thought and turns out to be worth it. Men, women, and dogs share most of the tables. Discouraging ooh-la-las, the women wear shapeless frocks made for Queen Elizabeth. One, lisping like a devotee, shares her lunch with a squeaky lapdog. Diners, their elbows boring holes in the table, drag deep on Gauloises, ignoring the *défense de fumer* signs. Pear shapes predominate, and bottoms envelop the plastic chairs they sit on. After forty, Frenchmen think, a man has the right to let down his belly. Only once have I seen a jogger.

Windmills, creaking like castle doors in old horror movies, stand about the Beauce Plain on the outskirts of Chartres. Tall above the wheat fields, the cathedral called for Our Lady shows its profile from a distance and, once seen, isn't ever forgotten. Pilgrims trekking south thought they saw the towers of the New Jerusalem. Twin spires thrust at heaven, not a Norman thing to do, but these are twins with a difference, like the stone Gemini carved on archivolts beside the church doors. The north tower is the new one, finished four hundred years ago. Its stonework, like lace stitched with hammer and chisel, is all about joie de vivre. On your right as you face it, the old spire, less flamboyant, dares more. Sprung from a square tower, the steeple makes an octagon, smooth as a skating rink and narrowing as it goes up. Pointed gables, thrusting it up, hide the transition, and you feel that what you see is what you get. Rising toward heaven, it rises from earth, a limitation and the source of its power.

As I enter the nave, Gene the tour guide is at it, giving "jam to the pigs," *la confiture aux cochons*. He says that quarries at Berchères, five miles away, furnished the ceiling stone. A miracle that they got it up there, and he points toward the great blocks under the roof, "115 feet over our heads." He has a lot to say about the Holy Camisole, this church's most celebrated relic. Mary, Christ's mother, wore it next to her body at the Annunciation, or maybe at the Nativity, and its travels from Palestine to medieval France make a story he likes to embroider.

All the natural world comes crowding in at Chartres, fish and birds on the "vuissoirs" surrounding the arches, on the rood screen the lion St. James says we are yoked to, and the serpent, engineer of our fall. May, the merry month, his winter hat discarded, carries a hawk on his wrist. July is for reaping, and a bas-relief peasant mows down the wheat with his scythe. Winter waits around the corner, and February finds him frozen with cold, warming his feet by the fire. He does this on the north porch, north for winter darkness and the dark age before our new dispensation.

In last things Chartres is simple, an affront to Gene's little gray cells, but where the waters are limpid he roils them. His model artist, setting up a strawman, fakes out the reader. Or he himself is fooled, and the reader, deconstructing him, unpacks his hidden intention. This is what happens in the well-known essay Gene's reputation depends on, "Sophocles contre Lui-Même," proving that Oedipus suffered from an Oedipus complex. He really meant to kill his father and marry his mother, but the author didn't know that.

Gift shops around the church set out copies of the Christmas crib and the shepherds in their fields by night. Jews wearing their funny hats stand for the old law, and turn up on the west portal. The ox and ass come from the rood screen. Medieval people thought the Old Testament forecast the birth of Christ, "recognized in the midst of animals," so invented this ensemble for their nativities. Infinitely touching, it has its practical side. You had to have the ass to carry Mary to Bethlehem, the ox coming along in order that Joseph could sell it. That was how he paid for the journey. Justifying all that "copia," stone- and glass-workers supposed we came to God through our senses. They wanted the whole story and a sense of air about it. At Chartres two midwives appear on Christmas day. Sometimes you see them washing the child in a tub.

Hierarchies organized the world outside the church, but the low man on the pole equaled the highest in the sight of God. On the royal portal Aristotle, a writing desk on his knees, pen at the ready above it, bows his massive head in thought. Beside him a shepherd raises the panpipes, ready to play. The mason has bored out the pupils of his eyes, and he looks on vacancy or perhaps is witless. But like the master of those who know, he fills a place.

When I lived in Paris in the sixties, I read St. Augustine on the two cities, one God's, the other the world's. The Bishop of Hippo runs on, to say the least, and his eye, more than mine, is on the world over yonder. But his two cities partake of each other, and the one in heaven has its sympathizers on earth. "Sojourners," he calls them, biding their time until the resurrection. This bit in the meantime gets my attention. Even the bishop, a great salvationist, said he wanted to be saved, "but not yet."

While I read I smoked cigarettes, one after the other, on the table beside me a glass of oily liqueur. All these years later, if I open *The City of God* I smell the acrid smell of Gauloises, mingled with Marc de Bourgogne. Weekends with my son I trooped around to old churches like St. Germain des Près, the oldest of all, on the Left Bank close to the river. It might have been unexceptional except for its spire, cone-shaped like the hat Jews wear in old paintings. Looking at it, your eye travels up, not all the way to heaven, though, and this church sanctifies the mundane.

Descartes, a philosopher who cared about the forest more than the trees, is buried in the south chancel. He took his cue from early icon smashers, but where they broke things, bad enough, he looked through them. Getting rid of flesh and blood, he turned Euclid's spatial figures into algebraic equations. Some countrymen of his were "Cartesian" long before the word was coined, and some are still with us today. Pairs of Romanesque arches support the square tower of St. Germain des Près. Four pairs in all, a sacred number, they keep the church from flying apart. In my next life I want to live within sight of the spire.

My son, who thought an altar was where you sacrificed beasts, liked the gorier side of old churches. St. Bartholomew, flayed alive, appeared in bronze or marble holding up his own skin, and St. Lawrence the griddle he burned on. When we first encountered them, I was no older than my son is today. Best was headless St. Denis, decapitated but cradling his head in his hands, gingerly, befitting a relic. His likeness survives in the church Abbot Suger built, still standing in a northern suburb of Paris. On a Sunday morning, wanting to see how time has been treating it, I make the journey again.

The northern suburbs used to be Communist and working-class French, but the people riding the Metro are mostly Third World, black African, West Indian, Oriental, and Arab. Loafing and chaffering around the cathedral, the men wear jalabas, and a street market like a souk covers several square blocks. Gaudy canvas awnings shade the booths from the sun but keep the smell of skewered lamb and the sweat of its customers from wafting away on the breeze. Though modern St. Denis has come down in the world, Sunday Mass is packed. Many are suited up in their best, some devout, others passing the time. No dogheaded worshipers, like the ones old travelers saw in the East, but otherwise this congregation evokes the one in Vézelay's narthex. Both are catholic, not the sect, the amalgam. Full of good hope, appropriate to Sundays, I imagine my favorite century staging a comeback on the scruffy outskirts of the city.

Decorating the arch supports around the doors of the church, the seasons of the year and signs of the Zodiac tell of time passing and returning on itself. The middle door, embossed metal, does the Last Judgment, reprobate and elect, angels and elders of the Apocalypse, demons dragging in their prey. Above this *omnium gatherum* the Son of God holds out his hands. Nothing human was alien to him, and the spectrum of humanity covered the whole of creation. Sentimental he isn't, though, and granting mercy to some, he withholds it from others. But his discrimination, aloof from race, creed, and color, is moral.

Jews keep their heads down in this quarter of Paris. Unexpectedly, though, I come across them in St. Denis. Suger himself supervised its construction, dictating themes and stories, and in a stained-glass window Christ crowns the church with one hand, unveiling the synagogue with the other. Old and new law made a pair like the twins in the Zodiac, not identical, only fraternal. At least it was like that when Suger built his cathedral. Tolerant he could hardly be, not in the Age of Faith. He was provident, however, the next best thing, and Jewish heroes, twenty of them, appear on his portals. You know them by their hats, conical or shaped like a melon.

At just this time an Italian banking family gave the papacy a Jewish pope. St. Bernard, speaking for the establishment, called him an antipope, and historians still follow his lead. A power struggle with the establishment turned out badly, and he isn't much remembered today. But that is only because the other side won.

5

The Scotsman's Return from Abroad

Margot Fonteyn was dancing at Covent Garden the year I lived in London. When they weren't doing ballet they were doing opera, and I cut my teeth on Verdi, the "Anvil Chorus" in *Il Trovatore*. It made my heart leap when I was young. Also that year I discovered Mozart. Crossing the river, I paid a shilling to hear him at the Festival Hall. If I waited until the last moment, I could see a play of Shakespeare's for sixpence. Thinking about that time, my annus mirabilis, I smell coal smoke on the air, mingling with the smell of Woodbines, a cheap cigarette.

Before leaving the States I had got married, too young, I realized later, but many in those days did as I did. After the incandescent time it was all "You said," "No, it was you who said that," and I cringed for the man I'd turned into. Sad how the perfect thing always bids us adieu, youth and its expectations, romantic love, not least the "beautiful physique" that goes with it. But time, though intolerant of all that, as Auden's poem tells us, has a soft spot for writers. Unlike athletes, whose professional life is finished when their legs go or their Ted Williams vision gives way to bifocals, they have a hole card. This is their writing, and if they stick to it, it gets better as their body gets worse.

Young writers look inward, at their navel. If you believe them, the world began today. Age, perhaps understandably, disputes that. But if wisdom comes with it, the yield is a skimpy one, like 2 percent on your investment. There is this to say for getting older, though—it forces you to realize that you aren't one of a kind. Before you came crying hither, others acted out your scene, smarted with the same fears, quickened with the same hopes. Knowing that induces humility, something I hadn't been big on.

Like most Americans, I set my face toward the future. What happened in the past, of interest to antiquarians and the DAR, wasn't of interest to me. But age is a great mixer-upper, running together yesterday and today. As the past turned into the present, "old unhappy far-off things and battles long ago" became signposts on my road, pointing me back to the beginning.

I never knew my grandfather Russell, stern patriarch of my father's family and dead not long after I was born. The stock market crash wiped out his business and cost the family their place on East Hampton. But copybooks he'd made, inflected with "the strong Scots accent of the mind," were still there in the attic for a small boy to wonder at. In a precise, even elegant hand, he wrote out lesson plans in civics and geography for his nine children. He made them memorize the Bill of Rights, America's rivers and mountains, the capitals of our forty-eight states, all the presidents down to FDR.

Grandfather died embittered, "turning his face to the wall," my mother said. I'd like to redeem his misery, and so gratify my newfound affection for the ancestors. Not by fiddling the truth, of course, as when we hear that the good end happily, the bad unhappily. Gresham's law holds for life as much as economics, and the not-so-good drives out the good. But in the ideal country where every writer lives part-time, a man's reach is honored, never mind that his grasp always falls short.

I am the Scot I write about, but my title is secondhand and comes from the poem by Robert Louis Stevenson. Living much abroad, at the end of his life in romantic Samoa, he grew up in Edinburgh near Charlotte Square. Coolly classical buildings stand around the square, the work of Robert Adam. Stevenson's poem breathes a different spirit, though, and its comic hero is a music-hall Scot. Gargling his English, he swallows some letters, elongating others. "Noo," he says, when they ask him for money. Borrowers and lenders alike come to ruin, "an' they themsel's ken it weel."

But Jekyll needs Hyde, and the closefisted man has a wild streak. Returning to Scotland from "far outlandish pairts," he greets the hills of home, birches in the Highlands, the bonny kirks—

> But maistly thee, the bluid o' Scots
> The king o' drinks, as I conceive it,
> Talisker, Isla, or Glenlivet!

Single malt liquor is this king he swears by, and like poetry it sends him
stumbling through the dawn, chanting lays of love and old war cries. My
elegant walking stick, bought in the Highlands but made in Taiwan, has a
hollowed-out compartment under the crook where you can keep a dram,
if so minded. I haven't cared to do this, feeling about Scotch whiskey the
way William Faulkner did. "As between Scotch and nothing, I'll take
Scotch," he said.

But in the Fraser country west of Inverness, I tip my hat to all things
Caledonian. "Scots wham Bruce has aften led" lived in the glens and braes.
A piece of luck if their descendants are standing beside you when you have
to stand up and be counted. Sandy Arbuthnot is one of them. His mother
called him Alasdair, but John Buchan's intrepid Sandy gave him his nickname. Buchan's character backed up the hero in those long-ago novels that
didn't think twice about the world beyond the Channel. "Bit of a Dago,
isn't he?" Sandy inquires, in *The Three Hostages*. "Not at all," Hannay tells
him. "Family been here for centuries. Ancestor rode with Prince Rupert."

My friend has a guardsman's mustache but the abstracted air of a don.
"Rusticated" from St. Andrews for disrupting a university lecture, he
drifted down to London and scribbled lies for the *Daily Mail*. "But truth
will always out," and when it got him the sack, he crofted for two years in
the Orkneys, renting a boggy acre from the laird. Now he runs Speyside
Heather in the Grampians near Dalwhinnie. Not far from his plant nursery is Prince Charlie's Cave, hiding place of the Young Pretender after the
defeat at Culloden.

A yen for the bagpipes threw us together in the Outer Hebrides, four
hours at sea off the west coast of Scotland. Hunting German subs in the
Second World War, the Royal Navy once sailed out of Stornaway, but these
days its harbor sleeps in the sun. I take the car ferry from Ullapool, the
last stop on the mainland before the road, turning north, peters out in
empty space. More sheep live on the land than people, posing a problem.
The locals have resolved it, and a splash of paint on the rump distinguishes
meum and *tuum*. Buttercups and daisies brighten the highway, and on the
hills the heather gathers the light. When Highland clans went to war, they
"took to the heather." It gets along well with the soil it springs from,
the two together suggesting the subtle cloth women weave on Lewis and
Harris. Still good as new, the tweed jacket I bought in London when
young is the work of their fingers, and like an old salmon has followed me
upstream to its source.

Stowing my car, I climb up to the aft deck for a last look at the water-front as we cast off. A scurf of garbage floats on the swell, and seagulls, swooping over it, shriek like klaxons on the boulevards in Paris. The wind rising, I duck into the lounge, wall to wall with tobacco smoke and drunk, exuberant young men. They are the only playboys of the western world and, having bested Dingwall in the soccer finals at Inverness, are going back to the Hebrides and home.

Getting in the night before me, Sandy comes by plane from Fort George on the Moray Firth. Inland from the firth and this side of the River Spey is his plant nursery, stocked with Highland plants and flowers and packets of wild heather seed. Seethe heather in boiling water and its fumes are strong against "megrim," Sandy says. Partly a herbalist, he is also a crank.

In his early days a Communist, he fell from favor when he joined the Scottish Nationalist Party. These enthusiastic patriots meant to liberate Scotland from the English "yoke" but weren't keen on exchanging West-minster for Moscow. An independent spirit didn't charm them in the SNP either, and they expelled Mr. Facing-Both-Ways. Sandy today is a party of one. Any party that would have him isn't a party he wants to belong to.

The only town on the Isle of Lewis with a bespoke tailor, supermar-ket, and Established Church of Scotland, Stornaway is civilization's thin red line. Its stucco houses are gray, though, not a color but its absence, and the lace curtains at the windows have given up the ghost. Ascending from the pier, the main drag through town hangs a left past three pubs and a dingy store front, local home of the Nats, short for the Nationalist Party. Beyond the roundabout is the Caberfeidh Hotel, Gaelic and proud of it. The polished bar simulates a Viking longship, fine china and old silver clut-ter the public rooms, and dead animal heads look down from the walls.

We sit in the TV room while the piper fingers his chanter, warming up with "Amazing Grace." Not marching us to war, he plays the small Irish pipes, suitable for hymns and slow strathspeys. Our entertainment is the ceilidh, Gaelic for concert. Last in a series of musical evenings, this one takes place on Saturday, a prelude to silence like the road out of Ullapool. Mostly in the islands people keep mum on Sunday, unless at church, once in the a.m., again before dusk. Church means the Free Church, whose parishioners are known as Wee Frees. When it split away from the estab-lished church in the 1840s, it refined the liturgy according to John Knox, boiling off the last bits of sweetness.

For a week in late summer, pipers in Stornaway "cut" one another, asking the vote of their peers. The most famous of them, known from John o' Groats to Hadrian's Wall, are almost as famous as rock stars. Set to music, "old unhappy far-off things" bring some in the crowd down to tears. Almost five hundred years ago, English at Flodden Field massacred the Scots chivalry, led by their King James IV. "The Flowers of the Forest," a grand lament, faintly dissonant, harks back to this battle. "I've heard them lilting at our ewe-milking," it tells of the lasses whose men won't come back. But its heart remembers the dead, fallen flowers. "Sae bon-ny was their blooming, their scent the air per-fum-ing, But now they are wither'd and a'wede a-way."

In the west and north of Scotland, many speak the old tongue, an enduring legacy of "the Forty-Five." When Scots bid for independence in 1745, English went on a killing spree in the Highlands. Rooting out Scottish customs, they targeted the language, and in the schools only English was spoken. But Gaelic survived, going underground, and here in Stornaway the air is full of aspirants, slurry like chuckling.

The piper wears the *breacan,* parti-colored cloth, a red flag in the eyes of John Bull. After Culloden, you broke the law if you went kilted, and they put you on a ship to Australia. *Pibroch* is their word for the art of playing the pipes. What they play, variations on a theme, is chiefly martial. For the soldier's music—reveille or the call to arms—they use the Great Northern pipes, loud enough to wake the dead. The piper's office passed from father to son, like the office of the bards who sang the epic poems of the Highlands. Just behind the chief when "the front o' battle loured," he thrummed the three bass pipes called the drones. A "rant of thunder," says the old poem, describing this wild music. It stiffened the sinews, and fighting men, hearing it, stepped over their dead and kept coming.

In the dining room off the bar, we choose from sea scallops, freshwater fish (trout and salmon tonight), also lamb and beef, homegrown and -slaughtered. "He that shall complain of his fare in the Hebrides has improved his delicacy more than his manhood." Dr. Johnson said so in *A Journey to the Western Islands,* and the menu leads off with his praise. Warmed by the wine, Sandy journeys back in time, recalling the House of Stuart, Scottish kings who won the throne in England, then threw it away. Charles Edward Stuart, grandson of the last king, hoped to regain the throne. He was the Young Pretender, and in the Forty-Five the Highland clans—not all of them, mostly those who couldn't resist a lost cause—rose with him. The waiter, filling our wine glasses, fills the glasses beside them with water. "To Bonnie Prince Charlie," says Sandy, and passes one glass above the other. "The king over the water."

I am bound for the Lowlands and my plane out of Scotland, Sandy for the Highlands and his plant nursery on Speyside. Twice a year he takes the train from Dalwhinnie to Glasgow, where he and his supplier sit down with the inventory between them. We are halfway there already, and having placed a phone call, he makes up his mind to go with me. The road from Lewis to Harris, one island with two place names, isn't the same as the M-1 out of London. Megaliths at Callanish tell of people on the land, but they have gone away ages since. A dozen gray elders stand in a circle, outside it more standing stones pointing northward. In the center of the circle, a chambered tomb forms the hub of this desolate wheel. Tiny, it suggests a king's son, dead in his nonage.

In the silence we move noisily, and cattle grids, draining the narrow road, clank when our car passes above them. Crofts, bits of arable land, dot the fells, plums in their pudding. Faced with stucco or local stone, the crofters' cottages look like pieces in a board game. Hugging the soil, they merge with it, and from a distance are only bumps on the board. Some, agglutinating, turn into communities. At Barvas on the coast, cottars, peasant farmers, are bringing in the sheaves, discharging their Protestant function. I wave a hand in greeting, but they don't wave back.

Near Arnol we pass a "Black House," its long narrow rectangle topped with green sod. Ropes and large stones secure this carpet on the ceiling, and a hole lets out smoke from the fire. "Leodhasach," early natives, thought peat smoke did wonders for the roofs of their houses, and dispensing with a chimney, let it filter through the thatch. Underneath the roof, men and cattle stall together, only a thin partition between them. Like a social worker, I sympathize with the plight of these poor folk. Sandy, his pursed mouth telling me to forget it, says they weren't poor in Scotland, not that they knew, but marched to a different drummer than we do.

Peat smoke, wrinkling our noses, leaves a sweetish telltale on the spongy air. Where the peat used to be, the land gurgles and sucks like a sink full of dishes. But the bog is alive, friendly to bog myrtle, yellow bog asphodel, and cushions of grayish-white sphagnum moss. One variety makes a poultice, sovereign for tired limbs. Sandy, having said farewell to political action, has turned to homeopathy, which is a distinction without a difference.

Telephone poles strung with wire divide up the emptiness, and wire fencing hopes to keep the sheep off the road. Ruminating, they move slowly, their chewing deceptively like thought. Border collies, black and white with a grin full of teeth, move them along. Dun Carloway, a north-facing tower off the A-858, remembers the Iron Age. When raiders came by sea, men and animals piled into this stone *broch,* their home away from home until the storm blew over. Parts of the double wall, rising thirty feet, still test the wind off the water. No trees break its fury, all but a few having disappeared with the Norse raider, Magnus Barelegs. Scorching the earth, he left Lewis as bare as his shanks.

But Harris, thick with Scotch pine, has a profile, its brawny hills cupped by lochs that wander inland from the Sound of Shiant. Thistles, small pink flowers atop a tall spiky stem, poke up in the hummocky fields. "Monument o' a' they were" in Scotland, "the thistle rises and forever will," says their dialect poet Hugh MacDiarmid. On a darker day, however, he said how "thwarts o' weather o' *grun* [ground] or man or 'ither foes" conspired to limit its freedom. The limitation made it more sweet.

Two sea lochs meet at Tarbert, where the ferry for Skye brings us across the water to the village of Uig. Bonnie Prince Charlie traveled this way, fleeing the wreck of his hopes at Culloden. English spread their net by land and sea and would have snared him, but for a lass of Skye. She was Flora MacDonald, who dressed the prince as her maid and brought him off by boat, stage one on his journey into legend. Disaster in Scotland, an ill wind, blew good to some. Scots with a love of learning, going out on the roads, civilized "far outlandish pairts," and a women's college in the American South is named for the heroine of the Forty-Five.

Portree is the "King's Port," recalling a royal visit when Scotland still had its king, and our modern hotel annexes the past in its present. In the old inn it hitches on to, Flora MacDonald said her goodbyes to Prince Charlie. After this, taken by the English, she went into captivity. He escaped to the Continent, first to France, then to Rome, where he rented a palace on the Square of the Holy Apostles. Frescobaldi played the organ in the church across the square. Time passed, and the Young Pretender grew old and took to drink. Once a darling of the ladies, he lost the power to charm them. Sometimes a visitor or member of his retinue sang a Jacobite favorite like "Lochaber no more," and he wept. He lived on for forty years but never spoke his thanks to the woman who saved him and never came back to Scotland.

The road threads high hills, purple against a sky that settles earthward like wet canvas. Squared off at the top, MacLeod's Table is one of the hills. Chiefs of Clan MacLeod ruled from Dunvegan Castle, where the road ends at the sea loch. The castle, sitting up in the air the better to overawe us, bristles with gun ports and crenelated towers. Below is the Sea of the Hebrides, and in summer "magic casements" open on the foam. Inside, however, Victorian pomp inundates the past, bringing in a tide of bric-a-brac. Portraits of the stately ancestors take up the available wall space. The old men on the walls, their bulging eyes like poached eggs, imitate C. Aubrey Smith, crusty colonel of the Bengal Lancers in movies I saw when a boy. Clan chiefs in name only, they survive into modern times as landlords.

Gardens, stimulating the senses like Skye's Talisker whiskey, surround the castle walls on the land side. Above the cotoneaster, orange berries that might be elfin lanterns hang from mountain ash. Potentilla, coming up to our belt buckles, explodes in showers of gold, and the rhododendrons are as big as the trees. Though Skye is a northern outpost, the Gulf Stream is a girdle insulating the island, and its jagged peaks are blurred with softness. Is not this an emblem of Scotland the brave? Sandy wants to know. "A rock above the water," it warms itself with the blood of its heroes. When magpies chattered "elsewhere"—he means to the south of us, where the Sassenach live—great poets sang in Scotland. One of them wrote how the fear of death confounded him, *"Timor mortis conturbat me,"* but he wasn't afraid, only pious.

I think he is whitewashing the past, and say so. True, he tells me, old chiefs in the Highlands lifted their neighbors' cattle and made a religion of blood feuds. But they poured French wine at table, loved women well, wore lace at their wrists, and spoke Latin.

Sandstone and limestone flank the road going south, and mist shrouds the hills above it. White water, whipped by broken scree, makes a glamorous curtain standing out from the hills. Boswell in his *Tour to the Hebrides* called them mountains. Pointing to one, he remarked on its great size, but Johnson saw "no more than a considerable protuberance." On our left hand, the high ground shelves away to Loch Ness, another bone of contention. Four hundred million years ago it thrust up its waters, deeper,

says Sandy, than much of the North Sea. Free for the taking at the tourist
stop outside Invergarry, the colored brochure estimates the probabilities
of a Loch Ness monster, rating them better than even. Tourists are stocking up on presents in the gift shop, coin purses like sporrans, toy bagpipes,
tins of shortbread. Colored slides show ruined castles, and stenciled tea
towels a likeness of the Fair Maid of Perth. Silver-plated bar pins resemble the whinger, a short sword favored by Highland swordsmen. Inserting
a windup key, the salesgirl gives it a twist, and the plastic "Nessie" hums
"Flower of Scotland."

   "Charlie's m' darlin,'" Sandy says savagely, putting on his broadest burr.
"Will ye noo come back again?" Smiling uneasily, the salegirl looks away,
and for a moment it seems he means to sweep the counter bare. Slowly,
however, his hands fall to his side. "A's no' gold that glitters," and do I
know MacDiarmid's lines for Bonnie Prince Charlie? The fire he kindled
in our "lyart" hills, not a living flame, turned out a will-o-the-wisp in the
end. Throwing a baleful glance at the salesgirl, the ex-member of the SNP
addresses the roomful of tourists. "He keeps his meed o' fame, though,
more than can be said for Scotland."

   On the Road to the Isles, tawny-colored Highland cattle that might be
ancient mastodons clump together against the sudden cloudburst. Under
the curled horns, shaggy, matted hair fringes their eyes like a valance.
Evergreen forests border the loch, and pine dusts the hills, making room
in the upper glens for oak and aspen. Streams, jumped by old stone
bridges, crisscross the bottom land. In ground shaded by oak trees, you
find the yellow pimpernel. Sandy, growing up, knew it as *seanhair Mhuire,*
the gentle grass of Mary. "Quaking aspen" supplied the wood for the cross
that stood on Calvary, and its quaking means to signal repentance.

   Nature in West Scotland takes its cue from Romantic paintings that go
heavy on impasto. When the rain stops, a ray of light shoots out of the
clouds and, slanting across the hillside, gilds the rocky beach beside the
loch. "Scotch mist," dropping from heaven, falls on guilty mortals like
mercy's gentle rain. In the somber cleft at Glen Coe, once a killing
ground, they need it. Three centuries ago the English had a Glorious Revolution, deposing their Stuart king. Highland Scots bore only grudging witness to the new king, Dutch William, and he made them pay. Singling out
the MacDonalds of Glen Coe, he said "all must be slaughtered," all under
seventy, including the "cubs" of the clan chief. An unsuspecting host, he

brought the king's soldiers into his house, but in the wee hours of a win-ter's night, they rose up and did as instructed.

South of Ben Nevis, the road crosses the Moor of Rannoch, bounded by dark hills. Lonely country, it searches a man, alone with himself and his God. Scots, tempered, sometimes twisted, are men for the final exigent. In the world east of Suez and south of the Sahara, they know this. Rose-bay willow-herb as tall as sheaves of wheat grows on the verges of the road, but the fields don't invite cultivation. Like Flanders fields, where the poison gas still seems to swirl in pockets, they haven't shaken off the tor-por of history. Hangings, imprisonment, and transportation overseas fol-lowed the fall of Prince Charlie. Winter did its part, thinning out the glens, and many starved to death or died from exposure. Highland chiefs who rebelled died on the block or gallows.

The Forty-Five was still a raw wound when England, wanting an em-pire, recruited Highlands regiments to build it. Sending Scots soldiers to the ends of the earth had its uses, and Pitt, the prime minister, said equably that "not many of them would return." In the nineteenth century, life put down fresh roots, but the Highland Clearances, torching homesteads and whole villages, destroyed them. Traveling Scotland by car in the last century, the poet Edwin Muir saw a country emptied of history. Its people and spirit, art, intellect, character too, all were lost. Much of Scotland's history seems a gloss on this doleful verdict. But I wonder. Muir was profoundly a pes-simist, and my more sanguine temperament inclines me to a less gloomy view. Considering that all of us go down in the end, perhaps the only thing that matters is how we carry ourselves in the meantime. Sandy has an anec-dote that tells of a young Highlander who came back alive from the rout at Culloden. Picking up the fallen flag, he wrapped it round his body and bore it safely from the field. Ever after he was known as Donuil na Braiteach, Donald of the Colors.

Glasgow in its history almost to the present is a byword for bad times, that is, the Industrial Revolution and its horrors. But some elegance, even old elegance, redeems it. Before Robert the Bruce smote the English at Ban-nockburn, the twin towers of St. Mungo looked south to the Clyde. On either side of the nave its three arcades still aim at heaven, one rising on top of the next. John Knox, meaning to destroy St. Mungo, pulled down its statues, but men of the city's trade guilds interrupted the work of reform. Good Scots and thrifty, they elected to preserve the past in the present.

While Sandy tends to his heather seeds, I re-create the old quarter called Bell o' the Brae. Once the bell tower atop the rise or brae rang in triumph for Wallace when he took back Glasgow for Scotland. Though the past lies hidden under modern steel and concrete, hereabouts he ran up his battle flag, emblazoned with the cross of St. Andrew. Robert Adam, master of proportions, not omitting grace notes, left his mark on the eighteenth-century city. Walking west along George Street, I look for his domed Trades House, built for business but not altogether. The square takes its name from English George III, but I color it green, not red. The Celtic city was Glas Cau, the Green Place, and the modern city, where nature has made a comeback, recalls this. Cooling down on my park bench, I deplore the exhaust fumes and appreciate the leafy trees. Not taking umbrage, they give it.

East of George Square, the Italian Renaissance palazzo houses the city fathers, lovers in secret of the warm south.

Glasgow, known as the cultural capital of Europe, has other surprises and would like to detain us. But fifty miles away in Edinburgh, the International Festival is going full tilt. For both of us, the Tattoo is the festival's reason for being, and Sandy having managed a pair of tickets, we board the train for "Auld Reekie." *Auld* gives no trouble, Edinburgh going back a way, but *Reekie* makes me pause. Because it stank, Sandy says. This embarrassed Boswell. Walking the streets with Johnson, he couldn't prevent his friend from "being assailed by the evening effluvia," evening being the time when the locals threw their slops out the window. Progress isn't always a term of reproach, and as we climb the stairs from Waverley Station attendants with mop and wash pail are sloshing the stair treads and putting a shine on the handrails.

Edinburgh divides into New Town on the north and on the south the original city. A splendid stage for the world's work, Princes Street borders the first, separating it from the second. Hotels and art galleries, banks, gentlemen's clubs, and swank clothiers like Burberry's come down to the footlights. Below in the pit, public gardens, blooming madly, expel the last whiff of Auld Reekie. Making common cause, the white rose recalls the Jacobites, and the pansy "freaked with jet" the black cockade the English wore at Culloden. When I walked the battlefield on a day trip from Inverness, black and white flags showed me which army to cheer for.

Visible through the gardens, the Royal Mile, going west, climbs up to Edinburgh's Castle, descending the other way to the Old Burial Ground at the foot of Calton Hill. At the top of the map is New Town, new as in New College, Oxford—that is, old. The well-to-do have their houses, mainly Georgian, in this quarter, still infiltrated by country. Hills like yellow bolsters render to nature but don't ask you to notice. New Town improves on the natural world, and even its streetlamps are artful. In Charlotte Square the inverted glass globes balance on a slender standard, supported at right angles by a bishop's hooked crozier. The black cap on top of the globes is a French sailor's cap with a pompon.

New Town, despite its whimsies, is serious, coming out of the Enlightenment. But the name belies itself, if you will accept the impeachment from an admirer of Pope, Johnson, and Swift. Progress is the shrine the eighteenth century worshiped at, and it had little brief for things past. David Hume, one of its luminaries and a famous resident of New Town, never mentions the Declaration of Arbroath in his *History of Scotland*. Scotland's declaration of independence, it still shakes the heart seven hundred years after it was written. Hume thought that subsequent progress left it dated.

Lord Kames, the Enlightenment's most eminent jurist and another of those Scots who is praised for creating the modern world, believed that natural law informed all human society. He added a codicil, however. Kames saw natural law as mutable, not fixed. "It must vary," he said, "with the nature of man, and consequently refine gradually as human nature refines." That is, we get better and better.

On Queen Street close to Charlotte Square, the Royal Museum is rich in Scotland's antiquities. Mary, Queen of Scots, is the museum's hottest ticket. Thronging the exhibition rooms, crowds of locals and tourists hope to touch the hem of her greatness. Did she really sip wine from the silver-gilt drinking bowl, simple witness to a bygone age? Around the foot the inscription runs: "Money lost little lost, honor lost much lost, heart lost all lost."

Our hotel room on Leith Street above Princes Street looks out on Calton Hill. We have to climb it but not on an empty stomach, and adjourning to the Duke's Tavern over the way, we call for Scotch ale and the menu. Today's specialty is haggis, known to Robert Burns as "the great chieftain o' the pudden race." Chopped in bits, it makes a meal in itself, like spaghetti Bolognese minus the spaghetti. Turnips called swedes and

skinned tatties, or potatoes, garnish the sides of the platter. First you have
to have a sheep, though. Once in Rome, wanting more canneloni, I bought
a do-it-yourself kit from the waiter who served me. "Take a six-foot marble table," my recipe began. Haggis, not a simple matter, is like that.

Abstracting the sheep's stomach bag, you disengage heart, lungs, and
liver, mince and mix with oats, onions, suet, and the juice of a lemon. Sea-
soned for taste, these ingredients go back in the bag. Boil for three hours,
pricking with a needle when the bag starts to swell—a darning needle,
the books specify. Wash down with single malt whiskey. "When in Rome,"
Sandy tells me, and I do this.

Hard-drinking Scots have their opposite number, teetotalers who sing
psalms and pinch pennies. But in a time when every layabout lays his burdens down, they shoulder their burdens, rally round the flag, and pay their
bills on the first of each month. Near St. Giles's church in the old town,
a bench by the sidewalk, some citizen's donation, remembers "Janet (Aun-
tie Jessie). She always did her best." His country, Sandy says, pulls in
different directions, lavish versus miserly, the control freak and the hot-
blooded man. Pub and kirk make a pair, while the Anglophile, a word of
reproach, pairs with true-blue Scotsmen "who hae wi' Wallace bled." Or
rather, he corrects himself, not blue but white, like the white rose of Bonnie Prince Charlie.

The modern ruin on the crest of Calton Hill mimics the Parthenon,
the one in Nashville, Tennessee. But the Athens of the South finished what
it started, and in Edinburgh they have run out of steam, or the money ran
out, leaving a handful of columns. Lord Nelson's monument, compared
by some to a butter churn, mixes John Bull and devotional Christian. Seen
from on high, the tower of St. Giles looks like the crown of Scotland, but
to take this church's measure you have to see it close up. Its modern
stained-glass windows are recognizable, like picture postcards. Appealing
to realism against the hieratic figures in older church windows, they show
you saints and sinners who look like the people next door.

Under the hammer-beamed roof in the square, the Scottish Parliament
sat. It closed three hundred years ago, when the Act of Union created
Great Britain. Where Scotland's representatives used to decide things,
chaffering solicitors, bewigged and wearing gowns, wait their turn to split
fees in the law court. Ghosts populate the old town, but people still live
and die in its "lands" or tenements. Every day old, pipe-smoking men ren-
dezvous for a game of bowls on the grassy enclosure beneath the turrets

of Canongate. *Gate* is for the canon's gait, a walk or road, and leads to Holyroodhouse, once an abbey that owned a piece of the cross. Mary of Scots brightened the palace with her "joyousity," said the English ambassador four hundred and some years ago. He wrote home to his principals: "My pen staggereth, my hand faileth. . . . I never found myself so happy." Robert Louis Stevenson imagined the young Charlie aglow like the morning, holding levees in this royal palace. Both had glamor to spare.

James IV, who died at Flodden, built Holyrood Palace, the last residence of Queen Mary before she fled to England and her death at the axman's hands. In the main tower Rizzio—her secretary, some say her lover—died before her eyes. Dragged through the bedroom, he fell in his blood, stabbed fifty-six times with a dagger. Anecdote says that the stains are indelible, but carpet covers the floor, leaving this claim unresolved. Only ruins recall the old abbey, demolished by the Reformation. The little peak-roofed lodge survives, though. Over it Rizzio's murderers made their escape, and in its bathhouse Mary bathed in white wine.

Holyroodhouse faces Edinburgh Castle, at the other end of the Royal Mile. Each looks backward, remembering things past. In summer the castle mounts its famous Tattoo, employing as a stage the sloping Esplanade where the Scots and later the English burned witches. Floodlights pick out the emblem of Scotland, a white cross on a blue ground. From the topmost turret flies the Union Jack, its folds shaken out and snapping. This alfresco theater exploits its resources, and before we see the massed bands we hear muffled music in the dark beyond the portcullis. Then they are on us, clansmen in full dress, dragoons, crowned by black fur shakos, gigantic.

"The onset of the Highlanders was very formidable," said Dr. Johnson, thinking back to battles on which the blood hadn't dried yet. "Men accustomed only to exchange bullets at a distance, and rather to hear their enemies than see them, are discouraged and amazed when they find themselves encountered hand to hand, and catch the gleam of steel flashing in their faces." War, played by the rules, was a game, like Barry Lyndon's in the movie. You fired off a volley, then retired, and your enemies did likewise. Soldiers on the Esplanade make us feel that the game was in earnest.

Edinburgh's Festival keeps different balls in the air, and if you have earnest, you have to have jest. Offstage, commands are spoken, and we wait in darkness. When the lights go up again, the soldiers are gone. The two comics who replace them, both falling down drunk, wear the little kilt called the *philabeg,* and their broad Scots is good for a laugh. We learn that the excise man has doubled the tax on their whiskey. Cunningly stupid, they talk about this, thinking up ways to outwit him.

Coming into the home stretch, kilted warriors, introduced by the pipers, salute us. Leather boots shake the Esplanade, almost a stage in the round, and the boots are like the buskin worn by tragic heroes. As the soldiers march toward us, the leather and silver sporran they wear at the waist swings from one side to the other, mesmeric. Men of the Highlands, said an eighteenth-century reporter who saw them in battle dress, "looked as though they had never heard of original sin." I ask myself how this can be. All know that war is hell, its hold on us marking our fallen condition. But another truth says that war is a kind of life, perhaps of our essence. When Bonnie Prince Charlie lay dying in Rome, his favorite piper stood outside the door, playing "The Flowers of the Forest." Much to regret in "the lilt of dule and wae," but the heart lifts when you hear it.

The festival's costume man has done his homework, and the plaid, gathered in folds, falls along the body from the left shoulder to the knee. Sir Walter Scott, though promoting the old days, wore his across the right shoulder, and if he could do that, what else might he do? A silver brooch, studded with cairngorm stone, yellow quartz, secures the plaid, and the hose is tartan fret. Hugging the calf, the top of one stocking makes room for a tiny black knife. Two dags, claw-handled pistols, dangle from the belt. Bull's hide, worked with silver bosses, covers the target or shield. Steel spikes protect its surface, some twelve inches long.

Not everyone came in like that, "dressed to kill." Bringing up the rear of each Highland company, the wild and bearded "humblies" fought naked to the waist. The rest, when they charged, threw off the plaid, putting their trust in the basket-hilted broadsword. Double-edged like a razor, two inches wide and a yard in length, it hung from one hip. Hanging from the other was the dirk, half a foot of wrought silver. In the charge at Culloden, David Fraser of Glen Urquhart killed seven with his broadsword and dirk. Some of his blood, at least a scintilla's worth, mingles with my blood, and no doubt I ought to deplore him.

Some in the Jacobite army did without stockings, possibly for want of a needle. Tommy Dent, our soccer coach in college and a foot soldier in the First World War, went through the war without them. Mud from the trenches caked his kilt, however, and the stiff edges, slapping bare skin, left his legs scarred for life. Kilted men in the trenches provoked laughter at first. Later, Germans called them Ladies from Hell.

"They came running upon our front line like troops of hungry wolves." "Thomas Lobster," an English soldier, said this, describing the charge at Culloden. But for every Scot there were nearly two English, and God fought with the bigger battalions. Scots artillery was almost none, cavalry none, food and drink they did without, or were glad of a biscuit. They had marched all night from Nairn on the Moray Firth, greeting the sunrise dead on their feet. "None but a mad fool would have fought that day," said old Lovat, Clan Fraser's chief, before his execution.

When Bonnie Prince Charlie, crossing over from France, landed in the Hebrides in the summer of '45, they told him to go home again. "I am come home, sir," he said. Though only seven landed with him, he raised his standard and the clans began to come in. Entering Edinburgh in September, he routed an English army at Prestonpans, outside the city. In November he marched on London, getting as far as Derby. Panic gripped the capital, and the Hanoverian king, his bags packed, thought about leaving. Then, a mistake, Prince Charlie turned back. One more victory remained, Falkirk, east of Glasgow, but his army didn't follow it up. Going to ground at Inverness, he waited two months. On April 16, 1746, it was time.

Culloden House, home to Scotland's lord president, stands on Drumossie Moor, and near it Scots and English fought the last major battle in Britain. Things might have been different had Prince Charlie left the conduct of war to his lieutenant general, Lord George Murray. This experienced second wanted to fight on the soft and broken ground across Nairn Water. Commanding the English, William, Duke of Cumberland, was glad not to do this. A king's son, already plump, he turned grossly fat, and his cruelty earned him a nickname, the Butcher. The flower "sweet William" is called for Butcher Cumberland, and Handel acknowledged his soon-to-be acquired fame by writing "Hail the Conquering Hero."

Beyond the Moray Firth, thin snow spotted the mountains, and on the slopes of Ben Bhuiddhe the heather showed as black-brown. A sharp wind rose early, bringing rain, then sleet, blowing in the Highlanders' faces. To the south Cawdor Castle, whose murderous thane craved sleep but couldn't find it, dominated the countryside. Through this land of bogs and lochans, little lakes, English infantry, bayonets fixed, marched up to their knees in water. But as they neared the sticking point the ground changed to wide, bare moor, giving the horse maneuvering room and the guns a clear field of fire. Bannockburn, fought in early summer 1314, was the mirror image of Culloden. Outnumbered four to one, Bruce chose the higher ground, forcing the English in their heavy armor to ford a deep, wet marsh beside the burn. Scots won that day, and General Murray meant to copy their tactics. However, the prince, believing in his star or the wild fury of the Highland charge, overruled him.

Roused at dawn by the chanters, Scots marched up the braeside south of their camp, forming in line across Drumossie Moor. Thomas Lobster, looking through mist, saw the last feudal army in Europe. In the year of Culloden every Highland man and boy old enough to bear arms enrolled as a soldier in the regiment of his clan. *Clan* means children, and the clan chief led his children in war. Cadets of his family or chiefs of smaller septs served the regiment as company commanders. The head of each family, an officer or noncom, brought in his brothers, sons, and tenants. Father and son, brother and brother, stood together. Boys fought, or tried to. One, Murdoch MacLeod, aged fifteen, ran from his grammar school at Inverness that morning. Equipped with broadsword, dirk, and pistol, he sought out the men of his name.

Pride of race, a humble man's consolation, made a bond between the humblest and highest. All descended, they thought, from a single clan father, and in their veins ran the blood of Norse and Irish kings. Men not the same in rank knew the same obligation, each obliged to give his life for the other. Some fought from compulsion, the dictate of the chief. Or they fought from hatred, remembering their hero Wallace, tried by the English as a traitor, then hanged and his body hewn in fours. MacLean of Drimnin, his son Lachlan dead on the field, fought from hatred. "Come away!" they implored him. But the old man, turning back, cut a trooper from the saddle, wounded another, and died.

The best of them fought from a sense of themselves, like the Bruce, Sandy says, and has the famous words by heart. "It is not for glory we fight, for riches, or for honors, but for freedom alone, which no good man loses but with his life." Darker days followed the victory at Bannockburn, and the work seemed always to be done again. But he meant to keep at it "for as long as one hundred of us shall remain alive."

By order of Prince Charlie, all who mustered on Drumossie Moor wore the kilt. In their bonnets they wore the white cockade. The badge of kingship, it promised good luck, but they ran out of luck at Culloden. English cavalry galloped unopposed, their three-pounders in the front line fired by pairs, and coehorn mortars lobbed shells from the rear. Most died where they stood, awaiting the order to charge. The cry of "Claymore!" sent them forward. Shrilling war cries in Gaelic, they drew the huge two-handed sword, some flourishing scythe blades and axes. Put your ear to the ground, Sandy says, and you can still hear them.

As the line of Scots drew closer, English artillery changed from ball to grapeshot: canisters of nails, lead balls, and iron scraps. English firelocks volleyed and reloaded, rank by rank to the beat of the drum. Firing, the first line ducked and the second stood, followed by the third. No advance was thinkable, unless you were willing to climb over your dead. Men of Clan Chattan did this. Breaking the first English line, all died on the bayonets of the second. In less than an hour it was over.

Of the five thousand men who fought at Culloden for Bonnie Prince Charlie, at least twelve hundred, perhaps two thousand, are buried on the field. Granite boulders stained with lichen mark the grave sites, and each boulder is cut with a name: MacDonald, MacGillivray, MacKenzie, Grant, Chisholm, Fraser. Graveled walkways, crossing the moor, lead the tourist to other monuments, one for Irish soldiers. Serving France's king but volunteering to fight England's, they were the "Wild Geese." Dense with pine and birch, the hills beyond the battlefield are purplish in season. Heather grows on the field but not on the grave mounds. Visitors drop greenish-gray twigs along the mounds, and some drop white sprays, remembering the white rose picked by Prince Charlie on the shores of Loch Eil.

In the nineteenth century the authorities ran a highway through Drumossie Moor. They planted conifers for harvesting, spoiling the view. The trees are gone, however, and the highway has been rerouted. Cattle graze on the other side of the Inverness road, beyond it the firth, and even on cloudy days the light plays tricks on the water. The viewing platform, provided by the National Trust, looks across the moor toward the Black Isle and Ben Wyvis. Near it the rough stone cairn in honor of the dead calls to mind those ancient *brochs* that still stand in the west country, survivors of Scotland's prehistory.

6

Over the Sea to Skye

I had an epiphany half a lifetime ago, hitchhiking in the Mojave Desert. Coming south from Bakersfield, California, I caught a ride to Barstow, too far or not far enough. Viewers of the Weather Channel will recognize Barstow, where the temperature in summer goes off the charts. Forecasters say that except for Death Valley, it's the most depressed place in the country. Standing outside it on a day in summer, I didn't feel that good either.

I have friends for whom the desert strikes a mystical chord. The cloudless sky sharpens their awareness, and they can't get enough of the burning sand and stony soil, varied by the occasional saguaro. But what they call grandeur I call banality. The desert appals me, wearying in its sameness and empty like the void. I prefer my landscapes serried, broken by peaks and troughs and refreshed with running water. Inevitably there are trees, the more umbrageous the better, not only for shelter but to give a lift to the soul. Even more to my taste are human habitations, not made by nature, made by man.

Once in my time at Princeton the son of Sir Herbert Read, the English critic and poet, came for a visit. He came with an introduction to our great man, R. P. Blackmur, and Blackmur, doing a friend's office, showed him the sights. Young Reed, donnish and very fey, didn't look with favor on what he saw, though. "But Mr. Blackmur," he said, "where are your holy places?" America does without them, no ancient churches or manor houses, no pressure of form. The desert is like that, only raised to the ultimate power.

At the city limits of my way station on the road to nowhere, I stuck out my thumb and smiled hopefully each time a car sped by me. Night was coming on when I gave up and trudged back into town. Part of my dwindling stash paid for a motel room, most of the rest for a bottle. Lying in bed, I sipped away steadily, reading by the light of a gooseneck lamp. In a drawer in the bedside table I'd found a Gideon Bible, and flipping the pages I stopped at the Book of Job.

What with the poor light and the whiskey, getting the words to focus wasn't easy. Hemingway says his memory was most vivid when he'd been drinking and recalls how Turgenev's *Sportsman's Sketches* burned itself into his psyche. That summer's night in the desert the Book of Job was like that for me. "Only I am escaped alone to tell thee," I read, assuming the role of messenger. The tidings I carried thundered in a young man's ear. "For we are but of yesterday and know nothing, because our days upon earth are a shadow." Coming forth like a flower, we are cut down in our prime. End of story.

This awareness didn't make for depression, like the one Barstow is stuck in. The speaker wasn't bidding me curse God and die, nor were his words spoken out of the whirlwind. Flesh of our flesh, he told of the nothingness we come from and go back to. That was mournful, no question. But the words themselves, describing chaos, put it in chains, the way we lock up a malefactor. It occurred to me that the writer's job was like that. I had only begun to feel my way into the job and what it entailed, but already I sensed that it gave a shape to the pain and loss that go with living. The writer didn't console us nor palliate the truth. But presenting the truth with an unwinking eye, he made it acknowledge a form.

In the heart of downtown Aberdeen, the tearoom is the Tastie Tattie Shop. Today's menu features tatties and chili, and the girl I give my order to is wearing a stud in her nose. Aberdeen, the Granite City, looks built to last, but the modern world, disposable like plastic milk cartons, squeezes between cracks in the granite. Across from the cathedral the Upperkrust Katerer has a shocking-pink valance over the store front. At Marks & Sparks around the corner, platform shoes and leopard-skin short shorts are on display in the window.

The waitress, a chatterbox, grew up in the Granite City, on Castle Street near the printmaking museum. But her role models are English rock stars, and she thinks of herself as English. The royals, who walk in beauty, make her heart beat faster. Nearer to home, however, "Scotland is boring." Like living in a covered wagon, she says. I mention the Scottish Nationalist Party, whose slogan is "Independence Now," and she rolls her eyes comically. Maybe, I think, things happen when they should have or won't happen at all. Scotland should have got its freedom when the Highlands rose in the Forty-Five, but the clans went down to defeat at Culloden. Two and a half centuries later, few remember the past or regret it.

But hand-wringing won't change history, and you could make out a case that Scotland is better off, like Wales, even Ireland, united with once-terrible England. Maybe balkanization is our time's greater peril. The girl in the tearoom, evacuated to nothing, seems dreadful, however. Something must be done!

Edwin Muir, Scotland's best-known modern poet, has a poem about this girl and others like her, who don't know where they come from or where they're going but "are content / With their poor frozen life and shallow banishment." In the Scotland they live in, Wallace and Bruce guard a painted field. Another famous duo, Burns and Scott, are "sham bards of a sham nation." Fighting words, Muir's still flutter the dovecotes in Scotland. I know better than to quarrel with rhetoric, and will say only that Burns is bigger than an aphorism. But since Muir said his say, many years ago now, the sham is worse than it was.

My wife looks bemused as I turn up the stereo, listening to "Flower of Scotland." "We can still rise," I tell her, and be the nation again. "Terrible things happened in Ireland too," she tells me. But Scotland needs national status to recover its lost sense of itself. Ireland, full of self-esteem, needs it less.

Three hundred years ago, the English, pioneering the friendly takeover, turned Scotland into North Britain, a province known for whiskey and the comic Scots who drink it. Celtic and inferior, they didn't mind "the poorest and most simple fare," clinging "in the strangest manner to the habits and homes of their fathers." The Lowlander who said this served the Duke of Sutherland, Scotland's richest landlord, an Englishman who never traveled beyond Tweed. Both the landlord and his factor, out to make money, had their eye on the Highlands. Neither paid much heed to the Highlander.

English have always been good at cultural trashing, banning Chinese from Hong Kong's Victoria Peak, except as houseboys, or the dark-skinned friends of T. E. Lawrence from the clubs in Pall Mall and Cairo's Anglo hotels. "Taffy was a Welshman; Taffy was a thief." Supercilious but good-humored, the English joke about the kilt, the kirk, neeps and midges, parsimonious Scots. They are the sunny, seductive Greeks, intruders on our ancient Tyrian home, at the end of Arnold's "Scholar Gipsy." If the sense of self counts for anything, fly their greetings, fly their speech and smiles!

Such a misalliance! Fewer live in the whole of Scotland than in London alone, but it isn't the numbers, it's the posturing, uniquely English, that overawes the *puir* Scot. What is he to make of them, dressing for dinner in the tropics or building mock-Tudor houses in upcountry Burma. My black friend Cedric, taught by an English schoolmistress in equatorial Africa, remembers reciting "O, to be in England / Now that April's there." As he watched the movie *Zulu,* a tale of us against them, he wondered why he cheered for the redcoats.

Overawed like Cedric, upper-crust characters in the novels of Sir Walter Scott clip their vowels and salute the Union Jack. *Redgauntlet* has two of them, the hero and his friend, both adept in polite evasions. David Daiches knew young men in his boyhood who talked the way they do. Poor lads, they wanted to make themselves English, he said, but their nationality tugged them in different directions. Daiches himself, a redoubtable dinner guest, fluent in Russian and at home on both sides of Tweed, played many parts in one person. He wrote biography, criticism, travel literature, and a guide to Scotch whiskey. His life of Bonnie Prince Charlie, who led the last Jacobite rising, is both skeptical and absorbed in its story. But where Daiches was complicated, that is, civilized, the young he tilted at were only confused.

Confusion is writ large in Scott's novels, though sometimes it works out to our good. "It's a queer thing," says one of his characters, remembering the exploits of Rob Roy and William Wallace, "but I think the Hieland blude o' me warms at thae daft tales." He knew better but couldn't help it. At last, however, Scott threw in with the ascendancy class. With a straight face he said that since the last of the Stuarts, "four monarchs had reigned in peace and glory over Britain, sustaining and exalting the character of the nation abroad, and its liberties at home." These were the years of the Four Georges when England was cleansing the Highlands. Scott, doing his part, sanitized the Highlander, once a bugaboo to Englishmen and tamer Scots of the Lowlands. When English after Culloden proscribed the claymore, kilt, and bagpipes, he engineered their comeback, turning them into stage properties first. For King George's visit to Scotland in 1822, he designed a royal tartan. The king was German, but Scott dressed him like a Highland chief, complete with eagle's feather. His fictions à l'Écosse are like the European vogue of Chinese.

But when he renders the speech of the people, Scott's prose comes alive. In *Waverley* a Jacobite soldier has been telling his strict construction-ist landlady how his clan chief often played with the broadsword and tar-get on Sundays.

> "Lord forgie ye, Ensign Maccombich," said the alarmed Presbyter-ian. "I'm sure the colonel wad never do the like o' that!"
>
> "Hout! hout! Mrs. Flockhart," replied the ensign, "we're young blude, ye ken; and young saints, auld deils."
>
> "But will ye fight wi' Sir John Cope the morn, Ensign Maccom-bich?" demanded Mrs. Flockhart of her guest.
>
> "Troth I'se ensure him, an' he'll bide us, Mrs. Flockhart," replied the Gael.
>
> "And will ye face thae tearing chields, the dragoons, Ensign Mac-combich?" again inquired the landlady.
>
> "Claw for claw as Conan said to Satan, Mrs. Flockhart, and the deevil tak the shortest nails."

The priggish hero in *Rob Roy* does his best to kill this lively back and forth. Scandalized by talk of the King over the Water, he "comprehended" that the words "boded a general national convulsion," so kept his head down, satisfied with "regretting the promiscuous scene of confusion and distress likely to arise from any general exertion in favour of the exiled royal family." Professors of English mistake this for fine writing. What's all the fuss about, Rob wants to know: "Let it come, man—let it come. . . . ye never saw dull weather clear without a shower; and if the world is turned upside down, why, honest men have the better chance to cut bread."

Such sap as runs in the novels is owing to this common touch. No low or comic writing in the nineteenth century is better. I don't know any as good. What might Scott have written, had he not immersed himself in the warm bath of Great Britain?

For the history of the Highlands after the Act of Union (1707), what mat-ters is the bottom line. You could make more from wool, later from mut-ton, than from working a farm. There are other ways to look at this. Maybe the farm deserved protecting for the sake of the virtues it nourished. English ruled in Scotland, however. Sheep bringing in more money than people, the Clearances followed, and that was all there was to say about that.

At the time of the royal visit to Scotland, the glens were already emptying out. First the local landlord evicted his tenants to make room for sheep, then went the same way, replaced by Lowlanders and English. Highlanders, relocated to the barren seacoast, were told they might fish for a living. Slums like Glasgow's swallowed up many. Others left for the New World, some wanting to go, more of them forced to, and in Edinburgh's National Gallery a powerful painting by William McTaggart shows the immigrant ship standing out to sea. In the sky above the masts a rainbow hints at better days. On shore, however, left behind to die, are the old folks.

Stay-at-homes eked out a living as shepherds, or they reinvented themselves, becoming ghillies like Queen Victoria's favorite retainer. Cunning in the ways of roe deer and salmon, they helped English sportsmen turn the Highlands into a game park. Others took the king's shilling and won an empire for England. In Beulay west of Inverness, a monument to the Lovat Scouts honors the men of that outfit who died in the Boer War, a naked imperialist landgrab. I am moved but distressed that many bear the same name as I do.

Today the Highlands are haunted. The clan system disappeared with the people, a casualty of England's need to break the land to its will. Most of the men and women whose crofts were burned over them never saw their own hills again. *Cha till mi tuille* is the Gaelic of the pibroch that sang their departure, "We Shall Return No More." The word for this is *genocide*. It happened, says Prebble, the historian of the Clearances, "within the span of one man's youth and middle age."

The Clearances are hard, but the wearing down of national pride is worse. It began in the early years of the seventeenth century when James VI of Scotland came to the English throne, succeeding the first Elizabeth. If a Scots writer wanted to be noticed after the court moved south, he dropped the authentic speech of the people, once spoken by king and commoner alike, preferring polite Southern English. The poet William Drummond, born in Scotland, sounds the same as his English friend Ben Jonson. That was how he wanted it.

After a while they were all English under the plaid, like Smollett and Hume, eighteenth-century Scotsmen but you wouldn't know it. "Adopt the English idiom and pronunciation," said Smollett. That made sense to Hume, who thought Scotland's native tongue "a very corrupt dialect" of English. This chauvinism in reverse came at a price. I tried *Humphry Clinker* again a year ago, and have always meant to finish Hume's *History of Great Britain*.

A pedigreed Scot, John Buchan is much livelier, but Englishness trumps Scottishness in his adventure novels, like *Mr. Standfast* (1919). The English ascendancy has been doing a number on West Scotland, hard on the people who live there. Hannay the hero knows what's going on, so does the author. Citing a parallel case, his footnote refers us to the Duke of Sutherland, who expelled his crofters and took their land for sheep runs. Like the hero who speaks for him, Buchan deplores this. A pity about the crofters. But progress requires that we "break down a multitude of molehills."

When progress was only a cloud in the sky, Rob Roy MacGregor rallied his clan against it. In the old Hollywood movie Errol Flynn plays the hero, and the happy ending has him making a friend of King George. This scenario, good for laughs, is almost believable. The gap between classes in prelapsarian Scotland, though wide, was only a matter of money. The king on his throne in Edinburgh had a lot of it, the commoner who cheered him only a little. In the Highlands, however, the commoner or crofter was already joined by blood to his clan chief. No patent of nobility grander than that. Money couldn't augment it, nor a lack of money make it less. The poorest clansman spoke his name like a talisman, sometimes with his last breath. "Though poor, I am noble," he said. "Thank God I am a MacLean."

Modern Scots would rather be rich, and who will blame them? But a tide of vulgarity washes over Scotland today. "By appointment to H.R.H.," a personal piper performs for Queen Elizabeth II. At my hotel in Edinburgh, a piper in full fig stands in the doorway, piping in a contingent of Japanese tourists. Expecting a sound and light show, they aren't disappointed. The manager, English with that trademark complexion, pink shading to florid, ushers them into the lobby.

Edinburgh, first stop on the tourist trail, is popular for its pastness, the castle on its ramparts "beetling over" the Old Town, at the other end of the Royal Mile Holyroodhouse, once home to Scotland's rulers, now to Queen Elizabeth II when she comes north for a visit. The Burberry tartan has a building to itself on Princes Street, and clan scarves and badges rake in a lot of money. You can buy your own *quaitch,* or drinking vessel, with your clan crest embossed on the side. Mine has a motto in Gaelic, the national language, long since driven out of the schools. If your drinking partner means to stick you with his dirk, the glass bottom of the *quaitch* lets you see what he's up to. In modern Scotland the past is mostly cosmetic. The young crowding Edinburgh's streets are innocent of history, and if they knew about it would reject it. Given what they are, they'd be right to. Some of them, color-blind, dye their hair purple. That sounds a little Blimpish, and I mustn't blur the point. It isn't that the present is so much worse than the past. But the past, unlike the present, had edges.

Not so long ago, you crossed to Skye by a ferry from Kyle of Lochalsh. When I was a boy I cycled down from Inverness, a long diagonal over rough country. At journey's end, with a sore rump and stout heart, I trundled my bike up the gangplank to the ferry. Now a bridge spans the water, easier on tourists. But the distinction between the Highlands and Islands is gone. Before you reach the bridge, Eilean Donan, a majestic relic of the past often pictured on scenic calendars, looms up on your left hand. English cannoneers did their best to knock it down in the Jacobite rising of 1719, but from a distance it looks as it used to, mist recomposing its ruined towers. Going back to Skye a year ago, I wanted to stop and clamber over the ruins. To take the measure of the past, I find that foot-soldiering works best. Cars have their own rationale, however, all about getting there, and I kept going.

Bonnie Prince Charlie, escaping to the Islands after Culloden, could have made it over the water without ado, had our modern technology been available to him. As it was, he was five months on his way. Everyone knows how Flora MacDonald helped him cross in an open boat, disguised as her maid, Betty Burke. A Jacobite song tells about the two of them.

> There is Flora so bonny
> a floo'r abune ony
> and one that is tall maist comely withal,
> Put the one for my king & the other for my queen,
> and they are aye so welcome to Skye again.
> > Come along come along
> > wi' yer boatie & yer song,
> my ain bonny maidens my twa bonny maids,
> For the night it is dark & the redcoat is gaen
> & ye are dearly welcome to Skye again.

The crossing to Skye from the Outer Hebrides was perilous, but all accounts say that the young prince's spirits were high. He had no inkling of the waste of years before him, nor could Flora have known what her courage would cost. In a more nearly perfect world, Prince Charlie would have marched into London at the head of his men, loyal men if ever there were such, and taken back his father's throne from King Geordie. Flora would have been with him, the white cockade in her bonnet. Who knows, they might have married. Romantic fiction would like that.

For a little while all things were possible, true for every one of us. "Rally in the name of God," cried young Charlie, as he watched the debacle unfold at Culloden. "Pray, gentlemen, return. Pray, stand with me, your Prince, but a moment." The cry went unheeded, and after that history took over. Flora endured her captivity, went to America, returned, raised a family, outlived a husband, and died on Skye, an old woman. You can drive out to her grave in a lonely place on the northern tip of the island.

Over Prince Charlie's subsequent career I draw a veil, as older writers liked to put it. They weren't squeamish, only tactful, and what happened to him doesn't bear telling. But he had his moment, and RLS captures it for us, both the pathos and the wild surmise.

> Sing me a song of a lad that is gone,
> Say, could that lad be I?
> Merry of soul he sailed on a day
> Over the sea to Skye.

Possibility is of the essence in the story of the Forty-Five, and still open in the Highlands and Islands. The land is pristine, the burr on the tongue still faintly roughened. Life's edges, sandpapered down elsewhere, still feel rough to the hand. Tourist-trap Scotland, including greater Edinburgh and running north to Perth, west to Stirling, is Disneyland over the water. At Stirling William Wallace beat the English of Edward Longshanks, and nearby is Bannockburn, no ground on earth more hallowed. In June 1314 Bruce, routing an English army there, sent it homeward "tae think again." Suburban-style housing sprawls over the battlefield, nothing wrong with that: people must live. But the Wallace Monument, knocking its head against heaven, is Victorian chest-thumping. Doing both at once isn't easy, but have a look and see if it doesn't.

At Scone Palace outside Perth, Scotland crowned its kings for centuries, some seated on the Stone of Scone. It makes the hairs rise on my head to know what that stone was, literally the pillow on which Jacob dreamed his dream of angels descending the ladder to earth and going up the ladder to heaven. Shakespeare's Macbeth travels to Scone "to be invested," but Edward I carried off the stone, and in the sixteenth century Knox's rabble destroyed the palace. Victorians rebuilt it for the earls of Mansfield, whose seat this is today. Unlike Lord George Murray, a neighbor to the north and Prince Charlie's lieutenant general, they served the Hanoverians, brought in to run England when the Stuarts lost the throne. Queen Elizabeth II descends from these German princelings.

Murray, loyal to the Stuarts, forfeited the family seat at Blair Atholl. The Mansfields, loyal to their bread, hung on to Scone. Over the years they filled it with bric-a-brac and animal heads, bits of armor, silk on the walls, and period pieces cordoned off in public rooms, like the writing table made for Marie Antoinette. Tour buses in summer decant foreign visitors at the entrance stairs, so many visitors that you have to wait your turn behind ropes. Guides attached to the palace move the crowd along briskly, though. You can hear them fluting before you set your foot on the stairs. "Mind the ropes!" Unlike Tony Blair's, their accent isn't homogenized but harks back to Oxbridge when it favored the "superfluous *u*."

Americans in the gift shop, everybody's destination at the end of the tour, say *superfloo-us*, however. Most are weary from threading the maze, spruced up with photos of the earl's family playing tennis or patting a prize Angus bull. In 1745 the Young Pretender slept at Scone, and not far off in a country churchyard is the grave of Rob Roy MacGregor. No road signs direct the tourist to this tucked-away place, and not a dime has gone to its upkeep. English, wary of Rob Roy, tried to root out his name, forbidding Scots to use it. But the inscription on the stone reads: "MacGregor Despite Them."

En route to Fraserburgh—nothing to write home about but piety mandates a drive through—I stop in Newburgh on the coast north of Aberdeen. The heart of this community is the Free Church, whose parishioners split off from the Established Church of Scotland. Like establishments everywhere, it tugged its forelock to the ascendancy class, assuming that churches can do that. Ministers, knowing who footed their bills, preached the gospel of progress. Honor to churchgoers in Newburgh for refusing to worship false gods.

But Newburgh, while saving its soul, has lost the physical world, without which the soul is a specter. If you arrive in town on a Sunday, as I did, eyes you don't see look you over from the windows of gray, skimpy houses, their stucco coating like a rash. Sundays are for prayer, but I don't know what the people are doing, only that the narrow streets are empty. Any minute now, air-raid sirens will sound the all clear. Like the girl in the tearoom, this evacuated place asks a question that had better be answered. Failing an answer, the last angry man in Scotland can shut out the lights when he leaves. Politicians and commentators, their ilk always knowing what is to be done, have the answer. Less assured, I am old King Lear, waving my arms in a vacuum. "I will do such things," I tell them. "What they are, yet I know not."

But I know what I'd do, if the option were mine. I would fall in with my clan on Culloden's field, throw down my musket, and go forward with the claymore alone. This time, since I am writing the script, the outcome will be different. See them standing tall in Scotland, and the cross of St. Andrew flying once more over Edinburgh Castle. But all that is finished. In the melee at Prestonpans when Jacobite fortunes crested, I hope against hope, while aware that Bonnie Charlie won't come back again. Goodbye to the King over the Water. Let the dead bury their dead.

Being sanguine, however, like Celts except on their melancholy side, I can hardly let this ending stand. Casting about for a better one, I hit on the words of Arbroath's famous declaration. In the spring of 1320 nobles loyal to King Robert the Bruce met at Arbroath Abbey on the North Sea to speak for themselves and for Scotland. They appealed to liberty, an abstraction but fortified with flesh and blood. While life remained to a handful of them, they said, "we shall never in any wise consent to submit to the rule of the English."

A red sandstone ruin, the abbey in its founding remembered the martyrdom of St. Thomas Becket, childhood friend of Scotland's king, William the Lion. In the rib-vaulted sacristy the monks kept a relic of St. Columba, borne before the army when Scots went into battle. Light blazing from the great rose window, Arbroath's Round O, served as a beacon for ships out at sea. The lower half of this window is still visible above the rounded arch of the doorway, but the stained glass disappeared a long time ago. Likely, it showed the Last Judgment or the Wheel of Fortune. Both were popular in churches like this one, and both honored a god who worked in mysterious ways.

Since the time of the Declaration of Arbroath, Scotland's fortunes have fallen, then at the nadir begun to pick up. "We can still rise and be the nation again"? No chest-thumping from me. A few things I can say for sure, though. The Wheel continues to turn, God's last word has yet to be spoken, and the past remains alive in the present.

Some liberal friends who have my and their well-being at heart suppose the path of things always runs upward. This makes it easier to dispense with the past, seen by them as gratuitous, at worst pernicious. Belittling the past, "dead white European males," all that, they think its out-of-date ideas must contaminate the present. That is why revolutionaries, a step up the political ladder, generally summon us to violence. Send the past to the stake, they say. Consume it to nothing. I am a revolutionary too, though not a violent one, and on my more hopeful reading the past empowers the present, relating to it like a giant with a dwarf on its shoulders. North of the Great Glen, what I call the good old way persists fitfully. I don't speak of ancient loyalties, to throne, church, or clan, but of the character of the good man that gave them all substance. Maybe, filling different molds, it will beget the next revolution in Scotland.

What the Forty-Five was all about was revolution. Of greater power than economic or social protest, its animus was aesthetic, accounting for its fierceness, and its appeal to a better time, outside history. Andrew Lang, a scholar and man of letters who isn't much remembered, is its spokesman:

> A wind that awoke on the moorland came sighing,
>> Like the voice of the heroes who perished in vain:
> "Not for Tearlach alone the red claymore was plying,
>> But to win back the old world that comes not again."

Tearlach is Gaelic, once a living language in Scotland, for "Charlie."

The last revolution, led by Knox, was moral, and its results are still with us. When fire damaged my grandfather's factory on Union Square in Manhattan, a man from the insurance company came by with a proposition. Winking, he said he would build up the damage report, and they could split the settlement between them. Grandfather threw him through the plate-glass door of his office. That was how you dealt with a claims adjuster.

But something more is wanted to complement the moral bias that goes with being a Scot. You won't find it in Newburgh. Inland from the coast, though, "the air smells wooingly," and grace that comes unbidden dowers the great houses, Craithes and Corgarff, Cawdor and Blair Atholl. Doing my duty and pleasing myself, I pay a visit to one of them, west of Aberdeen. Castle Fraser, while faithful to old conventions the tower house had to follow, honors the native genius of its local masons, and corbelling, turrets, dormers, gables, and chimney stacks make a once-and-for-all composition. Frasers of Inverallochy, the North Sea hamlet they came from, lived in the castle and kept the good old way. Of course they were Jacobites. But all trace of the old cause and its supporters is gone from Castle Fraser, leaving tourists with the feeling that history began about 1800.

At Haddo House, home of the Gordons, the genius of the place is or was Palladian. Covenanters burnt down the original house, but William Adam, the father of Robert, rebuilt it, honoring that symmetry the eighteenth century rejoiced in. Curving flights of stairs, left and right, sweep upward to the first-floor balcony, and until the late nineteenth century that was how you entered. Elegance makes a political statement, however, and a new facade replicates and fudges the old one. Portraits of men wearing redcoats crowd the walls. The men are handsome in the corpulent style, and their complexions match the clothes they are wearing. Tour guides point out the bed Queen Victoria slept in.

Haddo House has a painting by Lawrence and Castle Fraser one by Raeburn, but no portrait survives of the young laird who fell at Culloden. If true to type, however, he cut a modest figure and laid up his treasures in heaven. Like his antecedents, different from his successors, he measured his worth not in money but men. When he called them, they turned out, more than five hundred for the last battle. In time of need they could call on him too.

But he wasn't like my rich uncle, the one who gave me a silver christening spoon. The relation between him and me, I blush to say, was pretty much a matter of greed, my parents'. Ten to one, the young laird wasn't big on liquid assets. Still, he disposed of more than his dependents. The tie that bound them was a blood tie, but it needn't be that and can hardly be that anymore. All in this little world, on one side a microcosm of ours, acknowledged a mutual dependence, however, and it made them ampler of soul.

That is said too easily by apologists for a class system. Having an ax to grind, they don't want us to know that money is only less important than love. Scots, to tell the truth, never had much of the former, a reason they are apt to pinch pennies. But when they kept the good old way, a man's essence counted more than his purse. I mustn't kid my reader, much less myself. The clan system, valuing the essence of things, no longer exists. I need a surrogate to replace it, an unusually comprehensive one, for the essential thing, though always of the spirit, is sometimes of the flesh. Nationalism won't do, neither will an access of black bile—kicking an Englishman as some patriotic heavies did, after seeing *Braveheart*. My surrogate is multifaceted. One facet is manliness, different from brute strength, belonging as it does to man the thinking animal, another the form or style that gives a shape to chaos. Without it, life leaks away.

Signaling one another, Scotland's great houses are much like those well-branched firs and copper beeches you see on the hills as you climb up to the Highlands at Ballater. Scale is part of the Scottish thing, as in our phrase "on the human scale," and the houses we remember aren't "built to envious show." Big they may be, but they mustn't impose. Even Blair Atholl, though spreading itself, seems to grow naturally, the way leaves grow on a tree. The unnatural thing, asking us to clap off our hats, is a nineteenth-century import.

This alien growth fastens on modern Scotland like a tourniquet, clamping off the life's blood. For example, the Scott Monument on Edinburgh's Princes Street or those fussy hotels where the waiters wear winged collars. But Corgarff Castle, once home to that Earl of Mar who raised the standard for the Old Pretender, is simple. The two cubes of the house, one on top of the other, seem slabs of rock left behind by the glacier. Around it purple heather glows in season. Best not to give nature the palm, though: this house is man-made, nothing inadvertent about it.

Blair Atholl is grander, but looking at it you don't get a crick in the neck. Giant rhododendrons, beautifying the nearby kirk of St. Bride's, some junior son's sinecure, might have borne witness to the death of the Bonnie Dundee. He took a bullet in the pass at Killiekrankie. On the grounds of the great house a European larch, as big around as the gatekeeper's lodge, offers a point of vantage to a large goshawk. Its black and yellow eyes are expressionless but blaze like a gilded bull's-eye. This bird of prey, all brute strength without the considering part that gives life its interest, is a killing machine. Soaring along great planes of sky, it banks sharply with the aid of its rudderlike tail. Slate-gray feathers cover its back, and white and black bars, like prison garb, its underbelly. Keen of eye, it scans the parklike floor below, and if a creature is stirring it will drop from its perch like a stone.

The huge larch tree it perches on put down roots before Prince Charlie came to Scotland. Though his quest for the throne ended in defeat, bringing to an end the royal line that began in the time of Robert the Bruce, the larch is still there, asserting connections. If I cite the Bruce and others, that isn't because I read history as romance. My history is a tightly woven skein including heroes, villains, and spear-carriers, also ideas, and the ground on which they were tested. Romantic novelists like Scott downplay the middle term, and ideologists, in the saddle today, the first and last. Take out one of these components, however, and the skein unravels.

Trees are important for the skein of history, like the avenue of limes leading up to Cawdor Castle. Old as the hills, they only seem to remember Macbeth, thane of this castle in Scotland's prehistory. Cawdor, without Shakespeare, would be little more than a blip on the screen. There are plenty of castles in Scotland. But with or without Shakespeare, Cawdor would matter, even if no tourist ever knocked on the door. Pains have been taken here, seeing to it that nature doesn't run wild. Art, collaborating with it, civilizes the countryside, not a tyranny, a blessing.

Scotland, land of crags and torrents, sometimes gothic in its violence, requires reining in. Formal gardens like Pitmedden's in Aberdeenshire fulfill this function. From the belvedere at Pitmedden color stuns the eye, thousands of annuals mingling to create a Fauvist painting. The original Fauves were wild beasts, however, not fit for society. Their thing needs refining, and boxwood hedges plus the four sharply demarcated parterres take order with the riot of color. This formal envelope doesn't banish wildness, though. Vitality is the child of wildness, and the sine qua non of every liveable place. But without a wary eye it turns into destructiveness, and you have to keep shaping it up.

7

Peter at the Crossroads

The cold war hadn't thawed when I went to Russia in the sixties, part of a team that negotiated the cultural exchange. Before I left on the trip, they handed me a file of documents stamped "For Your Eyes Only." It sounds more glamorous than it was, and what the government called hush-hush you could find in the public library. Try telling that to my mother, however. I couldn't go out the door without her sketching the sign of the cross over my head and whispering "God go with you." Naturally I let her think that I was cloak-and-dagger, parachuting behind enemy lines.

My taste for melodrama showed itself at an early age. In college I strummed along with Pete Seeger, singing Spanish Civil War songs like "Freiheit!" This was the official hymn of the German Communist brigade, known to me as freedom fighters. Having failed to achieve power in Spain, they succeeded later in Germany. The East German Republic or DDR, of all the Communist states the most repulsive, was their offspring.

When I got to Harvard, I stood at Armageddon and did battle for the Lord. That is, I signed on with Henry Wallace's presidential campaign. At rallies I waved placards with such slogans as "Workers for Peace!" and "Friendship with the Soviet Union!" I picketed the draft board in Boston, drawing the attention of a boisterous crowd. After the catcalls came a volley of sticks and stones, and I was glad to quit the picket line and duck into the subway. Later at UCLA, where my teaching career began, I joined a socialist study group that meant to build Jerusalem in Venice, California. Our discussion leader, Carlos, an old lefty, dreamed of power in the barrel of a gun. Shaking my hand, he wanted to know which side of the street I stood on. Back then I stood on the right side, meaning the left. What I was beyond that meant nothing to Carlos. I remember his eyes, cornflower blue and empty of personal feeling.

An epigram I liked reciting gave my young man's point of view. "I'd rather be called a Red by a rat than a rat by a Red!" Mike Quin, who said this, ran the Transport Workers Union, but his epigram, as I thought about it later, seemed to lack traction. It didn't tell us what this Red was like, that we should be mindful of him. Did he bring to the world an equable perspective, or was it blotted by anger, merely personal to him? Perhaps he wasn't a working stiff at all, but one of the abstracting tribe who looks at the world through a lorgnette.

People say that as we get older, we get curmudgeonly, and this may explain why the arrow in my political spectrum has swung over from left to right. But it's not that I don't like lefties; some of my best friends are lefties; it's that labels, like epigrams, don't comprehend my old man's sense of the truth. As with skin color, they leave us on the doorstep. When I estimate a man. I have a question to put: Would I want to buy an authentic old master from this man?

Princeton, when I moved there, was much nicer than Venice, California, in the shadow of the oil wells. Each year in the spring the alumni, wearing orange and black, returned en masse for the annual P-rade. I marched in this parade as a marshal, escorting the class of "oughty-ought." To those who are oriented in terms of the new millenium, that's oughty-ought as in 1900. To complete my outfit the alumni office gave me a Da Vinci cap, black velvet with orange rickrack. Like the grace that falls from heaven, it confirmed my bona fides.

Everyone who was anyone belonged to that class or its sisters on either side. The governor of New Jersey graduated with one or the other, also the senior senator, the secretary of defense, the secretary of state, and his brother, our nation's number one spook. If you wanted something done, these were men who could do it for you. They were likeable too, but I sensed a whiff of coldness about them. Like Orson Welles in *The Third Man,* they looked down on the world from the top of a Ferris wheel. Seen from that distance, people don't matter much.

The way my second trip to Russia began makes me happy. I am standing with other passengers at the rail of a transatlantic steamer, heading up the

Neva into St. Petersburg. Suddenly music comes over the water to meet us. The band, facing the river on the English Embankment, is playing "I Left My Heart in San Francisco." A rude glissando on the trombone changes the beat, and the ragged, foot-stomping men segue into "Muskrat Ramble." In Leningrad as it used to be, "Tea for Two" was as hot as it got. Half a lifetime ago, boarding the train in Helsinki, we chug-chugged all day through the snowy taiga. At nightfall we came to Leningrad's Finland Station, where Sovietskis in red epaulettes scowled while they looked through our passports. No jazz band piped us into the city.

The hammer and sickle doesn't fly any longer over the old capital of Russia. Retreating at full throttle from the proximate past, it is once again St. Petersburg. But rumple-faced men still ply the river in dinghies, and the Neva is still the city's highway, breadbasket, and scourge. Less than fifty miles long, it runs down like a granite chute polished with rushing waters from Lake Ladoga on the east to the Gulf of Finland and the Baltic beyond it. Germans controlled the Baltic in the Second World War, but Lake Ladoga stayed Russian, and over its frozen surface a motorized life-line—the "Way of Life"—kept starvation at bay. When the ice goes out in spring, the freshwater current in the river brooks no argument, and you can still see it a mile from shore, churning up the salt waters of the gulf.

Fishermen take perch, bream, and pike from the Neva. Armed with murderous teeth, the pike is cannibalistic, like Russia's rulers from Czar Peter to Stalin. Hoisted to power on the backs of his colleagues, Stalin killed them when he got there, and Peter killed his own son. Everybody knows about Stalin, but for sheer brutality Peter the Great runs him a close second, lacking for mass murder only our modern technical know-how. Chief among his victims was Alexei, the czarevitch. Others, who pitied the unfortunate youth, fell in Peter's dragnet, like the bishop of Rostov, broken with hammers and left to die on the wheel. Lopakhin, brother of Eudoxia, the wife Peter "put away," died on the block, made to lay his head down in the blood of those beheaded before him. Glebov, the captain of Eudoxia's guard and her lover, lay for three days on spikes, while a sharp wooden stake in his rectum slowly gouged him to death. Peter, relishing these proceedings, took part in many. One story has it that he was his son's deathsman, lifting the ax with his own hands.

Perhaps I am hard on Peter the Great. Life in the old days was mean and nasty at all levels, and compassion had yet to be heard from. Ivan the Terrible said, "A state without terror is like a horse without a bridle."

When the terror relaxed, the horse grew unruly. Infected with French republican ideas, a group of young army officers, members of the Imperial Guard, revolted against the czar in December 1825. Had the censor been more vigilant, this might not have happened. Most were softhearted liberals, though, and of course they botched the job. Later that year, ironically on France's Bastille Day, the ringleaders were hanged outside Peter and Paul Fortress on the Neva.

In August winter is coming on, and men are stacking cordwood on the far side of the river, along the University Embankment. A line of small maples marches with the embankment, the leaves already starting to turn. Storm clouds bringing rain roll in from the Gulf of Finland, and soon falling snow will create a winter wonderland, but like the flower that hides the serpent beneath it. Often when it snows you don't see the river until it is under your feet. This aspect of the city wasn't lost on Osip Mandelstam, the century's best Russian poet. He said living in St. Petersburg was "like sleeping in a velvet coffin."

Neva in Finnish means swamp, and wraithlike vapors, simulating reality, flicker over its surface. Choosing unstable ground for the site of his capital, Peter the Great built it on the bones of a hundred thousand men. Carytids, they held up the mighty edifice of his bureaucratic state until it crushed them. Before this happened they filled in the swamp, dragging earth from far away, sometimes in the hem of their pitiful garments. When they died, of exhaustion, hunger, or disease, they were buried in the clothes they wore, in the earth they had carried. Their bones aren't inert, though, but quicken in death, breeding spectral shapes from decay. Yevtushenko saw all classical Russian literature originating in St. Petersburg's white nights and dreams, "swirling like the mystical vapors on the marshes."

On both banks of the river, columns topped with architraves face the elegant buildings, painted in muted pastels. Pale red and apricot, like marzipan pastries, yellow, lime green, and robin's egg blue, they overlie the harshness of the north land. Turn back the clock and you see it as it used to be, when gloomy forests ringed the burgeoning city. Wolves came from the forest into its streets, and an account of the time tells of one who seized a woman in broad daylight and ate her. But Peter, taking the wish for the deed, called St. Petersburg "this paradise. Truly," he said, "we live here in heaven." The glowing pastels that beautify its facades help foster the illusion. Perhaps all art is like that, plastering over the void, and St. Petersburg is a great work of art.

Deposited on the English Embankment with nary a glance from Customs (they don't scowl any more but snooze on their benches) I feel a hand twitching my shirtsleeve. "Speechki?" the man is saying. Have I got any matches? From my pocket I fish a matchbook, courtesy of the ship's bar, and he lights his evil-smelling papirosa, dragging deep.

"You English?"

"American," I tell him. He likes Americans, and when he speaks English, tries for an American accent. "Tries," wrote the teacher, grading my daughter in home economics. "I am Pavel," he says, showing crooked teeth and a self-deprecating grin. "What you in America call a toot."

"You toot your own horn?" I ask him.

"I give tips and drum up business," he says. "I am—"

"A tout!" I say, and he nods in agreement.

Different from the squat and jowly Brezhnevs and Khrushchevs, Pavel is a skinny Russian, whose long face and smoldering eyes recall Solzhenitsyn's. His muscled hands are a peasant's, though, almost wristless where they join the arm, like a football player whose head sits on top of his shoulders. To emphasize a point, he stabs you with a blunt finger, driving the air out of your chest. Waiting at dockside, Pavel hopes to pick up some change from the tourists. "My native city," he says, taking it in with a sweep of his hand from the Admiralty Arch, where Nevsky Prospekt begins, all the way to the lavra that gives the city's biggest thoroughfare its name.

The lavra is a monastery, one of the important ones. St. Petersburg's remembers a Russian hero-saint, Alexander Nevsky, victor over the Teutonic knights in a famous battle on the ice. Prokofiev, whose music glorified the battle, likened these early invaders to Hitler's. Russians, standing in the breach, have saved the West more than once, when barbarians sought to destroy it. In our own time they have done this again, driving their own barbarians out of the Kremlin. I think it may be left to them to save us from rampaging Islam. More than most, they know about the threat it poses. Perhaps they feel the pull of its seductiveness, having lived in the monochromatic world for so long.

Pavel knows the city "from nuts to bolts," and perhaps I would care for a guide? I don't want a guide, but after the horde of well-heeled shoppers on the cruise ship, hot for *beryzka* dolls, fur hats, authenticated icons, and hand-painted boxes, I wouldn't mind someone to talk to. Not much younger than me, Pavel will have seen a few things, unless blind. He isn't blind, and we strike up an acquaintance.

His job, "if you could call it that," is restoring old paintings. He works half days, all the work they will give him, at the Russian Museum on Mikhailovsky Ploschad, earning, he says bitterly, about the same pay as the babushka who hangs up coats in the cloakroom. This is standard in "Peter," his name for the city, and the price of living in paradise. Whether he means to be ironic isn't clear. Later I understand that in most things he tells me irony and the unvarnished truth go together.

For instance, the name of the city he lives in, mutable and the same, like the people themselves. "First it was St. Petersburg, named for you know who. Well, actually, his patron saint. Then, during the First War when German was verboten, it turned into Petrograd. Now that we've seen through Lenin, we're back where we started. But the name doesn't matter," he says with a touch of pride. "Whatever the world wants to call us, people who live here call their city 'Peter.'"

As we walk along the embankment toward Senate Square, we talk about the founding father and his "Window on the West." The Baltic Sea it looks out on laps another universe, different from Russia's, says Pavel. Civilized when St. Petersburg had yet to be dreamed of, islands like Goteland stand over the sea, and cultivated port cities surround it, to the south Tallinn in Estonia, Copenhagen to the west, Stockholm to the north, to the east Helsinki, close except in feeling. Before it went down to defeat at Poltava, imperial Sweden controlled most of this land. Its feeling is German, part medieval, part baroque, but the czar wanted something new. Notoriously, he started from scratch.

"Strictly speaking," I say, "that isn't an option." Pavel agrees, and says that the czar's window, like a mirror, gave him back what he looked at. It wasn't old Europe, America either, where New York was already a going concern, but a fairy-tale city of gilded hemispheres and pylons. Peter, who dreamed this city, had the imagination of a poet. Travel to foreign lands stirred his imagination, and in Amsterdam he saw a city built on islands, separated by canals and stitched together with bridges. Overlooking the canals, the tall gabled houses didn't spread themselves, however. This detail Peter modified. A giant, he craved low ceilings. They made him look even bigger than he was, and his buildings are less tall than wide.

He had a "phobia," that all-purpose modern word that purports to describe everything while getting at the quiddity of nothing. I use the word consciously, Peter seeming to me like the famous riddle wrapped in an enigma. His phobia was the fear and hatred of the other, and he meant to redo the world in his own image. Struggle obsessed him, against the Swedes or the past or the backward-looking clergy. As czar he toughened his people for the struggle to come. It was always looming, the one thing they could count on. When he lived in Holland as a young man, he visited a dissection theater. His Russian comrades cringed at the sight of cadavers, but he made them bite off a dead man's muscle with their teeth. Pavel compares him to those gargoyles you see on the walls of old churches. "They scare you, at the same time make you laugh." Emceeing the big dinner after Poltava, he sang with the priests, beat time for the orchestra, set off the fireworks, and carved the roast oxen himself. "Like Bottom in your Shakespeare, he wanted to play every part in the play, even Thisby's."

Turning away from the river, we pass the czar's Senate and Synod, color of old ivory. In these twin buildings state and church conducted their business. Both were creatures of the czar. When the Decembrist rebels drew up their troops in Senate Square, the senators looked out the windows in horror. Swearing allegiance to Nicholas I, they nipped rebellion in the bud. By six o'clock that night, it was over. A baroque arch ties the two buildings together, and a long colonnade curves round to meet the embankment. It directs your eyes upward, to statues of angels and abstractions like Justice, personifying the work that went on here. "They weren't all that angelic," says Pavel, following my gaze, "and justice didn't always prevail. The buildings are nice, though, and if you like poetry better than truth, St. Petersburg is the best of all cities."

Peter used the church the way Stalin did, he tells me. He took away its power but let it feed at the trough, and it kept his people in line. Clergy worried about the form, while the czar looked after the substance. I think about this, thinking how most of my liberal friends identify form with the surface of things, as when we speak of the "dress of thought." Form to them is superficial. But the questions that come up when you worry the surface aren't superficial; on the contrary they tease and stimulate thought. Trying to answer them puts truth in your way. With luck, you stumble over it.

Nice distinctions are a pleasure of mine, and in my bookcase at home I have the Nicene, Ante-Nicene, and Post-Nicene Fathers of the Christian

Church. Sometimes I take down these old volumes, and what I read in them widens my eyes. In Peter's Russia they asked themselves: When you made the sign of the cross, did you hold up the traditional two fingers, symbolizing Christ's two natures, or the three fingers that stood for the Trinity? Bored by all that, Peter left the hairsplitting to churchmen. He thought, says Pavel, that the people cared more for their security than forms.

But the forms are the prop security leans on. The words of the marriage service, their sound and syntax, like the ceremony itself, help keep the marriage from coming apart. The King James Bible puts successors to shame; the Gettysburg Address beggars paraphrase. Change the content, if you have to. Whatever you do, though, don't change the form.

Dominating Senate Square, Peter's forbidding silhouette, a man on horseback sculpted by Falconet, tramples a serpent. This image out of the Apocalypse surmounts a granite monolith, shaped like the crest of a wave. The sun is bright today, and seizing the day, a good idea in Russia, brides in white wedding gowns are arranging themselves around the base of the statue. The photographer, setting up his traps, tells them to look at the birdie. Like Moscow's Red Square, this huge public place is an emptiness, without benches or chairs to sit down on.

Atop the monolith Czar Peter, his right arm outflung, summons the future. He couldn't have predicted the Communist future, and Pavel says he would have hated its godless ideology. He wasn't an ideologue. But like his successors he docketed experience, making it tractable, and put every last thing in its place. If things didn't fit he stretched them, or he cut them shorter. Pushkin called him "the Idol." In his poem "The Bronze Horseman," the czar, spurring his dark stallion, pursues the bedeviled hero through the night until he dies.

"Of course he did what he did for the good of the people!" As usual, Pavel's truth wears a lopsided grin. The facts he enumerates, stabbing with his finger, add up, however. Before Peter, he says, everything in Russia was a law unto itself. He made everyone serve someone greater than himself, the serf under the landlord and the landlord under the czar. Everyone had to soldier, go to school, climb the ladder of success. Three ladders, each with fourteen rungs, gave a man access to the three kinds of service, military, civil, and service at court. The society Peter dreamed of, where birth didn't count, only brains, sounds attractive to me, and I say so.

But Pavel has a different take. The czar's ad astra per aspera staircase led to the world's biggest bureaucracy but made little of personal allegiance.

Men whose eyes were on the stars lost all sense of where they came from. Most didn't have time for today. They weren't idiosyncratic, "like the man your Shakespeare tells of, 'in his habit as he lived,' but two-legged ciphers." He has an example, one Ulyanov, grandson of a serf but the son of an educated man, a schoolteacher, "wouldn't you know it?" Climbing Peter's staircase, the father reached the fourth stair from the top. His goal-oriented life exacted a price, though, turning the man into the achiever. "Hey, hey, I'm on my way!" Pavel sings mirthlessly, doing a little jig.

Ambition in the son, more impersonal than in the father, bred a devotion to abstract ideals, like liberty and equality. Fraternity the young man went light on, caring little for Tom, Dick, and Harry. Friends were tissue paper, tossed aside when he'd used them. Loyal to no country, he grew up in no particular village, not that he remembered. Like a character in an old-fashioned novel, he came from ___ in the province of ___. "Fill in the blanks yourself," Pavel says. "They don't matter." In pursuit of his ideals, the man from nowhere shifted from one place to another, occupying the same rooming house in the same squalid corner of an anonymous city. When his elder brother died, he inherited the title and signed himself "Nobleman Vladimir Ulyanov." Later he changed this name to Lenin.

South of Senate Square, St. Isaac's Cathedral overawes the city, as if God and his czar were looking down from the roof. In the afternoon Pavel is busy at the museum, and I go back there alone. I know a pair of saints named Isaac, early Christian fathers who cared little for the things of the world, but there is nothing early Christian about the cathedral, and its focus is decidedly worldly. Immense granite columns, admonishing all outdoors, tell of power, but only as sensibilities whose capacity is limited conceive it. Inside, pains have been taken. Four hundred kilograms of gold and sixteen thousand of malachite plus tons of bronze and meters of lazurite, porphyry, and marble spruce up the walls and pavement. More than a landmark, the gilded dome is to the city what St. Paul's is to London and St. Peter's to Rome. The cathedral, grand from a distance, turns grandiose up close, though.

During the war, when Leningrad-as-it-was lived through a German blockade, the green lawns around the entrance became a vegetable garden. I imagine the granite columns looking down haughtily on the cabbages and humble potatoes. Though the columns are real—I have read somewhere what each of them weighs and am staggered—they give the effect

of being lowered from the flies. Mass-produced statues crowd the interior, and its mosaics, work of "the golden smithies of the Emperor," knock
your eye out. "Voila, quelque chose!" I hear a French tourist say.

The last time I saw St. Isaac's, some decades ago, the Communists had
decommissioned it, converting the interior to an atheist museum. Instruments of torture stocked the museum, evoking the Dark Ages before our
enlightened age. This medieval period, a bend in the road of history, witnessed the heyday of religion. That will mean different things to different
people, austerity in early America, dourness verging on hysteria in Spain,
in Italy of the Renaissance a state of mind more laissez-faire than regulated
by the catechism. Before the Revolution, religion in Russia aspired to create the City of God on earth. It wasn't down-to-earth like Bethlehem or
Tower-of-Babylonish like public buildings under Stalin, and it came in two
models, old Corinthian inoculated with modern macrocephaly or Byzantine that owed something to the Prince Regent's folly at Brighton. Stupendous St. Isaac's follows the first model.

The Resurrection Church on the other side of Nevsky Prospekt follows the second. Blood soaks the ground it stands on, like the bleeding
head Rome's first architects discovered on the Capitoline Hill. What did
it augur but the headship of Rome, unless it augured Rome's end in a
bloodbath? Exploding in your face like a giant pinwheel, the Resurrection
Church rises on the spot where the liberal czar, Alexander II, was murdered. Terrorist bomb throwers recognized their enemy in the man who
abolished serfdom. He might have made the Revolution de trop.

Histrionic Russians know his church as the Cathedral of the Spilled
Blood. Transcending his terrible death and the wasted lives of the men
and women he liberated, it acts out a crazy fantasy of onion domes and
writhing turrets, gilded or stippled, some whipped like gobbets of cream.
Looking at the cathedral, I feel a long way from the white "Congo"
churches of Protestant New England. How does its wildness that just
escapes being Disney harmonize with that dour Russia where the standard
retort is "nyet"?

In the flea market beside the church, one of the vendors, sly but good-
humored, wants to barter with me for my Aussie cowboy's hat, bought
from a tourist shop in Visby on the Baltic. He offers in trade an "antique"
samovar, genuine silver plate. The vendors are friendly and get a kick out
of winching you up, when you think you've gone as high as you want to.
But the great city isn't people-friendly. Thundering traffic bears down on

pedestrians, like the Horseman in Pushkin's poem. On Nevsky Prospekt hordes of citizens on the sidewalk are auditioning for *Ten Days That Shook the World,* the movie. In the street a frantic press of sardine-stuffed trolley buses rushes through the lesser flotsam of Moskvas, Fiats, and so on. The spirit of the place doesn't care if you grow old and gray while you wait at curbside, getting your nerve up to cross.

Like London after the war, before every man's castle had a garage, St. Petersburg is an imperious city, its psychology still that of the knight on his charger. Peasants get out of the way. Monumental, a bad word in my thesaurus, it reminds me of our nation's capital, a cenotaph on the grand scale, nobody there if you knock. Or it is like Paris, after Baron Hauss-mann got through airing it out. Haussmann, the foe of alleyways and cul-de-sacs, tutored Louis Napoleon in crowd control. City planners in St. Petersburg took note.

The spacious boulevards that radiate outward from the Admiralty and the Winter Palace don't meander like something in nature but run straight as a broomstick. Sighting along them, the czar's palace guard had a clear line of fire. If a crowd from the city took it into its head to petition the government, the soldiers knew how to disperse them. On Bloody Sunday in 1905, two hundred thousand people converged on the Winter Palace. They brought their children with them and carried their icons, singing "God Save the Czar" as they came on. Firing from ten to twenty yards' distance, the palace guard killed five hundred, wounding thousands more. Survivors remembered the blood on the snow.

From my vantage point between the Admiralty and the Winter Palace, I look south like a soldier along the plumb line of Nevsky Prospekt, then turning on my heel, north across the river to the fortress named for Sts. Peter and Paul. St. Petersburg's first settlement grew up around the fortress, like the hut on the Palatine where the she-wolf nursed Romulus and Remus. To see it, I cross the Neva by the Trinity Bridge. Men fishing from the bridge lean over the rail or against the filigree lamp standards, designed by the same Eiffel who did the famous tower. In the foreground sun worshipers are lying on the sand that slopes down to the river. Behind them the spire of the cathedral inside the walls thrusts like a stiletto at heaven.

Built to repel the Swedes, Peter and Paul Fortress never had to do that. It kept busy all the same, though, lording it over the city. In its prison "politicals" regretted the day they were born, among them Alexei, son of

the czar. Dostoevsky slept here. Malingerers went to the prison's "Dance
Floor." Lashed to a stake, they stood on sharpened piles, shifting in their
agony from one foot to another. From a distance, they might have been
dancing.

Romanovs, beginning with Peter, are buried in the cathedral. In this
morning's *Pravda,* a more-or-less liberal daily resurrected from the dead,
I read that the ashes of the last of them, Nicholas II, are due to arrive any
day now. As the world was falling to pieces around him, he received the
British ambassador, who begged the czar to go to the country. "Do you
mean that I am to regain the confidence of my people, Ambassador, or that
they are to regain my confidence?" Nicholas asked him. He wasn't much
for humor, not a prerequisite of czars.

On July 16, 1918, at Ekaterinburg in the Urals, Nicholas and his wife
and children were shot by a firing squad in a cellar. The sickly czarevitch
didn't die at once, and a revolver had to finish him off. Anastasia, the
youngest daughter, lingered also, dying from the thrust of a bayonet. Then
the children's pet spaniel was killed, and the bodies, dumped in a mine
shaft, were doused with vitriol and burned.

Outside the fortress, the right bank of the river, bending north, takes
me past the battle cruiser *Aurora.* Behind it I come to journey's end, the
Finland Station. On a high summer day like today's, holiday crowds pack
its platforms, waiting for a train to the seashore. The guns of the *Aurora,*
still pointing at the Winter Palace over the water, fired the first salvo of
the Revolution. "Such a little boat!" a visitor says, in the joke they tell
hereabouts. "Little or not," says Second Banana, "this boat has made more
trouble for the world than any other boat yet." But its guns didn't really
begin the Revolution. That happened earlier, on April 16, 1917, the day
Lenin got down from the train.

Allen Dulles, who used to run the CIA, didn't have much more humor
than Nicholas II. Once he cracked a smile, though, at his own expense
too, and from him I know all I know about Lenin the traveler. The day in
early spring, 1917, must have been unseasonably warm. Young Mr. Dulles,
attached to the U.S. Embassy in Bern, had a tennis date, he told us, and
was eager to be out of the office. "There's a young man in the anteroom
waiting to see you," said his clerk. "Name of Lenin. Says he has something
important." "I can't see him now," said Allen Dulles, hurrying out the door
in his white flannels. That night the Germans put Lenin in the sealed boxcar

and transported him from Switzerland to the Finland Station. Then they turned him loose, "like a plague bacillus," someone said.

The morbid side of Lenin's legacy—morbid as in sick, sick—was obvious enough when I first went to Russia in the sixties. Nobody smiled! Brezhnev, their head of state, wore a scowl so perpetual as to make me yearn, almost, for the hypergelastic world of American TV. In every city on my itinerary—Leningrad, Lvov, Kiev, Novgorod, Moscow—the same stony faces were on the plaform to meet the train. Their shapes and surnames were different, but those suits and overcoats were generic. Though they didn't promise to bury us, like Khrushchev a little later, they looked forward to the day, not long now.

Lenin himself was less optimistic, and didn't expect to see the Revolution in his lifetime. On the outbreak of war, trade was booming in Russia, and a reforming head of state, having balanced the budget, was well into his program of handing over land to the peasants. Lenin's party, the Bolsheviks, wasn't the voice of the people. Rejected by both the peasants and workers, it lived a hand-to-mouth existence on the fringe. In elections for the new Constituent Assembly, it pulled less than a fourth of the vote. Against all odds Lenin triumphed. He was more resolute than most, he had fewer scruples, and messy life didn't distract him.

The Man of the Century was short, plump, and balding, indifferent to appearances, poor but not minding this, either/or in his thinking, cold in his person, prissy in his habits. If you wanted to smoke, he sent you to the toilet. Democratic principles provoked his contempt, but terrorism got his approval. Boosting his splinter group above the majority, he used force if he had to, and when the vote went against him, he dissolved Russia's first free assembly. Out of power, he made his name as a tribune of the people. In power, he repealed the right to strike, shut down the press, resurrected the secret police, imposed the death penalty. Objections to it, he said, were "inadmissible weakness."

Lenin's icy face, an archetypal schoolmaster's, rises before me, and I lift a hand instinctively to swat it away. "You wouldn't dare!" he says nervously. "Watch me!" I tell him, hooking my thumbs in my ears and waggling my fingers. Laughter is the best antidote to the gloom he engenders, and I will myself to laugh. Peeling away the leaves of the calendar, I drift back in my mind to all those dittos marked "Top Secret." I was sure the fate of nations rode on their contents! "Double Oh Seven," the head of our Secret

Service, had admonished me. "You must get those documents by heart before you destroy them." Actually, he was a she, a Ms. Fishbein who ran the Xerox room at the Government Printing House, and what she said as she handed me the packet was "Have a nice day!"

I meant to do as told and would have, except that our itinerary on the way out called for a stopover in Paris. I might have stayed in my hotel room turning pages, but I opted instead for a night on the town. The last leg of the journey found me on the train from Helsinki to Leningrad. I spent most of the journey in the men's room, shredding papers in a panic and flushing them down the water closet. I never did learn what was in them.

It seems funny in retrospect. But from the day Lenin took over, St. Petersburg began to crumble. He and his confederates never laid eyes on the city of domes and spires. Their X-ray vision cut through particular things, and they saw an abstraction behind them. Promoting the subway, they didn't spend a dime on the palaces Rastrelli built, the paintings in the Hermitage, or the cathedrals where their forefathers worshiped. Maxim Gorki, a socialist writer close to the people in power, saw them let the past run into the ground. In 1917 he addressed a manifesto to the citizens of Petrograd. Take care of your heritage, he said. "Take care of the palaces, take care of the pictures, the statues, the buildings. . . . Citizens, do not touch one stone; preserve the old things—all this is your history, your pride." But for upward of fifty years no one listened.

The best watering hole in St. Petersburg is the Astoria, kitty-corner across the square from St. Isaac's. Pavel and I arrange to meet there for our Saturday's trip to the country. When I walk in, he is seated on a bar stool, contemplating an etched champagne glass. Moisture beads on the surface, and the champagne, working up through the orange juice, pops and fizzes above the rim.

"Another mimosa for the gentleman," he tells the bartender in English. To me, he says, "You're buying."

During the war Nazis penciled the Astoria Hotel in their date books. This was where they planned to celebrate the city's surrender. For the gala dinner German General von Leeb had the invitations engraved beforehand and all ready to go. After the war they turned up in a box in Berlin.

I drop a bill on the bar and follow Pavel out the door, taking a diagonal in the direction of the river. Men on horseback are conspicuous in St.

Petersburg, and our path is blocked by an equestrian statue, patrolling the intersection between the hotel and the rear of the cathedral. Casting a cold eye on the hoi polloi, Nicholas I spurns the red salvia under his horse's hooves. This autocratic czar liked shooting down dissent, and Pushkin, a poet with a conscience, kept coming up in his gun sights. Also he decreed that no building in the city should be taller than the Winter Palace, where he lived. Pavel cites this as an instance of the ill wind that blows good. According to him, St. Petersburg's skyline, most of it on the human scale, is owing to Nicholas I.

Walking toward the embankment, we guide on the weathervane, shaped like a frigate, that turns atop the Admiralty's spire. "We too take ship O soul," Pavel says, quoting "your American poet," Walt Whitman. "Hoist instantly the anchor! Cut the hawsers—haul out—shake out every sail!" In midflight, however, he bursts his own balloon. Where the ship of state is going isn't clear, he admits. "It could be we're heading straight for the rocks."

The Winter Palace belies that, imposing order on the south bank. Beauty is order, Communism to the contrary, and its pale blue and cream facade abashes the rocks and forbids the waters to rise. Copper-green statues stand on the roof. Looking into eternity, they turn their backs to the great sweep of colonnade where the general staff meditated battles. The Alexander Column in the middle of the square is the pylon, the archway of the General Staff Building sketches the hemisphere, but an entablature crowns it, surmounted by a winged glory. Bronze horses draw her chariot, and weren't born for death. "Where is thy sting?" said the architect, a rhetorical question.

No ensemble to compare with St. Petersburg's, not the Brandenburg Gate in Berlin or even Paris's Arch of Triumph. "How would I describe it?" Pavel asks me. "Magnificent? Chilling?" "Both of the above," I tell him.

Centerpiece of the table is the Hermitage Museum, built into the palace by Catherine the Great. Ten naked Atlantes, only a loincloth saving the proprieties, hold up its portico. Pavel calls them the Dark People, his version of Russia's mute, anonymous millions. I see them everywhere in St. Petersburg, supporting the balconies and bay windows that jut from buildings on either side of the Neva's canals. The buildings are composed, with the elegance that only the eighteenth century can manage, the wrought-iron balconies are delicate as lace, but the half-bestial termini that take their weight have barely crawled up from the slime.

"What price beauty?" Pavel asks, not a question that occurred to the empress. Living alone in the Winter Palace, she said she had the mice for company. Together they viewed the pictures in her made-to-order collection. The Dark People didn't get past the front door.

If I lived for seventy years, Pavel says, and spent eight hours every day going from room to room, I might do the Hermitage. No time for coffee breaks, however. I get started the same afternoon I check out St. Isaac's. Yards of Rembrandts, Leonardos, and Renoirs go by me, and there are whole roomfuls of Cézannes and Van Goghs. Though I give a pass to the museum's 1,000,000 coins and medals and 224,000 works of applied art, I am running on empty long before the bell rings for closing. Gratefully, I prop an elbow on a convenient mantelpiece, and I then press a Wash 'n Dri against my forehead. Suddenly angry hissing sounds in my ear, and a red-faced babushka bustles up, wagging a finger. Even the mantelpiece is precious.

Opposite the museum on Palace Embankment, a small crowd has gathered, waiting while the hydrofoil noses into its berth. We are on our way to Peterhof, "Peter's Court" in Dutch, where the Romanovs camped out for the summer. The greatest of them built it to glorify his Baltic conquests, incidentally, says Pavel, to outdo the French king's palace at Versailles. Building Versailles cost France a full year's income, plus the deaths of many thousands, all of them expendable. Peter the Great put the Sun King in the shade.

As the Neva, running west, widens out toward the sea, sullen blocks of apartment houses materialize on both banks. They don't make the traveler think of Versailles. Wherever Communism planted its flag, outside Tallinn in Estonia or Moscow on the way to Sheremetyevo Airport, the landscape is like this. Concrete is of its essence, but the feeling it communicates is oddly insubstantial. Plunked down on the riverbank, not growing out of it, this complex of buildings makes a city to itself, except, as they say, there's no "there" there.

Peterhof's is an illusion but hugely compelling. In dappled shade under the big hornbeam trees, refugees from the city loaf and invite their souls. Strong-scented limes, elms, and Norway maples fan the glades. All this is a setting for the pleasure dome of the czars, fifteen hundred cultivated acres, glittering with palaces and pavilions. Nature, forced into a straitjacket, has had its revenge, however, and millions of gnats, spawned in

geared to impress you, and behind the columns the Zoological Museum looks like a temple in Karnak. *Rostra* in Latin is "prows." Sawing them off Carthaginian warships, Romans embedded them in their triumphal columns. Russians, notorious copycats, followed suit. "Don't tread on me," they warned foreign sailors, venturing into the Neva. After much bloodletting Russians have come down in the world, though. Buffeted by history, perhaps they are tired.

In the late afternoon sun I sit on my "shooting stick," a collapsible camp stool, saying "Das-vee-dahn-yah" to the statues on the roof across the river. My view is edited, a blessing, and I can't see the stony high-rises and industrial chimneys of the modern city or its gleaming supermarkets, hell on the eyes. All that is extramural, outside the walls, not walls of bricks and mortar but invisible, the contours that matter. Old "Peter," a northern Venice, opens before me on its half a hundred islands, threaded by rivers and canals. This is the city of Montferrand, builder of St. Isaac's, Rossi's Alexander Column, the Admiralty of Zakharov, Rastrelli's Winter Palace. A Johnny-come-lately as the world's great cities go, Peter antedates human history, however, and the stuffed mammoth in the Zoological Museum, found in the northern permafrost, is forty-four thousand years old.

I am looking at my pocket watch, wondering where Pavel has got to, when I sort him out in the crowd on Birzhevaya Ploschad. Taller than others, he is swinging his arms stiffly, as if arms and hands were soldered together, like the Tin Man in *The Wizard of Oz*. They have kept him overtime for once in the Russian Museum, at work on Briullov's famous painting, *The Last Day of Pompeii*. Here and there the canvas shows signs of cracking, he says, and the surface, thicker than it should be, needs cleaning. St. Petersburg, I tell him, is like this.

I don't mean the cracks and the muddy impasto but the part about the Last Day, not much they can do to fix that. "Open your eyes and you can see the volcano, almost ready to blow."

"Look around you," Pavel says, protesting. "People are smiling."

"Point taken!" I say. "At least there's that."

"There's not only that," he says. "They wear suits that fit them, even shoes that don't curl up like canoes."

"Lots more cars on the street too," I answer ironically. "Some things haven't changed, though. Have you noticed the plastering above the doors of public buildings?"

"Yes," he says, conceding a point. "The hammer and sickle."

"A block from St. Isaac's there's a plaque to Lenin's police chief," I continue. "Wherever I look, I see soldiers and cops. I get the feeling you could
throw a switch and we'd be back in 1980. I tell you what I think, St.
Petersburg is at a crossroads."

But Pavel remains upbeat. Rarely will I notice "The Three Beards" anymore, meaning Marx, Engels, and Lenin. On the walls of the city, blank
patches say where their portraits once hung. Pretty soon pollution will
make the walls all one color, and the bad old days will sink without trace.

"Maybe you haven't noticed," I say, "but billboards are filling in the
blanks on the walls. They want you to buy toilet paper and hair oil. Not
far from where we're standing, in one of the old mansions on University
Embankment, you can see where some landlord has cut plate glass windows into the upper story. Things like that couldn't happen, if this city had
a conscience."

"I guess we thank capitalism and its greed," Pavel says easily.

I don't agree. On my reading, the culprit is loss of memory. "Capitalism hasn't got a memory to lose, only a yen for dollars and cents."

"Communism is different?" he asks me, wrinkling his eyebrows.

"Communism is more efficient," I say, surprising him. "It has a program. It wants to get rid of history and begin from scratch."

"Change is the law of life," Pavel says. "When 'they' were in charge,
Nevsky Prospekt became Avenue 25 October, Leningrad replaced St.
Petersburg. They renamed the university for a Party hack. What's in a
name?"

"Names are the keys to memory," I say. "The place where we store up
the past. If you want to get rid of memory, change the name."

In front of the Zoology Museum, an ancient of days is peddling soft
drinks from a traveling kiosk, mounted on a pair of bicycle wheels. Jingling coins in his pocket, Pavel calls the old man over and buys us each a
kvass. "It's warm and not quite beer," he says, "but it only costs a few
kopeks."

We sip from our plastic cups for a moment, but Pavel has more to say.
"There have been worse times in Peter," he tells me. "I didn't live through
the Blockade not to know that the city won't fold."

Too young to serve in the war, he stayed home and watched his family
die. His city came close to dying, he says, hunger and cold accounting for
almost a million. "But the theaters never closed, even though the actors

were starving. Children never stopped going to school. In winter, trucks brought supplies across Lake Ladoga. Hundreds went through the ice, their drivers still at the wheel. But the Way of Life never snapped." Pausing, he looks down at his erector-set hands. "We're not ready yet for the Last Day."

Over our heads the sun, moving west, fires the buildings on the embankment. The sky is almost empty, most birds in the city having fled the approaching cold. But the crows we have always with us, and on a stanchion by the river I spot a solitary siskin. A breeze has sprung up, and sailboats, their sails freshened, needn't tack between the south bank and the Petrograd side on the north. Like an old lizard warmed by the declining sun, I turn my face in its direction. But the breeze is off the water, and I feel the coming fall in my bones. St. Petersburg's fishermen, fixtures on the bridges all summer long, are nowhere to be seen, gone for the year, Pavel says. When the ice melts, however, the sparling, a deep-sea fish, runs upriver to spawn and die in Lake Ladoga, and the fishermen return again. Pavel says I mustn't miss the running of the sparling, but if I'm to see it, I'll have to come back in the spring.

8

Proserpine's Island

I discovered early that we are all loners. Pop worked in downtown Manhattan and was gone right after breakfast, not to return until dark. We didn't play catch together, and he never took me out to the ballgame. When Mom bent down to kiss me goodnight, I smelled her scent, "Lily of the Valley," a lily, coolish and white. Once a week on Fridays, she went to the movies, Loew's on Kings Highway. I remember her walking away, down Avenue M to the bus stop. She was Myrna Loy to the life, her thick black hair crowned with a pillbox hat worn at a rakish angle, and I wondered if she would ever come back.

When still in grade school and wanting to please her, I got in the habit of going to church every morning. This was before they replaced the Latin mass and the formal structure that had imposed an order on the day. But at the same time I found the order constricting, like a tightly wound scarf. The world I lived in felt that way too, as if it were choking me. Indians were out there, and I dreamed of building a fort in the Badlands, with crenels for guns and walls thick enough to withstand them. It took a long time before I realized that there weren't any Indians. But the menace was real, though not personal to me. Today I'd call it existential, an all-purpose word for the ills flesh is heir to.

Like many youngsters without a cause, I was an omnivorous reader. Already in my teens I was reading the five volumes of Freud's collected papers, hoping to discover what ailed me. Effects got second place to caues. An early paper on the defense of neuropsychosis kept me on pins and needles for a nine-hour bus trip through rural Mexico, en route to the capital city. This was meant as a summer holiday to take me out of myself, said my parents. Mexico D.F. when I finally got there seemed less a city than an embodied chaos, foxy men with brilliant hair who looked like Cesar Romero, sexy women heavy on eyeshade, traffic wilder than the Circus Maximus in the days of Ben Hur.

I won't soon forget the rickety conveyance that brought me to the city. People and animals shared it, an open urinal ran down the middle of the aisle, and a hamper of chickens squawked in the luggage rack overhead. At some point in the journey I became aware of a wet substance dripping down the back of my neck. Looking up in alarm, I saw that a gunny sack of rice had split open and was aiming its soggy pellets at me.

But I kept my eyes glued to the page, hunting order. Unconcerned with that and me, my fellow passengers smoked, snored, and sang, the chickens squawked, the urinal smelled, and at last the bus creaked into Mexico City. To my astonishment, I felt as if I'd been there before. I was seeing it, of course, through the lens of American movies. Foxy men with brilliant hair looked like Cesar Romero, women had ropey hair and went heavy on eye shade, and traffic was wilder than the Circus Maximus in the days of Ben Hur. But in the midst of chaos, sleepy-eyed paisanos sauntered along the sidewalk as if they owned it. Living in chaos, they gave no sign that they noticed. How astonished they were! I imagined them strumming popular ballads, "south of the border, down Mexico way."

They couldn't have had more than a few pesos in pocket, reason enough to be glum, though only they seemed to hear a melody in the meaningless static around them. Our raucous sound and light show conspires to defeat all meaningful communication, and hearing the melody isn't easy. But order is the condition of life, and if you meant to grow old, you must latch on to it. Otherwise life reduces to sound and fury. So, cocking an ear, I listened.

Not knowing enough to come in out of the rain, I walk the ramparts of Enna's castle, built seven hundred years ago and looking its age. Rain was falling all over Sicily the first time I came to the island, en route to a *borsa di studio* in Rome's American Academy. *Borsa* is "purse," and they filled it with lire, grimy bills held together with scotch tape. The old *Vulcania*— teak paneling and brass fittings, little boys in Philip Morris suits striking chimes for tea and bouillon—lay over for most of a day in Palermo, where

Mike Kelly waited at dockside. Attaché without portfolio at the U.S. consulate—that is, Langley spook—this former college chum promised a day to remember.

Our afternoon's rubbernecking ended with dinner at the Villa Igiea in Acquasanta, outside the city. For starters they offered artichokes, new to this callow traveler. Nobody cuing me, I ate mine to the last bite, leaves, prickly needles, and core.

That was then, and I have learned to deal with artichokes. However, I haven't packed an umbrella. The telescope on the battlements is protected by a wooden cupola, though, and sheltering beneath it, I make out Lake Pergusa in the near distance. Brackish dead water, it discolors the plain like a bowl of dark Jell-O. No tides ruffle the surface, and not even the geodetic people can say if the lake has an outlet. Ancient Sicilians thought it covered the entrance to Hades. Pluto or Dis ruled this kingdom of the dead with his queen, Proserpine, snatched from the land of the living. Each year in the spring she left the underworld, assuring the rest of us a new lease on life. "Lease" was all it was, though, and in the fall death reclaimed her.

The great rock jutting out northeast of the castle is named for Ceres, the corn goddess, Proserpine's mother. Milton remembered the rape in "that fair field of Enna." His account has Proserpine gathering flowers when "gloomy Dis" carts her off in his wagon. The story as he tells it brims with tears, a version of the fall of man. Broken towers still ring the castle, and from the tallest, Belvedere della Sicilia, the view rates three stars in my guidebook. But rain blots the fair field, and the lake Pluto came up from looks "Stygian" where you see it at all.

Enna on its pinnacle enjoys a bird's eye view of history. This fosters detachment, and from up on top intruders on the plain below clump together. If it's A.D. 500 they must be Vandals. Characters in this costume drama keep changing, and history on the island notes their entrances and exits. When Byzantines ruled Sicily, Arabs called Saracens, a wave flooding from Africa, broke against the city on its eagle's perch. Later, Normans, a new wave, drove these Arabs back to the sea.

The fortress-city used to rule the interior, where pickings are slim and scrawny little towns like Prizzi and Corleone call attention to the emptiness around them. When the rains come in winter, yellow *cavoliceddi*, mustard flowers, dust the land, but the summer sun burns them away. A hundred years ago poor folk in their tens of thousands cleared out of these towns, seeking a better life in the New World. They brought along their dark turn of mind, and modern-day Americans know about Corleone. Gorgeously colored in *The Godfather* movie, it looks like an Impressionist painting. The movie's young hero finds an ideal helpmate in this earthly paradise, but violence, on the prowl, takes her from him.

No longer "Sicily's navel," Enna (pop. 28,000) sends its young men north to Turin and Switzerland or south to the petrochemical refinery in Gela. Italians in the north, all for cheap labor, look with contempt on these southerners. They have a saying: Europe ends at Naples. In the main square named for Victor Emmanuel, the little king from Piedmont, shop windows are shuttered and traffic is nil. Splendid but damp in white gloves and white helmet, the cop on his podium has nothing to do but kill time.

Turning left in my Fiat out of the square, I bump forward slowly into Piazza Crispi. The bronze fountain copies Bernini's *Rape of Proserpine* in the Villa Borghese, Rome. This sculptor handled marble as if it were bronze, and if you look closely at the original you see the dints in the flesh left by the god's brutal fingers. Terrified, the maiden shrinks away, but he has her, and a marble tear falls from her eye. Crispi, a local hero who spoke for reform, made his way to the top in the new Italian state. Becoming prime minister, he meant to do good but left his people worse off than he found them.

Shapes loom out of fog as I descend the hill of Enna and rejoin the modern world. The *autostrada,* a concrete ribbon wrapped around the island, runs east to Catania and ends at the Ionian Sea. Going the other way, it ends at Marsala, Arab Mars-al-Allah, the harbor of God. But long before the Arabs, Phoenician traders dredged the harbor and put down fresh roots on the coast. Homer's rootless heroes sailed the waters to the north. Lurking in this Tyrrhenian Sea, Scylla and Charybdis dragged some of them under. Near the Gulf of Gela, washing southern Sicily, the poet Aeschylus died, brained by a tortoise shell dropped by a passing eagle.

Trinacria, ancients called the sea-girt land, like a tricornered hat on the waters. Its peak looks toward Africa, visible on a clear day. Trinacria's emblem, stitched on aprons for the tourist trade, shows a three-legged figure, the twisty legs angling out from a disembodied head. Palermo on the north coast is Sicily's head. Like John the Baptist's it sits on a platter, the littoral, cut off from the past when its splendors put Rome's in the shade.

Blank walls, a stage set embellished with statues, box in Palermo's four corners, Quattro Canti di Città. The city's four *mandamenti* swear by these statues, one appointed for each jurisdiction. But the patron saints on the walls turn a deaf ear on their constituents. In the warren of tiny streets that move out from the center, raggedy today merges with yesterday, and tomorrow doesn't look any better. Men and women in Palermo take no thought for tomorrow. Not masters of their fate, they don't use the future tense. "I have to go," you hear them saying, leaving "shall" and "will" to others.

Palermo as it was in its heyday lies within a mile's radius of the Quattro Canti. You can make the circuit by bus but have to buy your ticket at the tobacconist, often *chiuso,* out to lunch. Traffic is *pazzo,* as in *Marzo pazzo,* "crazy March," and drivers, coming to an intersection, play chicken. Nobody wears a seat belt, machismo forbidding this. With time to spare, I set out to keep my appointment on foot.

Along Via Roma, Japanese tourists have buried the dress code with their late emperor. Young men peddle Zippo lighters or swipe at car windows, hoping to wash them for a few lire. A sign fastened to a lamp standard promotes a local clinic specializing in *dosaggi ormoni* ("guaranteed to pep up your sex life"). Further south in Pretorio square, the rococco fountain strains at its moorings like Donizetti's balloon. Nymphs, tritons, and river gods, some minus a hand or a couple of toes, attitudinize in the circular basin. Their missing pieces are thanks to the *menefreghisti,* the don't-give-a-damn ones. At night they roam Palermo's streets, and what time's tooth has spared they make up for.

Pausing for breath, weary Palermitani sit on the raised curbing, their backs to the fountain. Mike Kelly, where he said he'd be, doesn't need a name tag. Redheaded and taller than others, he licks the ruins of a sweet from his fingers. "Pasta reale. Marzipan to you." No longer our man in Palermo, he has come in from the cold looking shop-worn—red hair streaked with silver, chinos and scuffed gym shoes—and when he gets up to shake hands, lists to starboard. A dose of *lupara* will do that, he says. *Cosche* favor this sawn-off shotgun, loaded with "wolf shot," ball bearings. Sicilian for the mob, *cosche* means a thick cluster of artichoke leaves, and if I have forgotten our long-ago dinner, he hasn't.

Life in Palermo agrees with his sweet tooth. He'd walk a mile for a tube of cannoli, fried pastry stuffed with sugar, ricotta cheese, bits of citrus, and chocolate. Marzipan is his passion. The best, *frutta di Martorana,* comes from the convent beside the Martorana church where the nuns make the almond paste, shaped and colored like apricots, rosy apples, and pears.

Mike knows Palermo better than the Blue Guide, but his city isn't Augustus Hare's, much less sedate than that nineteenth-century tourist's. Its churches, palaces, and temples back a ramshackle stage crowded with supers in a Mascagni opera. The opera always ends badly, but the supers don't pull a long face. Presents "from the dead" cheer them up on All Saints' Day, the dead getting their due on All Souls' a day later. On this "Giorno dei Morti" parents decorate the graveyards and hand out sugar dolls to their children. For the feast of St. Rosalie they set aside a full week in July. In the 1700s Lampedusa's prince, not the novelist, an ancestor, paid for the fireworks, glad to do this for the city's protectress.

Hoisted on a huge cart drawn by garlanded horses, she moves through the streets, where children fill the air with small paper disks like confetti. The bits of paper are *coriandoli,* coriander seeds. One of those fantastic church fathers I like to read at bedtime identified it with the manna from heaven. The manna doesn't always come down on demand, and St. Rosalie, like Proserpine, wears two faces. In a bad July when the wheat harvest fails, barefoot flagellants appear on the streets. Some curse the saint for not keeping her side of the bargain.

Niece to a Norman king, William the Good, she began early on to display religious symptoms and, leaving the world at fifteen, hid herself on Mount Pellegrino. For five hundred years she was never heard of, carried bodily to heaven, people said in Palermo. Eventually, though, they found her bones near the top of the mountain. The reliquary, a silver casket kept under lock and key in Palermo's cathedral, isn't often exposed to the public. But never mind the churlish sexton, this Assunta church deserves a visit for its own sake. *Matrice,* or center, of the medieval town, it mixes Romanesque and Gothic under a neoclassical dome. Royal tombs in the south aisle remember Norman King Roger and the German emperors, "Holy Roman," who ruled Sicily after he did. *Assunta* is "Assumption," and remembers the Mother of God. Outliving her son, some say for three years, others for fifty, she went to heaven still clothed in the flesh.

The front tomb on the left is Frederick II's. German tourists, flocking in winter to the island in the sun, deck his tomb with anemone and laurel. Half-German, half-Norman, Frederick was *Stupor Mundi,* "Wonder of the World." He lived in Oriental splendor, kept a harem, wrote poetry, and patronized poets. Sicilians think he lives on in the flaming cone of Etna, waiting to come back in his kingdom's hour of need.

Americans, in a hurry when they bombed Palermo in the Second World War, opened the bomb bays and hightailed it for home. Monuments, houses, and munition dumps went up together, and fifty years later the holes in the ground are still there. Cottage hovels perch on the brink in the Albergheria quarter, southwest of the old Norman palace. But the bombing blew good to some, and where the slums used to be an open-air market claims squatter's rights. In Piazza Ballaro, the produce stalls and truck beds are heaped with pods of broccoli, some bigger than a man's head.

Limestone hills, the Conca d'Oro, cup Palermo's tangle of palaces and slums. Nineteenth-century travelers like Augustus Hare praised the view from this "Golden Shell," a vast garden of orange and olive trees. Urban sprawl has plowed under the garden, and the modern city, using up the littoral, straggles west to the airport, thirty kilometers away. Twin sentinels, Mount Pellegrino and Mount Aspra, "Bitter Mountain," guard the port on its seaward side. On Mount Pellegrino an enormous statue, St. Rosalie's, rises northeast of the summit. Zigzagging "old stairs," *scala vecchia,* lead to the top, but pilgrims today mostly prefer motorized transport.

Scooped from the bomb sites, anthills of rubble dot the marina, above them a rusty Ferris wheel, ghost of carnivals past. Arabs housed their elect, el-Halisah, in this dilapidated quarter, and a thousand years later the Arab presence persists in Palermo. Reconsecrating their cathedral, Normans sprinkled holy water on an old mosque. As you enter from the south porch, the left-hand column is inscribed with squiggly verses from the Koran. Behind the long facade of the Norman-plus-Saracen palace, the Palatine Chapel pays its respects to Islam. Down an avenue of granite pillars, God above the altar and the king on his dais confront one another, and geometry confronts the Word Made Flesh. Stalactites, not cherubs, hang from the cupola over the sanctuary, octagons on the coffered ceiling displace the heavenly host. Out of love with the "human face divine," Arabs dreamed their different dream, preferring an art of abstraction.

Crowned in the cathedral on Christmas Day 1130, King Roger ruled his city through a deputy, "emir" of Palermo. The emir was Greek and his title a holdover, evoking Islam, but neither Christians nor Muslims thought it unbecoming. On the ceiling of the Palatine Chapel, Muslim revelers appear, some wearing haloes. South of the Quattro Canti, the dome of the Martorana church quotes a Byzantine hymn, the inscription is lettered in Arabic, and the great campanile is Norman. In its shadow, the little red domes of San Cataldo only need a minaret to convert this Christian church to a mosque.

The mosque is long gone on Via dei Benedettini, "Street of the Benedictines," but Moorish Granada blooms in the cloister garden of St. John of the Hermits. Roses, jasmine, and red hibiscus perfume the garden, Wandering Jew grows where it wants to, and around the ancient *pozzo,* or well, philodendrons with long pods like bananas, kumquats, and locust trees bend to the hand. Clipped boxwood, severely formal, encloses the garden, framed by a double-columned arcade. This opulent place has its orders. Five domes surmount the church and a door at the east end opens on an older structure, empty like an anchorite's cell. From its *mimber,* or pulpit, the imam called the faithful to prayer. Palermo in its great age, accommodating Greek, Norman, and Arab, thought up this catholic style. It isn't permissive where anything goes but tolerant, implying decisions.

Mike is a history buff, not the pots-and-pans variety but "battles and leaders." Too young himself for the Allied invasion of German-held Sicily, he has it all by heart and wants to show me the east coast where the Allies drove the Wehrmacht back to the sea. Taking the scenic route, we drop south from Palermo, then pick up the highway, cut between hummocky hills. Not many live in the steppe lands, a moonscape of frozen curds like the one the camera captured when the astronauts went to the moon. Throats are parched in this *latifondo* country—large landed estates—and water leaks away through the thin crust of soil. If you mean to keep a cow, you need ten acres' grazing.

Lowering toward the sea, the plateau melts into farmland, but mountains, north and east, pinch off the subtropical coast. A single chain, they continue the Apennines, coming down from Italy, and Africa's Atlas Mountains, coming up from the south. Sicilians scrape a living between them. Etna, ready to detonate, overawes the east and much of the center. Snow scallops its peak and lies heavy on the flanks, taking up half the sky. Taormina to the east, domesticating this difficult neighbor, offers views. Tourists bored with Capri fill the grand hotels, one of them a Bristol, always a Bristol, and the streets and squares are lined with ceramic shops, pastry shops, and boutiques.

A twelfth-century Frenchman, exiled in Sicily, wanted to know who could live in a country "where the mountains vomit fetid sulphur," boiling up above the gateway to hell. Taken from the earth, men passed through this gate and descended, like Proserpine, "into the regions of Satan." Empedocles was one of these men, and he threw himself from Etna's summit into its flaming core. Disappearing without notice but sure to come back, he pretended to godhead. The volcano foiled this philosopher, though. Burning him to clinker, it tossed up one of his sandals, denying the resurrection and the life.

Not long ago, many Sicilians had never seen a wheeled cart, and when the little king died in Garibaldi's time it took several weeks before the interior knew this. Today's news, some of it newsworthy, gets through in a jiffy, thanks to the motorcar. Hill towns, built of local red stone, lie off its beaten track, Vizzini, for instance, on our right hand to the south. Verga the novelist, raised in Vizzini, brought it to gloomy life in his *Mastro-Don Gesualdo*. A.k.a. "San Giovanni," his hometown is blackish, rusted, without a shadow, its windows opening in the heat like so many black holes, the crosses of its church towers trembling in the sun-dark air. Most travelers omit it, and the motorcar, a cocoon, whisks them through homogeneous space.

Feathery papyrus grows on verges beside the highway, also deep green acanthus. Art in Sicily follows nature, not imitating it exactly, and the fleshy leaves of the acanthus glorify its churches, like Palermo's Palatine Chapel. Corinthian columns hold up the roof, and from their capitals the stone acanthus flowers in season and out. For Norman artisans form meant more than function, or function included gratuitous things. Just around the corner nature grew like topsy, and they took in its wildness while seeing how to make nature better.

Reaching Catania and the coast, we hang a right for Siracusa, in the rain and near dark not that different from its American namesake. A *zona industriale* stretches to the horizon on either side of the road. Crushed Coca-Cola cans and empty beer bottles, *nastro azzuro,* skitter across it. Our hotel when we get there is the Jolly, a big chain like the Holiday Inn. But gigantic fluted pillars line the sides of the *duomo* in the heart of the old town. Lifted from a Greek temple, they remember the Age of Pericles, and for two and a half millennia people have come here to worship. The Greek pillars are Doric, the cathedral's apse is Byzantine, and Normans, a warrior race surprisingly deft of touch, created the twelfth-century mosaics. Under the temple, sacred to Athena but converted to a Christian church in the early centuries, excavations reveal a cluster of huts. Pre-Greek, they go back to the eighth century B.C. This "hodgepodge," Mike's dismissive word, makes an order. Staying on here and teasing it out would attract me.

As the afternoon wanes, the *passeggiata,* a daily rite, forms up on the promenade that runs beside the Piazza del Duomo. Men linking arms with men and women with women pace solemnly by the water's edge under the ficus trees. Shading this Foro Italico, the trees are like bigger fig trees. Rich, poor, and middling, the men wear a flat tweed golf cap, the *coppola,* and the women are dressed to the nines. Sun whitens the cobbles, Aeolus, god of winds, having blown away the rain. No day without sunshine on the island of Ortygia, Cicero told them back in Rome.

Bridges link the island to the city across the harbor where the fishing fleet, in from the sea, rides at anchor. On the prows of the boats an unwinking eye, sky blue like the beads that shutter their coffee bars, wards off the evil eye. Business and industry, necessary evils, occupy the modern city, incidentally polluting the waters around it. Below the city proper, the river Ciane spills into the harbor. Pleasure craft, casting off from the Foro Italico, used to take trysting couples upstream to its source. Old olive trees, lemon trees, and the pomegranates lean toward the river, on its left bank a temple once devoted to Zeus. Proserpine, they say, might have evaded her captivity in Hades, but eating a pomegranate, forbidden fruit like the apple Eve pulled in the Garden, had to stay there. Though her handmaid, Ciane, did what she could to frustrate the rape, Pluto had his way, and this luckless intercessor watered the ground with her tears. Greek *cyane* is "blue," but waste darkens the spring, and you wouldn't want to swim in the river.

In the tropics memories don't linger, and 1943, when Kesselring's Germans and Patton's Seventh Army fought their duel to the death, is ancient history in Siracusa. But older wars, like light from a dead star, still throw light on the present, and past and present run together beside the Ionian Sea. The richest city of the classical age, Siracusa had a rival, Athens, over the water. Athens is the place we come from, and stands for the good society. I am "of Athens" and reverence its precepts, most of all the summons to reason. But in 415 B.C. it launched an unholy war. Thucydides, a participant, tells what happened. Tactful historians ought to imitate history—only the facts, no editorials—but all must find a lesson in this tale of pride before a fall.

"The men, not the walls nor the empty galleys, are the city," said Nicias the Athenian, spurring on his cohorts but speaking more truth than he knew. All Sicily came in on the Siracusian side, "and we who seemed to besiege others found ourselves besieged." Blocking the harbor mouth with a chain of boats and grapples, the defenders penned in the Athenian fleet. As the army of Athens fled south, they hacked it up piece-meal. "Both army and fleet and all that ever they had perished," said Thucydides. Coming with a purpose to enslave others, they went away loaded with chains.

Survivors, seven thousand of them, went to the Latomie, stone quar-ries northwest of the city. Most left their bones there, servitude taking the rest. Sun baked them in their prison house, a cauldron open to the sky. Nights they froze, and the alteration bred disease. Few of many came home to Athens.

The quarry pits in Neapolis, an archaeological park, rank high with tourists, but citrus groves and palm trees hide the deep cuttings and bougainvillaea hides their vertical sides. Hewn from the rock, a semicir-cular amphitheater overlooks the park and the base of a colossal altar, two hundred meters long. Broken pillars sketch the portico that used to enclose it. Sicilians live in the ruins but turn an indifferent eye on the past. Absorbed in the day's business, they let the dead bury their dead.

In the Quarry of the Capuchins, named for the monks who built the nearby convent, the vegetable gardens have gone back to nature. Lichen slicks the damp ground where the sun doesn't penetrate, and tufts of maidenhair root in the crannies. *Capelvenere,* locals call this fern, "hair of Venus," remembering the goddess who came from the sea. Above the Latomia di Santa Venere, the tomb with a Doric pediment belongs to Archimedes. Still thinking up inventions, he died by accident when Romans sacked his city in 211 B.C.

South and east of the park is the church of Santa Lucia, Siracusa's patron saint. Martyred on the spot—just here, tour guides say—she went travel-ing in death. Byzantines, great relic hunters, took her body away, and later Venetians stole it from Constantinople. Caravaggio, an exile too hot for Rome to handle, painted this saint's burial. I look for his work in the Museo Nazionale, a bone shop. Almost lost among tomb slabs, intarsia panels, bits of classical sculpture, church vestments, terra-cotta figurines, and a pair of old carriages, St. Lucy lies on the ground, awaiting interment. Caravaggio puts her front and center in the painting, but his eye is on the grave diggers, busy at their chores. One has a great brawny bottom swathed in cotton, silvery where it catches the light.

Down the street from Ortygia's museum is the Arethusa Fountain, a cistern sunk below the piazza. Eighteen hundred years ago a Greek traveler described it. "An isle Ortygia lies on the misty ocean over against Trinacria where the mouth of Alpheus mingles with the springs of Arethusa." Alpheus the river rises in Greek Olympia, dark with old sacrifice. Its indwelling god meant to rape Arethusa, but this wood nymph, plunging into the sea, emerged in Sicily, changed to a fountain. The god, taking the same likeness, ran her down, however, and now his spring and hers flow together. If you throw a cup in the river at its faraway source, it comes up again in Sicily, reddening the fountain with blood. Anyway, old chroniclers believed this.

Visiting Arethusa's fountain is a must for tourists, and I do as expected, wrinkling my nose. *Foul* is the word for this outsize laundry tub where ladies of Ortygia did their week's wash. Warned off by the iron balustrade, the ladies are gone, but algae films the murky water, ducks paddle its surface, and local fishermen, leaning over the rails, cast for bream. Papyrus edges the cistern, the same that grows beside the spring of Ciane. Some say it got here from Egypt, a gift of the Ptolemies, others that conquering Arabs introduced it before they went back where they came from.

I want to make a pilgrimage to Monreale outside Palermo, one of the world's holy places, and early in the morning Mike meets me at my hotel. The Grande Albergo delle Palme, a stone palazzo on Via Roma, is the work of the Inghams, nineteenth-century Britishers who introduced the world to the wines of Marsala. A stuccoed frieze of dancing girls runs the length of the lobby, Art Nouveau windows filter the light, and coyly erotic statues stand about in the corners. Wagner finished his *Parsifal* in the hotel, and his bust on a pedestal wants you to notice.

Cassaro Vecchio takes us west from the city, past the Norman palace and the cathedral on its green island, defended by a phalanx of saints. Seventeenth-century villas, nineteenth-century townhouses, and high-rise condos flank the main drag coming into Monreale. Outside the church,

mementoes of St. Louis, king of France and an unlucky crusader, are selling briskly. An urn on the altar has his internal organs and heart. But it
isn't for St. Louis that I have come here.

As we enter the church a fanfare of sound rolls up the nave, and the
Pantocrator looms out of darkness. The organist in the choir is fingering his
keyboard, and a thoughtful tourist has fed the coin box that turns on the
lights. Delphi, the first time I saw it, was like that, a thunderclap and startled doves beating the air above the oracle's cave. I thought they thought
God spoke in the thunder. The god in the apse has great staring eyes, and
the iris appears to float free. Wherever we turn, we are under surveillance.
Better to make a clean breast of it, if one of us has something to hide.

An artificial world pieced together out of glass, precious metal, and
stone, Monreale's is natural too. In a corner of the cloister south of the
church, lions, yawning but toothless, spill water in the Arab fountain. Atop
the twin columns that mark off the cloister, birds peck the spiral scrolling.
Writhing shapes like vines or creepers coil up the trunks of these petrified
trees, and the acanthus leaves look blown by the wind. Heads peer from
the foliage, Proserpine's among them. In touch with a darker world before
our new dispensation, she belongs in this pantheon, and maybe Christ's
mother, Mater Dolorosa, owes something to the pagan queen of sorrows.

In a god-obsessed time, somebody cared about the world and its business, and the church's mosaics mingle profane with their sacred. The carpenter and his adze have been at work on Noah's Ark, strewing the deck
with wood shavings. After centuries, you can still see them. In the ladder
that leads down to terra firma, you can see the nails that fasten the rungs
to the risers. Going up the ladder, animals, two by two, are glad to get
away from our doomed habitation. But going down again after the Deluge, both lion and lamb look reluctant.

Moving as the light moves, the blazing mosaics quiver like water, or like
a sun-besotted sky above the pillars that keep it from falling. Sages in the fire
recite the course of human history, beginning with the Creation and ending
with the last days. God hangs on the cross, but though dying he doesn't
die, and like the Emperor Frederick waits to come back to his kingdom.
Reserved for this Second Coming, the throne in the presbytery is vacant.

In the meantime things don't look good. Cain murders Abel on the
walls of the nave, and with this bloody fratricide history begins. Over the
main entrance fire licks the walls of Sodom. Lot and his daughters make
it to safety, but Lot's wife, looking back, is turned to a column of salt.

Forfeit to the underworld, she has her chance to escape. Like Proserpine, though, she can't seize it.

"Original sin" is the culprit, and contemplating it guiltily, all must say mea culpa. But Adam and Eve, eating the forbidden fruit, don't look guilty, only confused. Near the high altar he delves and she weeps with a shuttle in her hand. On the church's bronze doors an angel drives them from the Garden. Eve, reaching out to her mate, offers comfort, to him and the rest of us, unwilling legatees. But Adam ignores her. He is our surrogate, and throws up a hand in despair.

Christianity is a provisional faith, unable to answer the questions implicit in last things. To save us, it must rely on God's grace, a gift we can't earn or bid for, to save us. The "Greek thing," Pliny's phrase, is different. No riddle too thorny for these rational men, problem solvers like King Oedipus. Back in the beginning they colonized Sicily, opening the windows and letting in the light. Phoenicians, there before them, preferred a world like Caravaggio's, light infiltrated by darkness. Casting off for Gibraltar and the waters beyond, they left "Magna Graecia" to their successors. Wanting to know where I come from, I set out on their track, racing the sun as it wheels west from Palermo. Stowing his long legs under the dashboard, Mike climbs into the Fiat beside me.

Cellas, stylobates, and metopes are all Greek to him, but he responds to the countryside, "like California east of Barstow." Palms and giant carob trees bend away from the sea, then the road dips inland between the salt flats of Trapani and the plains of Castellamare. In the up-and-down country the olive groves go on forever until, without warning, the temple appears on its spur. Western Sicily's major city a long time ago, Segesta is deserted. Daisies gild the plateau, punctuated by goats, baaing sheep, and a woebegone sheepdog. Outside the café, its roof alight with bougainvillaea, unhopeful vendors make a pass at the handful of tourists.

Wars with Greek Selinunte kept this city on the boil. Today's winner lost tomorrow, then, the wheel turning, they went at it again. Arabs, strictly business, put a stop to their squabbles. Seizing Segesta, they made a Carthaginian peace.

You climb up by a path lined with bristling plants like oversize pincushions. Below in the fields, grapevines propped by stakes in long, symmetrical rows suggest a military graveyard. Wrinkled red fruit, the kind farmers feed their hogs, hangs from the cactus plants, and on the warty surfaces "Giuseppe" has scratched his name with a penknife. Fasces on a broken pillar remember Mussolini. Higher up, the Greek theater has seen better days.

But the temple still stands after two and a half thousand years. Unfinished, it lacks its cella or sanctuary, home of the cult god, and inside the portico the eye looks on vacancy. Weather, pitting the limestone columns, has cracked the metopes, square spaces in the frieze, and weeds and wildflowers widen the cracks year by year. Someday Mother Nature will bring the temple down. Archimedes could move the earth with a fulcrum, he said, but the force he disposed of doesn't hold a candle to hers. She isn't always maternal, and Selinunte previews the future. Farther south on the ocean, it lay in Hannibal's path when he came up from Carthage, bad luck to Selinuntines. But nature, not man, toppled their city.

Shattered columns lean against its building blocks, squared off like dice or rounded to cylinders. Honey-colored, the great drums weigh a hundred tons apiece. Some columns remain, survivors of the earthquake. Selinon, wild celery, pokes up through the sandy soil. This herb, good for seasoning, gave the city its name.

Putting Humpty Dumpty together again, archaeologists have reconstructed a pair of the temples. One, crowned with its entablature, rises from cypress trees, and ramparts of *tufa* stone, left over from old volcanoes, enfilade the approach to the other. At sunset a flaming sky glimmers through its colonnade, behind it the wine-dark sea where the black boats of the *tonnaroti,* tuna fishermen, ride low in the water. It really is wine-dark, like their local *vino rosso,* "Corvo," the raven. Marinella, a mile away, is built against the water, and the summer visitors who crowd it don't go home without seeing the ruins. When the season ends, however, Selinunte is left to itself.

Men and women in Magna Graecia claimed mixed descent from Greeks and Trojans. Segesta's founding father, Trojan on his mother's side, had a Sicilian river god for his father, like that Alpheus who pursued Arethusa. Aeneas, fleeing Troy, plowed the furrow that marked the line of the walls. En route to his destiny he stopped off on the island, and his adventures are part of its story. Virgil has him founding Erice, high above the sea northwest of Segesta. From the cloud-capped town, he looked back across the water to Carthaginian Dido and Cape Bon on the African coast.

Where the Norman castle broods over the sea, old Sicilians built a shrine to Aphrodite. Like Proserpine a life goddess but death-dealing, she showed an ambiguous profile, and pleasuring her lovers, tore out their genitals when sated. The mountain Erice sits on is Aphrodite's work, forced up from the ocean but left high and dry. At the base of the mountain the sickle-shaped promontory is Trapani, a Mafia stronghold. Snarling sounds of Vespas and mopeds drift up from its dingy streets. Anchises laid his bones there, returning to the arms of the goddess of love on whom he had fathered Aeneas. Off this coast she rose from bloody foam when Cronos, wielding a sickle, castrated his father and threw the severed member in the sea. Sicels, an ancient people, were first on the island, and Sicily is the land of the sickle.

The walls of Erice are "cyclopean"—that is, they don't need mortar to keep out the world. Blind facades of old stone houses tilt toward each other across the gray-cobbled streets, mostly empty except for broad-bottomed women. Making a beeline for home, they carry string bags heavy with pasta and goat cheese. But life goes on secretly in hidden courtyards behind the facades, and when spring comes to the mountain, nightingales sing by daylight in the gardens around the castle. A roller-coaster road, switchbacking through pine forests, takes you up to the top. "Mahomet's Mountain," Arabs called Erice, giving high marks to the beauty of its women. "The loveliest of the whole island—may Allah deliver them into the hands of the Faithful!" said Ibn Jubair, who liked his women substantial.

No Mason-Dixon Line divides the island, but you know you are south when you get to Marsala, astride the coastal road to Agrigento. Garibaldi and his Thousand entered the city in May 1860, step one on the road to Italy's reunification. The people broke out the tricolor when this hero came in, but most didn't know what his word *Italy* meant. Maybe it meant "La Talia," they thought, the name of their new ruler's wife. "South," a state of mind in Sicily and elsewhere, means taking life easy, passion that smolders, above all the implacable sun. Behind the coastal plain the entrails of the hills carry burning sulphur, and the leaves of the olive trees shimmer like wood burned to ash. Piddling villages snooze on the plain, a dustbin layered with the junk of our throwaway culture. On the outskirts the half-finished houses are "fruit of the emigrants." Sending money home to Sicily, they haven't sent enough.

Sun leaches out color in the arid west country, but Sicilians put it back again, and their houses, built of porous stone or cinder block, are daubed with tinted plaster. Blood-red geraniums, coming up to the windows, grow to the height of oleander bushes, and the oleander is as big as a tree.

Tomatoes in the market gardens want to be melons or squash. Sicily's Spanish masters brought the tomato from Peru, and the prickly pear cactus from the West Indies. Called Indian fig, it feeds the people and hedges the fields. The "leaves" of this all-purpose plant, like Mickey Mouse ears, stand straight up.

People in Agrigento favored the grand scale, and Plato, an early tourist, said they built "as if they would never die." But the city he knew has come down in the world, searched by war and earthquake. Nearby Porto Empedocle, nourished on the ruins, quarried its building blocks from the piles of broken limestone in the Valley of the Temples. This industrial seaport honors the philosopher, a native son. Working out his doctrine of the four elements, earth, air, fire, and water, he said love and strife kept them on the qui vive. Life dwindled whenever the temperature dropped, but disorder engineered its renewal.

Almond trees frame the temples, on a shelf below the modern town. Juno's, only a single colonnade and a few freestanding fragments, is open to the sky, and four Doric columns remember the Dioscuri's. This is a letdown, but the great temple named for Concord, alone on its rise and set off by the emptied-out country, stands foursquare like St. Peter's in Rome. Bernini, clearing out his huge piazza in front of St. Peter's, divorced it from life's distracting clutter. Around Monreale, product of a different psyche, dwellings, shops, and cottage gardens press against the walls, part of a living network. The Temple of Concord dispenses with these filaments, eager for takeoff like Donizetti's balloon.

Floodlights, illuminating the valley at night, leave its hollows in the shadows, and the temples from a distance look new as today. White stucco made from marble dust coated the limestone, but though this is gone, the tawny gold turns to chalk in the half-light. The ghostly colonnades, formed up like an army, hark back to the rational mind that conceived them. On to a good thing, this mind didn't bother to vary it much.

What you see isn't just what you get, though. In the near distance beyond vineyards and fields of artichoke, waves eat at the shoreline, and wind rising in the cypress trees tosses their plumes. From the manicured terrace of our hotel, I hear the soughing in the branches. Out there in darkness, something wants to get in. Aeschylus, on intimate terms with darkness, thought about this scary presence before the eagle laid him low. Vindicating reason, he patched a truce with the underworld, home of the Furies. These irrational spirits rose from the sea when Aphrodite did, sprung from the blood of our father, Uranus. On its official side Magna Graecia wants to disown them. No getting rid of the Furies, however, and the old poet offered them houseroom. According to him, they live in darkness, under the temples of law.

Magna Graecia disappeared nine hundred years ago when Greek Byzantium's last colonies fell to upstart Normans. Reggio Calabria, across the Straits of Messina, fell in 1060. *Addio* to their palaces and villas, they said, then for ages slept the sleep of the vanquished. In 1973 an offshore diver woke them up in Reggio. Exploring the waters six hundred meters out, he saw an arm emerging from the sand of the seafloor. This was how the world recovered the Riace Bronzes, older than Christendom and not much the worse for wear.

Lost in a sudden squall but waiting their time, they beckon from Reggio's provincial museum. Getting there isn't easy, but Mike has seen all the *pupi*—puppet shows—in Palermo and agrees to tag along. The new bill in Messina, *Orlando, Rinaldo, and Fair Angelica,* is worth an excursion, say the Sunday papers, and having done Reggio, we can catch the matinee.

On the Calabrian shore across from Messina's harbor, electrified pylons gather power for the lamps of Sicily, bringing light where there used to be darkness. Mountains on either coast come down to the water, the *traghetto* plying between them. Dropped off in Villa San Giovanni, we take the road for Reggio, *sempre diretto.* But driving "straight ahead," their best advice in Calabria, lands us up in a cul-de-sac. Where is the Museo Nazionale? The kibitzer at the curbside looks at us skeptically. "You're in front of it," he says.

On rectangular blocks packed with sand, two naked soldiers puzzle the crowd, among it a teacher, a gaggle of schoolkids, and a pair of *stranieri*. A helmet like a woolen cap covers the soldiers' heads, but the sea has worn holes in one of the helmets, and one of the soldiers has lost his right eye. Both, under the fluorescent light, look coppery green. Strife, the delight of Empedocles, keeps them alive, though, and I half expect them to step down from their platforms.

Memorizing the statues, I circle them slowly until the attendant plucks me by the sleeve. One of his sleeves is empty, and a military medal hangs from his chest. *Chiuso,* he says, time for closing. In the Kingdom of the Two Sicilies as they used to call it, time is cheap but money is dear, and the museum, short on money, closes promptly at noon.

Back in Messina, we locate the puppet show on Corso Garibaldi. However, the theater is dark. "Africa begins at the Straits of Messina," Mike says indignantly, waving the Sunday paper. Announcing a performance, it didn't mean to deceive us, but this is *settimanale,* their once-a-week closing, and a padlock and chain bar the door. Today we have no *pupi.*

Returning to Palermo along the coastal road, I stare from the window at felucca-like sails, but the men of Reggio blot out the wine-dark sea. Each held swords, the hilts still visible, also the bucklers strapped to the left forearms. The shields are gone, though. Thick beards, hiding the necks, curl and twist like their pubic hair and the shoulder-length hair that escapes from the helmets. Neither man has been circumcised, only a detail but important to the sculptor.

One of that famous tribe called "Anon," he lived in the best of times when Nicias sailed from Athens, living on to cope with the dark time that followed. Perhaps he survived the debacle at Siracusa. But he wasn't downcast, and his hand didn't swerve. Getting the muscles right—powerful deltoids where the arm joins the shoulder—he shows you how the ribs articulate in the rib cage. His heroes aren't superhuman, however, and it seems he knew this. Awaiting their fate, a fight to the death or a trip to the agora, they stand at the ready. One inclines his head slightly, the other looking straight at the camera.

9

Ɖaree *Bis*

A café in London's Soho introduced me to snails. With a show of confidence, I called for escargots. Secret in their little houses, they lay in a pie plate with bubbles let into the bottom. The idea was to winkle them out. The French have no problem with this, but on my first go the shell squirted loose from its clamp and went skittering over the table. The waiter sighed, and the girl I hoped to impress looked at me doubtfully. Things *française* might have ended right there. But I thought of the Old Guard that never surrendered, and kept at it.

My mother's father came from Marseilles, and many years later I lectured in that city, telling them what was wrong with their French Revolution. This ancestor, a painter who died young, spent the few years allotted him destroying his liver. From him I derive my fondness for drink, a strong man's weakness. At Princeton, when I was mewing my youth, I topped off lunches with a green Chartreuse. Also at Princeton I made a stab at learning French, tutored by a native speaker from Clermont-Ferrand. Polly X, as I shall call her, like those tactful old novelists who dispense with surnames, was the pretty young wife of a colleague in the Romance languages department. We sat together twice a week, turning pages in *Paris-Match,* until one day we read no more.

My then-wife, when I mumbled excuses, cut me short with an epigram: "O what a tangled web we weave, When first we labor to deceive." I wanted to reply with something Gallic and rueful, but my French wasn't up to the task. I blame the old dear who taught me the language at Dartmouth, whiling away the class hour with a stack of art postcards. The ladies on swings who showed a bit of petticoat were Watteau, and the fleshy goddesses were Poussin. What tongue they were speaking didn't concern us.

When finals rolled around, I went in panic to see the professor. "Relax!" he told me, lighting his pipe. He was that kind of professor. "*La vie est brêve, un peu d'amour, un peu de rêve.* Have a few beers, take in a movie." I did this, and next day flunked the final cold.

Reviewing the past, a habit of age, I can see why French gave me trouble. I wanted to reduce it to something other than itself. But unless for settling the bill or asking where the toilet is, anything worth saying baffles translation. That wasn't always clear to me. In my nonage I warmed to abstractions, like a son of the French Revolution: liberty, equality, fraternity, for instance. Now that I'm old I want more avoirdupois.

The mind of the Middle Ages gives me what I want. I like its habit of splitting hairs and share its taste for brambles and thistles. I like chewing them over. I believe that the name of a thing gives its nature, so think it important to get the name right. Don't call me a Monophysite: those heretics who said the Son of God was wholly divine, no scruple of humanity. I don't mind being labeled a Monothelite, however: to their way of thinking, the Son of God's nature is dual.

For modern Christians, words mean what they want them to. Their tendency is syncretic: we all worship one God, whose name doesn't matter. My tendency is to demarcate. I don't seek to abridge differences but to proclaim them. Vive la différence! as French people say. I fly to faraway places in the hope of finding the distinguishing thing. The frequent flier miles are a bonus.

Paris is like heaven, and you must climb the purgatorial mountain to get there. That wasn't true when I was younger. Perhaps things change for the worse? Clearly traveling, thanks to jet propulsion, has changed for the better. But as every traveler will tell you, that part of it that isn't airborne is worse than ever it was.

The first time I saw Paris I arrived via steamship. Aboard this floating palace, the upper crust dressed for dinner, black tie for the men, evening gowns for the women. Looking back, I see a painting by Edouard Manet. I was fiercely republican, a state of mind appropriate to youth, and thought that contrary to nature. Even the hoi polloi, living as I did in steerage, lived out of stand-up trunks with an ironing board that plopped open at the touch of a spring. That was close to forty years ago, and life has moved on, moving me in another direction. But Paris has been waiting its turn.

This second time over I fly into Charles de Gaulle, instant bedlam on the outskirts of the city. The flight is unremarkable, like sitting up all night on the subway. Taking off, we dawdle for an hour on the tarmac, the air-conditioner, referred to as "air," shutting down while we do this. Beside me, the young man in the tank top needs a bath. Midnight comes and goes with no sign of dinner, and the drinks cart is stalled behind the curtain marked "Executive Class."

Intending to make amends in the A.M., already P.M. Paris time, I head for the busy restaurant on the Rue Jacob, around the corner from my hotel. Stars like rosettes are dancing in my head, one, two, or three of them grading temples of cuisine in the Red Guide. The Tour d'Argent got three stars. How it marches today I haven't a clue, such places being out of my orbit. In the dear dead days, however, middle-class patrons could afford them and did. The tab for fine dining, like the price of a good wine, has increased exponentially since, and where once a modest salary, mine, for instance, could command both, now, though it has jumped tenfold, it commands neither. This suggests that the good life has been redefined. Today's middle class no longer identifies it with a table d'hôte dinner. It prefers an all-you-can-eat buffet, cheaper, and better suiting modern tastes.

When I last dined at the Tour d'Argent, a uniformed attendant took me up to the top for dinner. The bronze doors hissed shut, and the lift rose like an exhalation. "*C'est bien?*" it was saying, more statement than question. From a table by the window I looked down the Seine, past the flèche of Notre Dame, all the way to the Arc de Triomphe. Duck à l'orange was the specialty of the house, and the clientele, respectable *pères* and *mères,* plus the occasional tourist, tucked into it with gusto. An uncle like Daddy Warbucks, in town on business, took me along as his guest. I don't know what it cost him but doubt that I would have been staggered. Diners on expense accounts had yet to be heard of, and the Japanese in their thousands and tens of thousands were still lining up for takeoff.

Times have changed, and the restaurant of my choice sprawls over the sidewalk, like a fat man who has unbuttoned his trousers. Its outside tables are packed, promising a *bon répas,* but the gutters are choked with rubbish, and inside, the heat, thick with cigarette smoke, vibrates like the skin of a drum. A shouting match at the bar provides local color, language

salted with words like *ordure* and *merde*. Before you can say "Zut alors!"
however, two hard-looking flics in pale blue uniforms, their kepis left over
from the Foreign Legion, appear with batons at the ready. The meal takes
longer—not to eat, to serve. *Plus ça change, plus c'est la même chose,* and fast
food is still a no-no in Paris.

Sauntering up to my table, the waiter examines a spot on the ceiling.
The more things change, the more they stay the same. I ask about the
wine, perhaps a *vin de la maison?* He recoils as if stung, and I settle for a
bottle with a label. Dinner begins with snails, *escargots à la bourguignon.* No
bigger than bird shot, they taste like warm felt. The bread is for mopping
up with, but there is nothing to mop. Gripping the empty shells with my
forceps, I look in vain for the melted butter. Beef tartare, the entrée,
resembles a can of worms with a puddle of egg yolk, like a dying sun, in
the middle.

You can eat that way in Paris, and the famous way too. The "poetry" of
Bresse butter, slathered on thick tartines, delighted Henry James. But
though something kindly impressed him, "like the taste of a sweet russet
pear," he came away with a mixed bag, both sweet and sour. French taste
is often sour, and the cuisine reflects the national temper. The same is true
for their language, brandished like a sword.

Living in the city in earlier days, I hung out at the Alliance Française,
practicing *moues* with the *jeunes filles* in my French class. The old sandstone
building not far from the Luxembourg Gardens was sliced into offices and
smelled of lemon polish. Each chair in the schoolroom came equipped
with a folding-down armrest. Propping our copybooks on its ink-stained
surface, we ran through daily exercises, beginning with phrases like "La
plume de ma tante." Star of the class was "Mr. Eugenides," a Levantine
with oily skin and eyes that swiveled like ball bearings. Hateful to the rest
of us, he never made a mistake. The trio of leggy German au pair girls
were more agreeable. They were Lise, Helge, and Gertrude called Trudi,
and I eyed them over plume and papier, lust in my heart.

Most days we toured the neighborhood, letting our fingers do the
walking for us. At the charcuterie we bought a pork roast, at the patis-
serie, little cakes (*gâteaux*) laced with rum. The stationery store sold us
pencils (*crayons*) and erasers (*gommes à effacer*). Some purchases we turned
back on the salesgirl. "Non, merci, je veux celui-ci": I want this one.
Stumbling to my feet in the milliner's shop, I told the modiste that I had
no need of thread, "Je n'ai besoin pas de fil." But it didn't come out like

that. It came out *filles,* as in *jeunes filles.* Mr. Eugenides couldn't believe it, the instructor rolled her eyes, and my credit with Lise, Helge, and Trudi evaporated like steam from a kettle.

All that year I bathed in program music. The hero battled oppression, like Liszt's Tasso, or made love on the grand scale, like Don Juan in Strauss. At open-air concerts in the Luxembourg Gardens you could buy a chair on the grass for pennies. Warm evenings I sat on the edge of my chair, soaking up "Les Preludes" or the mournful strains of the "Love-Death." My loudest "Bravos!" went to Tchaikovsky and his "1812 Overture." Above the volleying cannon rose "La Marseillaise," a summons to charge the enemy and die on his bayonets. The cannon was real—I still recall the puffs of smoke—but my elation, like much else in life, didn't last. Mother Russia stood her ground, while the hero's star shot from its zenith. Napoleon was this hero, and I his loyal aide-de-camp. In one scenario I galloped up with tidings of the retreat from Moscow. "You're wounded, lad," the emperor said. "Not wounded, sire," I told him, "but dead."

From stalls on the quais I bought cheap reproductions of Ingres and Delacroix. Thumbed to the faded wallpaper over my bed, swag-bellied pashas flourished their scimitars, giaours reined in white Arabian steeds. You knew the odalisques by their lowering eyes. In the ensemble *Liberty Leading the People* got pride of place. Years later I came on this stupendous allegory again, folded in quarters in my old *Petite Larousse.* Bare-breasted and striding into the future, the goddess seemed more and less than a woman. As for the people, they were supers at the Paris opera, milling about at stage left.

A few days every week found me scuffling the dusty floors of old churches. I condescended to religion, "the opium of the people," and parading my emancipated views, hoped to annoy the devout. But I was a novice in the house of learning. Churches were my textbooks, and I conned them for matter-of-fact. To my surprise, though, much of what they had to tell me lived on the surface. As people say, it was only skin deep. Scrutinizing the husk, I looked in vain for the kernel, but in these old Paris churches I couldn't put my finger on it. Everything seemed circumference, and if like me you hoped to get to the point, you went away shaking your head. It took years before I realized that there wasn't a point exactly, or you were more apt to find it in the husk than the kernel.

Green Michelin in hand, I paced the nave and side chapels, alert to quoins, hood-mould, and squinches. St.-Eustace near the Louvre stuck in

my memory. Notably carnal, like many churches built in its time, it had a
stag's head beneath the gable on the facade. What did that have to do with
Christianity? The cross between the antlers made a big impression on the
hunter saint the church is named for, but the antlers were the focal point,
and the message, if any, was thin.

   Some churches had selenite windows, replacing the stained glass broken out by reformers in the Age of Reason. Selenite is transparent and
doesn't filter the light. That makes a difference for the way we see things.
In stained-glass windows the light is distorted, losing the chance for clarity. We see as through a glass darkly, and the type is refracted into particular versions. Oddly, I found them appealing. In the stained glass of Notre
Dame or Sainte Chapelle, Roualt-like cartoons with hallucinated eyes
heaped up treasures that rust didn't corrupt. My favorite was St. Nicholas,
patron saint of pawnbrokers. Donating a marriage portion to three young
virgins down on their luck, he saved them from a life of shame in the
brothel. There were the three of them, lying naked in bed like Lise, Helge,
and Trudi. Behind them the nice old man jingled coins.

   The art of our forebears, mine anyway, French on my mother's side,
does a number on airtight compartments. Time and place collapse, making everything foreground, and things invade things like the body snatch-
ers in the old horror movie. The crib Christ was born in was also an altar,
the site of his death, while Isaac, who carried wood for his own sacrifice,
was carrying the cross Christ died on. Past and present lived side by side
on a continuous plane, and the past kept coming around again. Upsetting
to a forward-looking young man like me, the only progress was a royal
progress, movement from one place to another.

   The God I saw in the windows wasn't the hairy Krishna you meet in
modern churches, nor disembodied like a voice from the whirlwind.
Sometimes I saw him "mewling and puking" in his mother's arms, or a
bestiary encircled him: lion, ox, eagle, and a man sprouting wings like a
bird. These half-human creatures symbolized the Evangelists, also the
Word Made Flesh. The winged man was St. Matthew, at the same time
Christ himself. Going up to heaven—that was what the wings were for—
he looked like the rest of us, formed from the dust of the earth. I knew
what God should look like, instructed by Michelangelo, whose figures
loomed larger than life. This one didn't fit the description.

   Living hand to mouth becomes a young man in Paris. My bed-sitter on
the way to Neuilly had a forty-watt bulb on a cord in the ceiling and hot

water on Saturday mornings. When you climbed the stairs at night, the hall was pitch dark, but a switch by the staircase triggered a feeble beam, lighting your way up until you reached your apartment. Frenchmen give money's worth but not a nickel extra, and you had to walk fast or the light went out before you got to the door. From the third-floor window you could see the Étoile and parts of two boulevards, spokes of its wheel. Colonel Dax, my landlord, lived on the farther one, Avenue Niel. I walked 'round once a week to hand over the rent. He liked getting it from me in person.

A thrifty colon in his long-ago youth, the colonel stood to attention for Algérie française. He had a bête noire, the radical in the Élysée Palace, de Gaulle. Having just expelled the American NATO contingent, the president was my enemy, Colonel Dax told himself, and the enemy of his enemy was his friend. An engraved dinner invitation, delivered à la main, spoke of his and madame's esteem for "you Americans." Not doubting my pleasure, it omitted the RSVP.

I showed up promptly at 8 P.M., in time to look twice at the small Cézanne on the sitting room wall. Intended for calling cards, the wash-basin by the front door was Sèvres. Pale yellow cretonne covered the sofa, yellow plush the dining room chairs. Madame waddled with style, like the fat soprano in the "Dance of the Seven Veils." When she sat us at table, invisible hands served up the *boeuf en daube* and the *fricassé de volaille* in its cream sauce. The wine had already been decanted in goblets, beaded bubbles winking at the brim.

After dinner, talk got on to the colonel's summer house, his pied-à-terre, he said demurely, on the Normandy coast. "Calvados country," and he topped up my glass. Though a chateau, it wasn't one of the biggies, not Chenonceaux, not Chambord, *non, non!* His French was better than my French, he'd been at it longer, and I took him to say that I might rent his country place for a mere bagatelle in the summer. We were winding up our agreement when understanding dawned. It wasn't the chateau he was offering, *non, non,* but that little swineherd's hut down by the river. My dismay and his outraged sense of my presumption looked at each other over the table. I never had dinner with the colonel again.

Paris twice or *bis* was different from the first time. *Bis* as in Nice, where the better off go in the winter. If you live long enough and are lucky, you get to join them. Loss goes with gain, though, and I no longer think of winning a black belt or drinking the night away with famous writers at the Ritz. Over the years age has clawed me with his crutch, and when I look in the mirror the man who looks back at me is like an older cousin, the ne'er-do-well who went to the bad.

Not that there aren't compensations. My juniors call me sir, and our friendly neighborhood banker is glad to shake my hand when he sees me. But deep pockets are wasted on the Geritol set. In Sun City, Florida, the restaurants open for dinner at four. They don't do that in Paris. Skipping the tine à l'eau with my coffee, I went to bed with the birds.

A lot of the time I spent in museums. Some were old standbys, like the Cluny on the fringes of the Latin Quarter. In this fifteenth-century "hotel," scraps and orts of the past compete with the modern grunge around it, no contest. Newer buildings had been lowered in place when I wasn't there to notice. The renovated picture gallery on the Left Bank, spelling the old Jeu de Paume on the Right, became a rainy-day favorite. But too many tourists have the same idea, especially on Sundays when the ticket price drops by half, and the Musée d'Orsay is wall-to-wall people. Imposed order in the picture frames casts its spell, however. The noon hour strikes, time for *déjeuner,* but the hungry sheep in the queue mind their manners. Admonishing its customers, the restaurant on the middle level calls itself the Café des Hauteurs.

Order doesn't mean to me what it once did. Starting out in the class-room—as "a rising young asshole," according to my wife, a product of the sixties—I couldn't handle a compliment from girls in the class without going all flustered or pompous. I stood on my dignity, paid for with a stiff neck. Like the law-and-order crowd, I kept a finger in the dike, fearing the rushing of waters. These days, when I get my shirts laundered, I ask them to leave out the starch. At dishabille, I draw the line, though. Visitors from Woolet, Massachusetts, expect to find it in Paris, everybody's Gay Paree, and some shiver agreeably at the prospect. But the City of Light is prima-rily that, with a moiety of shadow. Otherwise, its clarity wouldn't per-suade you.

Over lunch at the Café des Hauteurs, I thought about the old days, known as "good old days" to most in my generation. The food tasted bet-ter then, or my palate hadn't grown jaded. Today's travel, a step down from yesterday's, is what you get through. No native bearers tote your bags, and the American consul doesn't meet you at dockside. But the jet engine gets me places old Cunarders never dreamed of. A casualty of time, my armor-plated assurance has chinks in it now, and I look back with wonder at the savvy young man who got off the boat train to Paris. Hedging my bets, I tell my wife that we ought to go to church on Easter.

On the lower level of the museum, Ingres and Delacroix, youthful enthusiasms, are still asking the world to notice, and going down in the elevator, I renew old acquaintance. *The Lion Hunt* dazzles the way I remember it, light like first light, plus a vision of life at full tilt. A little awed by Delacroix and his big bow-wow style, I shake myself like a man dozing off. Compared to his brightly lit truth, my hole-in-corner truth seems murky. Sometimes it includes a comic dimension, like the lion on church portals, modeling Bert Lahr in *The Wizard of Oz*. Painters who aim to improve us generally exclude this dimension. If they risked it, the canvas might crack.

Also they tend to simplify, in the interest of making truth clear. Truth in old-fashioned art, if not many splendored, is certainly many layered. The king of beasts stands for St. Mark, whose Gospel tells of the lion's voice crying in the wilderness, a.k.a. John the Baptist's. At the same time the lion stands for the Word. An old wives' tale, connecting the two of them, says that he sleeps with eyes open, a lookalike for Christ in the tomb.

Most patrons on the ground floor head for Manet and his alfresco picnic, startling on a wall to itself. Heads turn toward his young woman, seated on the grass in the state of nature. My feminist friends deplore this painting, a male fantasy, one informs me. But a painter's eye appoints the decadent lunch, and masses of light and shadow, needing each other, put the sexy scene in perspective. *La vie Bohème* plus other things, it makes a composition, depending on particulars that aren't composed but lively.

Like many young men, I thought a good deal about life in the state of nature. It didn't cross my mind that being natural needs a lot of hard work. My inner life, a rich one, featured X-rated movies devoted to Tarzan and Jane. (Maureen O'Sullivan played Jane to my Tarzan.) In their bower of bliss, shalt nots were out, and they did and said the first thing on their minds. I knew what that was, instructed by instinct and Frenchmen with an ax to grind, like Jean-Jacques Rousseau. In the land of easy come, easy go, he lived a colorful sex life. Apologies might have been called for, but taking the offensive, always the best defense, he said we were most ourselves when we let it all hang out. In Manet's painting, however, though the woman is naked, the men who keep her company are dressed like fashion plates. Both are artificial, not a term of reproach, and their sense of order is managed by art.

Across the Seine at my feet and looking over the Tuileries, the turning carousel is orderly, but like the trains that run on time. Sitting in a gondola at the top of the wheel, you get a bird's-eye view of the city. What the bird sees below are little men like windup toys, moving through an evacuated Place de la Concorde. The city around it reduces to a surveyor's map, where the important features are thrown in relief. Marshal Foch, a cartographer, liked this synoptic view, clearer than the one from the trenches. "De quoi s'agit-il?" he wanted to know. "What is the essence of the thing?"

Glass doors line the museum's upper level, one framing the Sacré-Coeur in Montmartre. Before I saw Paris, I had the view by heart, familiar from paintings and postcards. The great dome, blotting out the sky, says that moribund beats lively. Renoir, Dufy, and others lived in little streets around it, and I picture their angry shades, Gallic and vociferous, worrying its dead-white pretension. Round-the-clock services honor the Sacred Heart, but the church is a cenotaph, nobody home.

Churches in the older time shared the little streets with their neighbors. Some elbowed the neighbors, wanting a place for themselves. As a young man I preferred wide-open spaces like Washington, D.C.'s, or the cleared-out piazza before St. Peter's, Rome. I thought you showed respect for the pièce de résistance by getting rid of clutter around it. Pope Julius II thought this. Very much a modern man, he knocked down the ancient church that stood for centuries where St. Peter's stands today. Michelangelo lent a hand, helping him build the new church, a city on a hill. Each liked setting the truth in relief.

On the Île de la Cité, old Paris, Ste. Chapelle struggles to lift itself out of the ruck of pawnshops, bistros, and bureaux de change. When were they going to bring in the bulldozers and send its crummy mise-en-scène to the dustbin? Michelangelo and Pope Julius asked themselves the same question. The second time around I took a second look, and the church's environs, admittedly less than grand, composed a net of filaments binding the house of spirit to earth. But putting it that way would come as a surprise to bakers, candlestick makers, and butchers in their blood-spattered aprons.

Ste. Chapelle, a jewel box, collects the light in its coffers. First of all, however, it means to teach us, and its eleven huge windows depict the history of the world. Paris's best, they blaze with holy fury when the sun is on the glass. In their version of history there is nothing new beneath the sun, and the past isn't put to shame by the future. Samson, carting off the gates of Gaza, looks forward to Christ, rolling back the stone from the tomb. St. Louis, a king of France, built the chapel in the courtyard of his palace. It hitched on to his apartments, or he used the apartments like a wagon-lit hitched on to the rear of the church. Going to Mass in the morning, he took the gallery between church and bedroom. Details like this were beneath my young man's notice, but I don't see the same church that I used to.

Close by, Notre Dame towers over the Seine. Napoleon had himself crowned in this church, hoping its glamor would rub off on a Johnny-come-lately. Little shops and tenements, still there in his day, infiltrated the colonnade or *parvis,* short for paradise. People said it had many mansions. In the age of St. Louis the open space before the church accommodated mystery plays, popular entertainments. Later times thought the church should stand alone, like the Eiffel Tower. Sharing this opinion, Baron Hausmann emptied the *parvis* and quadrupled its size. He was the same who laid out the boulevards, wide enough for a charge of horsemen wielding sabres.

Inside the church, however, nature abhors a vacuum, and side chapels between the buttresses deny the chance for wide open space. Guilds and rich donors paid for the chapels, each a local habitation. They make the great church provincial, full of cranks and byways like the Seventh Arrondissement just across the water. Though Notre Dame stirs the blood, it isn't St. Paul's, London, and there aren't any battle flags or heroes draped in togas. No Napoleon either, no Louis Quatorze. Even St. Louis isn't allowed over the threshhold. The ninth king of that name and the best-loved of any, he ruled the kingdom a stone's throw away, but no statue honors his memory. Missed by me earlier, he isn't wholly forgotten, though, and I find him outside on the church doors, kneeling in prayer like his subjects.

Napoleon, a boyhood hero, seemed everywhere in Paris when I lived there that first time. Street names recalled his famous victories, Wagram, Austerlitz, Marengo, and on the Champ de Mars near the École Militaire, my head buzzed with words like *gloire* and *honneur.* In this military school the Little Corporal studied the art of war, including its rhetoric, sometimes high-flown. He could call his men *mes enfants* without blushing. After the escape from Elba, they bought him a final turn on stage, and he played it for all it was worth. "Shoot if you will this old gray head," he told his would-be captors, words to that effect. Dyed-in-the-wool Frenchmen, they wept and kissed on both cheeks.

My last day in Paris, I go to pay my respects to the emperor. The long esplanade leading up to the tomb, vista piled on vista, is bordered by stately limes. Over the entrance an equestrian statue of Louis XIV looks toward the Seine, ready to walk on its waters. "Always remember whom you have loved," he instructed his mistress, then died. He was the Sun King, last of the big spenders, and helped usher in the Revolution.

Under Mansart's neoclassical dome, the sarcophagus, red porphyry on a green ground, is like an expensive centerpiece recessed in a circular table. Huge statues stand around it, twelve of them, making you think. Frenchmen are tactful, and don't insist on the connection to Jesus and his apostles. The body itself is hearsed in six coffins, like Russian *matryoshka* dolls, the outside coffin of oak. It looks tiny to my eyes, wearier than they were and a little creased at the corners.

Standing there in the late afternoon, ready to go home again, I ask myself whether the Frenchman's cynical *plus c'est la même chose* hasn't got it wrong, after all. But music, barely audible, cuts across my thoughts. A concealed tape is playing the *Eroica,* the part you hear when the catafalque passes through silent streets. Black-plumed horses and reversed rifles go with it, and the muffled crepitation of drums. Melancholy but stirring, the music is asking you to join the heroes in Valhalla. I don't want to die romantically, though. True, my body has played me tricks, and like the Ancient Mariner I am apt to recite a long list of woes, if you get within distance. But I wouldn't be twenty again, even for a house in Newark, New Jersey. Maybe forty, with a full head of hair.

Some things never change, like the pair of gamins who have sneaked past the ticket taker into the holy of holies. Teasing each other, they are playing prisoner's base above the sunken crypt, slapping hands against the railing. The mustachioed gendarme who patrols this hallowed ground is like the frog in the proverb, *aussi grosse que le boeuf,* puffed up as big as an ox. Wagging a thick finger, he lays it across his lips. "Shh!" he says. "C'est Napoléon!" Dancing out of his reach, the little boys ignore him. For all they know, the tomb might be empty.

China Boy

My family took me to the Catskills for my tenth birthday, the day after Memorial Day, when we decked the graves of our war dead. A black-and-white photo evokes that far-off time. The lake in the background is edged with pine trees, coming down to the water. Sun is on the water, and you know that fish are jumping. I stand in the foreground, a skinny malink in an undershirt and short pants, palms flat against my thighs, hair slicked back and parted severely. Beside me is my grandmother, known to us as Nana, a vigorous-looking woman in a shapeless dress, flowered hat, and black high-top shoes. The tip of her walking stick pushes into the sand, and her amazing smile is like President Roosevelt's.

Memory is notoriously selective, and the calendar-art setting seems too perfect even for a sunny day in youth. Not every day was sunny. I was much alone with no one to play with but my bratty sister, Marge. She's been dead a long while now, and I wish I hadn't felt that way about her. A dog would have cheered me, and I had one in my dreams, a friendly mutt named Spot, his tongue always licking my face. But Pop was death on dogs, and when I brought a stray home with me, he said, "We'd better put him out of his misery!"

The Depression wouldn't go away, and Mom let down or let out last year's pants and jackets, making them serve again this year. Pop, mostly a stolid man, seemed unusually jumpy, and I'd catch him looking over his shoulder. Though he kept his job, others we knew didn't. I remember grown men picking through our garbage can outside the house on East Twenty-sixth Street. They were hunting for something to eat.

The boy in the photo seems to have forgotten this, and all he needs to be a self-made man is more years on his back. He has that "Ad astra per aspera" look, especially in the jut of his jaw. Reaching for the stars, he means to put them in his pocket. He thinks he can move mountains, irrigate the desert, compel the ocean to go back from the shore. Should he sully his character, something the young are prone to, he can make a fresh start or be "born again," as people say now. He doesn't want to be told that a man's reach exceeds his grasp.

Body's wreck and the "slow decay of blood" were for the future, and I didn't huff and puff the way I do today, like a peasant carrying fardels. Books were the staff I leaned on. I read them with guilty pleasure long after my parents supposed I was sleeping, using a pocket flash with the covers pulled over my head. An anthology of the world's greatest poems was one of my favorites, read until it fell apart. Shakespeare was in there, the famous set-pieces, some of which I memorized. If we weren't all we might be, whose fault was that? I asked anyone who'd listen. "The fault," I answered, "is not in our stars but in ourselves." The speaker of the famous passage is partly a villain qualifying our sense of his words. But that Shakespeare intended the qualification never entered my young man's mind.

Books gave me my earliest heroes, Napoleon (in Emil Ludwig's biography), and Robinson Crusoe in the first novel I ever read. Both helped develop my view of life as a struggle whose outcome depended on me. I was the master of my fate and the captain of my soul. This self-reliant psychology came largely from my tone-deaf reading of Shakespeare. I heard him saying that we weren't fated but free, and our remedies lay in ourselves. What mattered was how we exercised our will.

But the story of Robinson Crusoe petered out, leaving questions unanswered. What fate befell the hero after he came back from the island and how much of it was owing to him? Did he slough his old self as the result of lessons learned, and acquire a new self? I wanted the ending to demonstrate cause and effect; otherwise, I couldn't accept it. Napoleon's biography was puzzling in a different way. Though it carried him from cradle to grave, I focused on the highs and glided over the lows, and when he lost the last battle, I was stunned. Just as Napoleon was tasting his triumph, Blucher and his Prussians came on the field. It seemed so unfair!

My ruminating on history, the preoccupation of a lifetime, must have got started with a first devastated response to the battle of Waterloo. It violated my sense of fitness that the hero's fortunes should have depended on a god-from-the-machine. A cheap trick of melodrama, I thought this reversal. But in the midst of my puzzlement, an unnerving thought occurred to me. I wondered whether the unlikely turn of events that lay outside our control was less stagy than part of life's normal round.

That first trip to China I was into Eastern religions. I held all life sacred, not just vertebrates like me. Bugs were God's creatures, and who could say what form they took in a previous incarnation. Picking them up on a three-by-five card, I dropped them out the window. "Shoo, little bug."

In the world outside the window the bad guys were making life hard on everybody else. But coping with them was the business of politics, no concern of mine. The world I lived in was only a halfway house on the way to something better. Striving to achieve it, I practiced nonaggression and turned the other cheek. Then came Tiananmen Square.

I still see the solitary student in the photo, standing up to the tanks as they get ready to crush him. If he isn't dead long since, he is dying piecemeal in one of their gulags. What his heroism added up to is a question I ponder at night. Did all that youthful ardor make any difference, or was it only whistling in the dark? Looking for the answer has brought me back to the scene of the crime.

"We couldn't do without China," says a voice at my elbow. "Since the breakup of the Soviet Union, you need a place like this to look down on."

The voice is Mr. Ciccarelli's. A mutt of a man with gray hair that sticks up like a toothbrush, he is special correspondent for the *Daily Express.* "Maybe you've seen my byline," he says, giving me one hand and waving a traveler's check in the other. "I'm in Beijing because my newspaper sent me. What's your excuse?"

"How can I help you, sir?" the cashier wants to know.

Mr. Chee, as I learn to call him, is fresh out of money. "I'll take it in yuan," he says, handing over the check.

The cashier smiles sadly. Today they don't have any money.

"Why is it I'm not surprised?" says Mr. Chee. An old China hand, he remembers when this city was still called Pekin, not that it made any difference. "Your basic China boy sleeps standing up, always has, always will. Has to do with the opium habit."

Bass chords boom, and an old Elvis standby bounces off the walls of the lobby. Stationed beside the hotel's revolving doors, the rock guitarist is a one-man welcoming committee. "You ain't nothin' but a hound dog," he tells us, turning up the dials on his amplifier. He is Chinese, and noise is his element. When you fly China's national airline, the little TVs that drop from the ceiling come at you like the Hallelujah Chorus. You can't shut them up, either, though this capitalist roader has tried.

Rock and roll to Mr. Chee is the corruption of the best by the worst. New Orleans jazz was the best, and rock and roll the worm in the apple. Growing up in Golders Green, northwest London, he spent his Saturday afternoons at the Palladium, listening to Dixieland. The trumpeter Humphrey Littleton, high priest in this temple, liked to light a fire under old Tin Pan Alley tunes. Illustrating, Mr. Chee breaks into song. "China Boy go sleep," he sings, his voice a gravelly monotone. "Close your eyes don't peep."

The clerk behind the counter looks up in alarm.

"Don't worry, son," says Mr. Chee. "Buddha looks down on you. Moon man loves you too."

The series of articles he is doing for the *Daily Express* will give travelers the lowdown on China's ruling clique and the network of prisons its power depends on. I wouldn't want to end up in Lop Nor. But what intrigues him most is the mystery food they put on the table. "If you want to make it home again, stick to rice and boiled greens."

I think of last night's dinner, regretting the times I turned up my nose at the Colonel's fried chicken. You don't order dinner in China, they do that for you. A waitress sets the platters down on a big lazy Susan, her aim unsure, her face expressionless, halfway to sullen. The entrées are bone and gristle, collops of fat, smelly fish, raw vegetables. Spinning the wheel, I send the vegetables on to my neighbor. He is slurping his soup, making great sucking sounds like jobs and money going down the drain after NAFTA. Out of the corner of my eye I see a small rat scamper across the floor toward the kitchen. When I am at home my discontent knows no bounds, and I go on about the tide of dreck, seeping east from California. Away from home I count the days.

But home will have to wait on the trip to Chongching. "If you could bring back something that put him before us, anything at all," said Myra, my cousin Ned's widow. "Sign the guest book for me at Stilwell House. See for yourself if the landing strip is as tiny as it looks in his pictures." What she really wanted was to be told that his sacrifice was worth it.

Some lose an arm or a leg. He brought back a dose of survivor guilt, and it scarred him for the rest of his life.

Ned was nineteen when he flew the Hump into Chongching, setting down his B-27 on a spit of land in the Yangtze. Unlike many, he lived to tell about it, even fathering a pair of twins when he was into his sixties. No one could have predicted this, and for most of his life he lived in limbo, waiting for something to happen. Near the end, however, he found a girl worth the wait. When she saw me off at the airport in San Francisco, I felt like a knight in those stories about the Round Table.

"Their beer isn't bad, I'll give them that," says Mr. Chee. "If you have an empty stomach, it's filling."

"Man can't live by bread alone," I say, pointing to the vase of carnations on the counter. In this Socialist country, someone has an eye for gratuitous things. The Japanese garden in the courtyard of the Holiday Inn is one of them, like cooling rain in the heat of the day. Mr. Chee doesn't stop to sniff the flowers. Italian on his father's side, English on his mother's, he goes off like firecrackers. "I have seen the future," he says, detonating each word, "and it doesn't work." If he could choose he would live in the past, Vienna, he thinks, in the heyday of the Austro-Hungarian Empire. "At least their secret police were corruptible." But Beijing is where the action is, and action is the name of his game. After doing the nation's capital, he is heading south for the Yangtze. I will have heard about their new dam, "bigger than any before it."

Born in the land where bigger is better, I remind him of the Hoover Dam. But Chinese, well before America, adopted the cult of bigness. When I pick up my room key in the world's biggest Holiday Inn, I leaf through a glossy advertising its Olympic-size swimming pool, tennis courts, and bowling alley. Thinking about it gives me a headache, and when I ask for an aspirin, Watson's Drug Store is there.

This "venture-capital" hotel, partly their money, partly someone else's, owes its existence to the spirit of progress. Unlike the cult of bigness, it has been slow in getting to China but is making up for lost time. As we begin our descent to Beijing, I look for the mud-brown houses that hugged their mother earth in fields outside the city. High-rises have engorged them. Rectilinear like filing cabinets, they sit on what used to be farmland. In man-made ponds like the water holes on golf courses, the winter wheat has begun to turn green, an old story. But traffic, something

new, begins to build as the city comes into focus, crowding out the bicy-
cles that swarmed like mayflies in trout season. Rising above the big gas
and oil containers, the sooty fingers are chimney stacks, squeezing off
rounds of white smoke.

In the airport an immense mural of the Great Wall makes me square
my shoulders. The Wall bestrides the mountains, hurdling them in seven-
league boots. Its job is subduing nature, all in a day's work. Old landscape
scrolls, like the one that hangs in my living room at home, carry a different subtext. An ancient with a walking stick and his young acolyte, both
dwarfed by the mountains above them, are crossing a bridge flung over a
river. Across the darkening sky flies a long-legged crane, symbol of the
longevity they hope for. Their road leads upward, and they take it a step
at a time.

A day trip from Beijing brought me out to the Wall, not long after
President Nixon had been there. "It's a great wall," he said, when they
asked his opinion. The mountains it straddles, stippled with evergreens,
look as if an old watercolorist had been dotting *i*'s with his brush. Chinese
painting gives the world a finished look, different from a patina. You feel
that the world isn't itself, until the painter completes it.

Standing atop the Wall, I am a solitary lookout, serving the Ming
emperor as his eyes and ears. Through crenels in the parapet I stare at the
desert. Out there, the barbarians are probing the Wall for a weak spot.
When they find it, they will pour into our heartland. That happened centuries ago, but the barbarians are still at the gates, and keeping them at bay
is a continuing struggle. It isn't always an us vs. them kind of struggle.
Sometimes the enemy, infiltrating the lines, is within.

The road into the city, like the one that runs with the Wall, is wide
enough for a troop of horsemen to gallop abreast. Leading the troop is
Basil Rathbone in *A Tale of Two Cities,* familiar from my youth at the
movies. He likes bringing down his riding crop on the backs of the hoi
polloi. These days he doesn't ride but drives a high-powered limo. If he
is among China's power elite, he drives a Red Flag, like the one that zips
by me on the road from their Capital Airport. People scatter to get out
of the way, but sneering like Ozymandias, he tramples them under his
wheels.

At the hotel's check-in counter I am given a packet of slick-paper
brochures. "In Beijing alone," I read, "over two hundred sights are worth

seeing." But the city of spectacular vistas freezes to the marrow on a blustery day in March, and wind from the Gobi Desert drives me along like the autumn leaves in Shelley. Skyscrapers that weren't there yesterday look like New York out by the airports. For three dollars and postage they will send you the blueprints. Corinthian doodads spruce them up, not an improvement. "A mule in horse's harness" is Mr. Chee's opinion.

But the mean-looking tenements that run like a baseboard under the concrete towers reverse the Disney model, where the grandiose thing is facade, backed by nothing. This Magic Kingdom is real, possibly predicting the future. A gloomy thought for a gloomy day, and to offset it I think of the USSR under Brezhnev. The monolith he sat on seemed in place for all time. Then wind shrieked, and it tottered and fell.

Blocks of flats for their huddled masses hark back to the fortress architecture of America in the sixties. "We're gonna tear this mother down," student protesters shouted, marching on the admin building. In Beijing, though the fortress is still standing, time has given its grim features a face-lift. Striped awnings like candy canes hang over the windows, and the day's wash, strung on clotheslines between them, says that people are living inside. Colored lights outline doorways, winking on and off like Christmas tree lights. Chilly day or not, crowds are out on the streets, the women in slacks, most of the men wearing sneakers and jeans. I see a few Mao suits, only a few. No more lockstep for Beijingers.

Trees are sprouting wherever I look, in pots at curbside and in median strips running down the street between lanes of traffic. I am happy for my environmentalist friends. The trees are all the same size, though, "regimented" trees planted at 2 P.M. on a Tuesday. Let there be trees, someone said, and there they are in their thousands and tens of thousands.

"Wangfujing Street," I tell the driver at the cab rank. He grins inscrutably, like the movies. "Goldfish Lane," he says, giving me my word back in English. "What are you looking for, Mister? I show you best places to go."

The cab lets me off in front of Sun Dong An Plaza, eleven storeys of shops and offices, packaged in a glittering container. A glass window at ground level reflects a pint-sized man I've seen before. Holding up an imperious hand, Mr. Chee is crossing the street against traffic. The paper his parcel is wrapped in says it comes from Louis Vuitton's. "50 percent off on leather goods," he tells me.

"Actually," I tell him, "I want something for two little girls."

"You're in luck," he says, steering me into Critterz-R-Us. A nest of cobras, guarding the door, hisses when I step on a button. "Everything from aardvarks to zed," says Mr. Chee. Ten minutes later I have a stuffed panda and a long-tailed monkey with eyes that open and close. My nieces in San Francisco will be pleased.

"Nothing much changes under the sun," says Mr. Chee. "Before the Revolution, Wangfujing Street catered to rich Westerners. Now it caters to China's richest Chinese. Makes you wonder what all the fuss was about."

The coolie on the street corner might be waiting for customers. Pulling a rickshaw, he stands between the shafts like a draft horse. Sunlight, glinting on the bronze surfaces, creates the illusion of movement. The coolie is as thin as a shoot of bamboo, and Mr. Chee takes notice. "You don't see any fat men in China."

Young Chinese, casual but elegant like American yuppies, have their cameras out, looking for the right angle. One hoists an infant into the rickshaw, another fingers the bronze pigtail, new in his experience. This stoop-shouldered coolie is part of their past, only a dim memory to most, though. After all, they made a fuss in China over something. With any luck children today won't know what life was like in the old days.

At the contagious hospital down the street from China World, the doctors and nurses are converts to hi-tech. Visitors are welcome, and the first thing they show you is their brand-new Olivetti computers. You tell the clinician your symptoms, she taps the keys, and the whole range of possibilities appears on a printout. "Fifty years ago, we did this by guess and by God." Impressed, I doff my cap to the gleaming computers.

Progress has its flip side, however. Chinese who make it the god of their idolatry act as if the past had never existed. No doubt it triggers bad memories, and you can see why some of them are eager to start out de novo. But it isn't only the downtrodden who want to smash the celadon and the blanc-de-Chine vases, rewrite the history books, and say goodbye to Li Po and Confucius.

I think back to certain students I'd known in the sixties, and one who got up in my class and harangued me. The string he harped on seems to vibrate at least once in an age. French revolutionaries harped on this string, when they beheaded the statues in Notre Dame Cathedral and dug up the bones of their dead kings and queens. "You have to get rid of the past," my student assured me. "If you don't, it will poison the future."

Beijing's sky in early spring is the same as it was the first time I saw it, a "white radiance of eternity" kind of sky, cloudless and washed of color. Golfball-sized balls of pollen still drift along the air. Children and some adults wear face masks, nothing showing but their eyes. Women with besoms are still sweeping the streets, brooming off the dust of time. My take on the dust of time is that it makes the future possible. "If your back cast is poor," says a fisherman whose counsel I value, "your forward cast will be a disaster."

Around the corner from Changan Avenue comes a quartet of Chinese workmen, plasterers by the look of their white-crusted aprons. Faces twisted, their gestures threatening, they are falling over each other like tumblers. One runs his wheelbarrow against the legs of another.

"A bit histrionic, wouldn't you say?" says Mr. Chee. "But your average China boy is at heart a perennial child. These fellows aren't really angry, they're only letting off steam."

I agree that Chinese are different from Mr. Chee's English. A billion of them fight each other for a place in the sun. This doesn't lend itself to good manners. Unlike the English, Chinese are no respecters of queues. Pushing up to the head of the line, they stomp on your feet and dig you with their elbows. Sexual discrimination is illegal in China, and the women are as bad as the men.

Like Scots, Jews, and Frenchmen, Chinese are cheapskates. Partly this is their provident nature, partly it comes from having done without for a long time. Standing knee deep in their alien corn, I keep my mitts up. Like the bully in the old Charles Atlas ad, they'll kick sand in your face if you let them. Valuing trivial things hugely, they value life hardly at all. As we land in Beijing, nobody tells me to fasten my seatbelt. The DC-7 is full, but there are lots more Chinese where these came from.

How many there are staggers the mind. Home to the emperor, Beijing's Forbidden City housed one hundred thousand of his personal friends, members of the imperial court. They had room to spread out in, nine thousand rooms, says my guide, who claims he has counted. The pagodas they lived in are positioned along a north-south axis, its center the same as the world's. (Chinese aren't behindhand in patting themselves on the back.)

Tiananmen Square, gateway to the Forbidden City, is bigger than a postage stamp. No trees break its paved surface, unrelievedly itself, like the sea. The modern age, dating back some hundreds of years now, has a thing for vacant space, not park space but emptiness, Red Square in Moscow, Chirico-esque promenades in Washington, D.C., the Zocalo in Mexico City. Tiananmen Square is the mother of them all.

Its immensity doesn't humble us, the way the mountains do in old landscape paintings. Like intergalactic space, it reduces us to nothing. When Chinese fall in for their big testimonials, they clump together like grains of cooked rice. The old canard has it right, and you can't tell one from another. But in a similar setting Westerners lose their identity too, like Italians in Mussolini's time, chanting "DOO-chay" in Rome's Piazza Venezia. Coping with the problem, officials number the paving blocks in Tiananmen Square, and each standee has his own block to stand on. This is different from private property.

Red flags snap in the wind around the granite obelisk, a monument to the People's Heroes. Youngsters of China's democratic movement, heroes with a difference, made this their focal point in the spring of 1989. I want to hear about them, I say to my guide. He is Mr. Yu, as in "Hey, You!" he says, goodhumored and talkative like Charlie Chan's No. 1 Son. Thrown by my question, he recovers quickly. He is sorry for the students who died in the late disturbance, but they should have gone back to their universities "to learn things."

What was broken has been fixed, and Tiananmen Square no longer sparks attention. Dublin's post office is still scarred by Ireland's long-ago Easter Rebellion, but no scars are visible here. The bullet holes in the obelisk are gone, and everything is back to normal, except for the surveillance cameras on poles and the pairs of red-tabbed soldiers. If you stop to tie a shoelace, they stroll up to you, just to be sure.

In the center of the square, Chairman Mao lies in a crystal sarcophagus, resting on a black granite slab. "Every evening," says Mr. Chee, "they lower him into an underground fridge. In the morning when the sun comes up, he rises."

The line of viewers, four abreast, splits in two as it comes to the chairman. It moves slowly, like a spreading inkblot. People at the head of each column pause to look for the full sixty seconds allowed them. Silence is the rule, and these hushed Chinese obey it. Outside the tomb, however, the crowds in the souvenir shops twitter like birds. "School's out!" and spirits are soaring.

From Tiananmen Square the roads radiate like filaments in a web, south to the Temple of Heaven, northeast to the Lama Temple, northwest

to the Summer Palace outside the city. Dowager Empress Cixi, the original Dragon Lady, built the Summer Palace in the nineteenth century,
with money earmarked for China's defenses. Her Stone Boat, an immove-
able object in the lake it can never sail on, has the charm of an absurdity
created in defiance of logic. But pagodas above the shoreline, dotting the
Hills of Longevity, rise from fragrant beds of peonies, wisteria, and lilac.
Crossing the water in a dragon boat, I am aware of nothing but the plash
of oars. Suddenly a pagoda, looming out of the mist, is upon me.

Too many Chinese cumber the park, and I wish they'd go back where
they came from. Most, only a while ago, were down on the farm, or they
lived in dank alleyways, *hutongs,* where the sun never shines. Bringing
them into the light is the price of settling the score with antidemocratic
Empress Cixi. It seems part of this trade-off that they stand in my light,
soaking up too much of it. Self-consciousness, the mark of civilized behavior, is outside their ken, and they stop and stare at me, mouths open. They
aren't xenophobic, only puzzled, as if a Martian had dropped down among
them. Some spit on the paved walks or blow their noses with two fingers.
There is a lot of preliminary clearing of the throat.

The Lama Temple is supposed to be hot stuff, China's Kama Sutra, Mr.
Hey You says coyly. But the truth of this is more than I can vouch for, a
Chinese bluenose having draped the statues with scarves. When sons of
the emperor who needed sex education came to visit, the scarves were
taken away. Not for my visit, however.

But I can tell you firsthand about the Buddha of the Future. Carved
from a single block of sandalwood, he stands in a pit, rising fifty-five feet
to the ceiling. According to Mr. Hey You, this is a first in the *Guinness Book
of Records.* The word for the Buddha is *Brobdingnagian,* remembering the
giants in Swift, huge of limb, coarse of feature. His eyes, wide open, stare
like Othello's, the Laurence Olivier version.

Devotees in the Hall of Harmony shuffle across the floor toward a trio
of Buddhas. Past, present, and future, they look the same, that is, like nothing in particular. In the Christian Trinity the Holy Ghost is unrealized, befitting a ghost, but Father and Son are made in man's image and likeness. Old
painters, depicting it, cared about superficial things, "that color upon cheek
or hair." Christianity is often said to be absorbed in the world over yonder,
but to me it seems tied to our delimiting earth, putting salvation in peril.

The closed eyes of all three Buddhas look within, like the wide open
but unseeing eyes of the Buddha of the Future. Their bellies are swollen,

as if they are practicing chi gong, the part where you expel your breath, letting the belly expand. But why are they laughing? Perhaps this is how an Immortal responds to our human condition. Borne on the Wheel of Life, I don't find it a laughing matter.

The devotees bring tribute, plastic flowers and fruit. Lighting joss sticks, they leave them to burn in a black copper boiler, shining with coins like the Trevi Fountain. I look for connections to medieval Christian churches or the great mosques of the sultan's architect, Sinan. Nothing. Restrained is a condition this temple never heard of. The torsos of its idols are lacquered with gold, and in the sancta sanctorum the reds are redder than fingernail polish. Why hide the light under a bushel?

But a bronze incense burner, shaped like the Buddhist holy mountain, Sumeru, smokes placidly in front of the entrance. Tiny bells, hanging from the eaves, begin to strike as the wind sets them going. This sound is upper register and seems to come from far off. Bassed by the deeper sound of a gong, it composes the unquiet spirit.

Plumy cypresses usher my way as I walk down the path in the Temple of Heaven Park. Here, said ancient Chinese, was the meeting place of heaven and earth. The trunks of the cypresses, some five hundred years old, have the writhened look of tree trunks in Chinese paintings. The old commonplace tells us that art imitates nature, but in the Temple of Heaven Park, nature imitates art, the artist having taught us how to see things. On either side of the path men and women of all ages are standing on one leg, raising and flexing their arms, one hand up, one hand down, "channeling internal energies," says Mr. Hey You. Off to my left middle-aged women are doing the fox-trot, most with women. Over the loudspeaker comes a dance tune, "Melancholy Baby." The women are retired, I learn from my guide, and come here every morning to dance.

Under the blue-tiled dome, going up in tiers toward heaven, the emperor prayed for good harvests. Chinese gargoyles, monstrous heads whose open mouths are rainspouts, ring the topmost tier, surmounted by a gold finial like a sheaf of corn. Blue and gold bands demarcate the umbrella-shaped tiers. I am ravished by the beauty of the great pagoda, like that "stately pleasure dome" Coleridge imagined. But a large placard in a fussy Victorian frame hangs on the exterior surface. Chinese characters, emblazoned on the placard, are like a neon sign above the restaurant door. "Hall for Prayer for Good Harvests," they say. No ghost from the grave needs to tell us, but the Chinese insist that we know.

Beyond the pagoda, the pile of rocks is thought by my guide to merit attention. "Found art," Chinese call it, only rocks left as nature disposed them. Supposedly, they evoke an image, like a megalithic cairn or the Rape of Nanking. The choice of the image is up to the spectator. Cultural democrats in the university town I lived in like this idea. Artistic intention seems to them a tyranny, also a delusion. The decor in their houses takes its cue from nature, and they prop a piece of driftwood on the mantel. Obliterating the distinction between nature and art, they ask the former to bear more than it can, while diminishing the latter to an impromptu performance. Chinese don't see why not.

The temple steps are easier on the way down, but there is still another lunar surface to cross, leading to another pagoda. Nothing detains the eye between points *A* and *B*. Imperial China made no concession to the weakness of the flesh, nor did its architects take pains with minutiae. Perhaps that is true wherever people are thick on the ground.

But Chinese painting is more delicate than scrimshaw, and the artists who created it would have gone to the stake sooner than tolerate slapdash. Steering clear of grandiose subjects, they favored trees, flowers, and birds. Even when the painting goes in for sublimity—"sounding cataracts" and the like—it makes room for men and women. Often they are tiny in proportion to the whole, and at first you don't see them way down at the foot of the canvas. They have to be there, though. Otherwise, nature means nothing.

Tiananmen Square and the city center are almost close enough to walk. But I have had my fill of walking, and the bus picks me up outside the western gate of the Temple of Heaven Park. As we approach the square I see the familiar gaggle of old men with their birdcages, like dogs on a leash. Craving the sun, the old men show up every day in the late afternoon. The first time I saw them, I thought they were sellers come to market. But no, the birds are pets, lovingly tended, and their owners, escapees from China's pressure cooker, have no business but kibitzing with friends.

Chongching is like Pittsburgh, built where two rivers meet and gasping its lungs out in a haze of toxicity. But Pittsburgh has cleaned up its act. Buildings in Chongching melt into air and water, like Parliament on the

Thames in the painting by Monet. Though the Jialing River is no wider than the Delaware at Washington's crossing, I can barely see the opposite shore.

Spring has come to this southern city, however, and under the smog rice is greening. The People's Hall, a huge pagoda up a staircase to infinity, will never look other than frigid, but pale red China roses have burst into bloom below it, and the magnolia trees are ready to go. In the People's Plaza citizens are taking constitutionals, "pierced to the root" by thirsty March. Grandparents walk infants, holding them by the hand or lifting them up in their arms. No strollers or baby carriages in China.

Red, buglike cars the size of Cinquecentos whip up and down the roller-coaster streets, trailing gray puffs of exhaust. On Sun Yat Sen Street, the parties involved are sorting out a fender bender. Chinese hurl themselves at each other like pellets from a gun but rarely come to grief, having eyes in the back of their head. Thirty million of them live in Chongching, the world's largest metropolitan region. Except for the war, I'd never have known it existed.

Crossing the bridge over the Yangtze, I do this on foot, wanting to memorize the scene for my reunion with Ned's widow, Myra. The bridge is a newish one, built or rebuilt since the war on concrete arches. A double row of lamp standards, doing what it can, adds to the grainy light of the sun. Office buildings and apartment houses crowd the skyline, barges with derricks work the river. I see a gas-powered sampan and a boat under sail that looks like a fishing boat, but that can hardly be. Below me on the Penghu Sandbar are the remains of the airstrip.

Thinking of Ned and the others in their flying boxcars, I ask myself how they ever made it down to that sliver of earth, water to one side of them, water to the other. Ned mostly stayed mum on the subject. If you pressed him, he was only "doing his job." A few times, however, emotion showed, together with something like joy. That was when he spoke of the men in his squadron, "this band of brothers."

The Stilwell Museum on Sixin Road occupies the same house the general lived in when he commanded the China-Burma-India theater. No soldier less theatrical, brainier, or tougher. History will give him a better press than MacArthur, who marched toward the whirring of the cameras. Stilwell was "Vinegar Joe" and didn't hide his contempt for China's Chiang Kai-shek. Papering over trouble, President Roosevelt took away his command.

A posted notice outside the house in Chinese and English praises "our American friends." Ferrying lifesaving cargo over the "snow-clad" Himalayas, they helped turn the tide of war. "Unforgettable" are the old days. The friendship between the two peoples is "precious."

Tobacco must have been Stilwell's solace, and in his signature image a pipe is clamped between his teeth. His homely, bespectacled face looks across the room at a blown-up photo of the Burma Road, snaking through jungle all the way to Kunming. The men who built the road and kept it open are remembered on the walls. High-fiving each other, or a 1940s equivalent, they salute a job well done. They have got rid of selfishness, the enemy within, and you don't see any "me" in their faces. Some, surprised by the camera, are unshaven, with tough-guy grins and sardonic eyes, a young man's affectation. Were they always gay, even when the sky was falling?

I sign the visitor's book and buy an accordion-roll of postcards and a paperback life of the general. As I turn to leave the museum, I do a double take. Above the rack of "Flying Tiger" T-shirts, the photo shows a group of young American airmen. In the second row, third from the left, is my cousin.

Years and decades have passed since the photo was taken, and the man who looks back at me is little more than a boy. If he were around today he wouldn't recognize the world he fought for. The armies of the Rising Sun are gone from China, but the chairs they sat in were still warm when the Communists came in on their heels. As to the precious friendship between the Chinese and their American allies, I hope it lasts forever but wouldn't bet the house.

Having done what I'd promised, I can leave Chongching when I want to. In the lobby of my hotel, another gleaming caravansary built with venture capital, the CAAC desk stays open twenty-four hours. "China Air Always Crashes," jokesters used to say the acronym meant, but China Air, like Pittsburgh, has turned it around. Next to the ticket desk sits Speedy, our "technology butler."

Tall for a Chinese, he has long, splayed fingers, and his hair is cropped close to his skull. The eyes are what you notice. Warming the room, they burn like lumps of coal. Speedy doesn't have a desk, only a card table that folds up at night, but the printed notices in front of him suggest that he knows what he's doing. "Mobile phone glitches? Internet access difficulties? Laptop misbehaving?" A large placard in boldface tells me what I must do: "Call Speedy the technology butler."

I doubt that he can help me and say so. Though I want to get in the swim, like people in the TV ads who solve all their problems by going online, I find the new technology user unfriendly. Anyway, I do my writing in pencil and my shopping at the neighborhood ripoff.

Not a problem, says Speedy, speaking English with an American accent. "Computers and such are only a means to an end." He doesn't say what the end is, but sweeps his notices into a briefcase. "Time to close up the shop for today."

Intrigued by his know-how and the easy way he wears it, I offer to buy him a drink. Young people in the bar move naturally from Chinese into English, the way upper-crust characters in Henry James break into French without warning. Leaning forward, they quiz each other, waggling their fingers and widening black inquisitive eyes. At the Yamaha in the corner a young man in a tux is playing Scarlatti. Except for me, everyone in the room is on the sunny side of thirty.

"It's not surprising," says Speedy. "Old people in China, like my grandfather, cling to the old ways. You wouldn't see them in a bar, maybe playing chess in the park."

Looking around, I don't notice the forty-something crowd either. If I had business with the state, though, I'd be sitting in one of their offices, doing a slow burn. The past they were born into doesn't exist anymore, but they haven't put down roots in the present. Footloose between worlds, with the short fuse that sometimes goes with this, they bear keeping an eye on. Then there are the young.

"Why Speedy?" I want to know.

"All my friends have English-language nicknames," he says. "My girl friend is Iris. Like the goddess of the rainbow? My nickname has the same sound as the first two characters in my Chinese name. Also it's good for my business."

He has more than business on his mind. To improve his English and because it pleases him, he reads Theodore Dreiser. Friday nights and Sundays, he plays chamber music. He is the cellist in a local group called Dare to Be Dull. Haydn, Beethoven, and Brahms, he says. Do I know the A Minor Quartet?

Speedy has a problem, keeping the brutes who run this country from looking in his direction. They mistrust "information" and take a dim view of people like him. He isn't a troublemaker and doesn't make waves. But I get the feeling that if they pushed him too far, he'd push back. Students

in Tiananmen Square must have been like him. How the future will play
out is a closed book to both of us. I'm tempted to say that it belongs to
China's young people, but that is perhaps a sentimental piety. In any case
the present is what we have, and how we live in it makes all the difference.
Not between winning or losing—in the end everyone loses—between
spending our talents or hiding them in a hole in the ground.

China Air will fly me direct from Chongching to Tokyo's Narita, first stop
on the long journey home. But the questions I came over with still need
their answers. Putting off to tomorrow what I could do today, I go for a
walk along the embankment. Shoe-shine boys, mostly women, sit on their
heels beside the river. Dawdling, I stop for a shine.

The woman buffing my shoes is young, no more than thirty. But time
and tough sledding have marked her, without giving her the privilege
of age. Some women who want to shine your shoes in Chongching are
in their late sixties. Last year the factories they worked in began to heed
a new imperative, the bottom line. "When the train of history goes
around a curve," said Lenin, still heroized in this country, "some must fall
off."

One yuan, she signals, holding up a finger. I give her a two-yuan note,
about twenty-five cents. Loosening her string bag she hunts for change,
but I wave it away. Surprised, her face opens in a heavenly smile.

"Overtipping is a bad idea," says a familiar voice. "That's how you spoil
them."

"I thought you were doing the Yangtze," I tell Mr. Chee. "The new dam,
wasn't it?"

"I leave first thing in the morning," he says. "By boat from the Chao-
tianmen Docks. Why don't you come along?" Seeing me hesitate, he
winks. "There are things I could show you. Seven A.M. on the dot?"

To board the *ban cheran,* a king-sized riverboat, we must cross a sus-
pension bridge over mudflats. Men and boys run beside us, wanting to
carry our bags. Two of them, spying lawful prey, take hold of my arms. I
shake them off indignantly, almost pitching into the water. On deck beside
the rail the crew are beating drums and chanting like Hare Krishnas. Some
bang clappers and shake bells with their toes. Getting in my face, a man
in a dragon suit has goggle eyes and long yellow teeth like the wolf's that
ate Grandma. He lights a string of firecrackers, "warding off demons," Mr.
Chee explains. "They do that when they pull up the anchor."

In the lobby on the main deck, red with plastic anthuriums, Muzak oozes from speakers in the ceiling. Like the TVs in hospital waiting rooms at home, they are high up so Luddites like me can't get at them. The Muzak is Mantovanni, and the TV in the hospital is tuned to Geraldo. Whatever happened to the East that was East and the West that was West, a twain that were never to meet?

As we motor downriver, black shale cliffs fence us in. Grain-storage huts, shaped like Quonset huts and covered with plastic, squat in the fields, some yellow with rapeseed. At the base of the cliffs black-suited Chinamen sit on the sand, staring at the water. "The Great River," they call the Yangtze, flowing almost four thousand miles to the sea. For centuries their life has been mortgaged to it, for the harvests that sustain them and the floods that leave them homeless. Scouring the land, they layer it with tons of black silt. In the spring the silt quickens, and the round of life begins again. China's rulers, opposing power to power, mean to break this circle, binding the river god in an adamantine net.

Small black boats in the river have little red triangles mounted in the bow. The boats are channel markers, moored in place while the river, like time, flows around them. Women, up to their knees in the shallows, are doing the wash, birds swooping over their heads. In crude, shouldering China, discriminations are subtle, and the cliffs do a fade-out, changing to arable hills. Plum trees blossom on the hillsides, and green shoots of rice poke up through the water, teal shading into pale green. In from the river are the Ba Mountains, one peak behind another, furred with mist and grayish blue like a gun butt.

Up there live the Ba people, says our riverboat guide, schoolmarmish Mrs. Hu. "Who is she?" she asks us playfully, poking herself with a finger, and answers, "She is Who." Do we see that old fisherman, standing barefoot in squishy brown gravel? When the Yangtze dam is finished, he and his fellow tribesmen will lose their ancestral lands. Numbers painted on the hills register the different levels the waters will rise to, 130 meters in three years' time, 175 meters in five. Meanwhile the village this fisherman comes from, though squarely in the gun sights, goes about its time-honored business.

"But what will the government do with the people?" asks Mr. Chee, launching a harpoon in Mrs. Hu's direction. In all, she tells him, a million and a quarter of them will have to "relocate."

"Hard lines!" he says, grinning like a death's-head.

"Not to worry," says Mrs. Hu. "There is plenty of land in Sinjiang Province."

"China's Wild West!" says Mr. Chee, cluing me in. "Trouble is, it's all desert."

"Plenty of land in Sinjiang," says our guide.

By late afternoon we reach Fengdu, City of Ghosts, on the north bank. Two thousand years ago a pair of hermits famous for their wonder-working settled this river port. "If you put their names together, they mean King of the Underworld," Mrs. Hu informs us, as we follow her down the gangplank. Waiting at the far end are the beggars. Most are missing body parts, some are blind. Crouched on the stumps of legs, they rattle tin cups and show us their sores. An orange tree, bright with globes of fruit, is growing out of the crud around them.

The ski lift charges fifteen yuan a ticket and brings us up to the top of the mountain, where vendors hawk demon masks and the temples have the feel of a theme park. Coming down, we run into Mr. and Mrs. Sierra Club. He is stringy, with a white beard, Mrs. a head shorter, tubby but solid. Both wear shorts and carry backpacks over their T-shirts, lettered with the words "I Climbed Mt. St. Helen's."

"It's a thirty-minute hike to the Otherworld," he says.

"Fifteen yuan isn't my idea of a bargain," she says. "Besides, it's healthier to walk."

We meet them again the next day, transferring to the sampan for our trip up an arm of the Yangtze. "White water ahead!" shouts Mr. Sierra Club, standing where he shouldn't be, on the raised upper deck in the bow. Two boatmen, springing forward, lift him out of the way. Each carries a bamboo pole tipped with an iron point like a spear point. Digging their poles into the foaming water, they work together like pistons, keeping us clear of the rocks.

"A bit dicey for a minute there," says Mr. Chee. Laying their poles aside, the boatmen stand at parade rest. I see people swimming, though the toilet in our sampan empties through a hole in the floor. Down the cliff face cascades a flood of garbage, tin cans, broken bottles, and an old metal bathtub.

"No Green Party in China," says Mr. Chee.

"Biodegradable," Mrs. Hu tells him.

At dawn the next day we have an epiphany, like the one when the Wise Men enter the stable, only ours is profane. The *ban cheran,* cuffing the waters, has been lording it over the river all night. Without warning, mountains thrust up around us, pinching in the current. We aren't center stage anymore but bit players. It happens with stunning swiftness, as if the tectonic plate has cracked open, forcing towers of limestone into the light. Pocked with caves, some are craggy, some rounded like dolmens. Canyons plunge through them, cratering the earth.

Frenzied, the river moves eastward toward the Yellow Sea, at the same time throwing back on itself. Whirlpools, circling rocks below the surface, mimic this contrary movement. Navigating the Yangtze took nerve and a strong heart—"still does," says Mr. Chee. He has seen dead bodies borne along by the current, like runners jogging in place.

Before steam power, the big junks needed manpower to make head against this current, and "trackers," harnessed to long hauling ropes, supplied it. Far ahead of the boat, they pulled to the beat of a drum, singing chanteys as they went forward. "Oh, it's hard to be a tracker," wrote a T'ang dynasty poet. At midnight and in snow and rain, they had to get back in harness. Often they pulled until daybreak. Some fell to their deaths from the towpath. If injured, they were left where they lay.

Long-tailed monkeys, real-life cousins of the one I bought in Beijing, pick their way across the walls of the gorge. High up in the walls, Ba people buried their dead. "Look!" says Mrs. Hu, indicating the rectangular holes in the cliff face. For the journey to the afterlife, she says they used coffins shaped like canoes. Safe harbor for eternity, Ba people must have thought, but didn't reckon with the dam.

At Sandouping Village, upstream from Yichang, we moor for a closer look. Construction is going forward just inside the last of the three greater gorges. Everything behind the dam site will disappear underwater, turning the river into a giant reservoir all the way back to Chongching. The authorities have arranged a conducted tour, and buses are waiting for us at dockside. Mr. Chee in the lead bus has his notebook at the ready. Mr. and Mrs. Sierra Club, hoping to save the river dolphin, are carrying pamphlets intended for the workers. I sit alone on the aft deck, riffling the pages of my Stilwell biography and committing the mountains to memory.

No one knows whether the dam will prove a boon or disaster, and you can make out a case either way. For men like the old trackers, it will cushion life's hardships. In fear and trembling trackers walked a narrow pathway chiseled out of the perpendicular face of the rock. Near Lijiang, just below Tiger Leaping Gorge, it isn't wider than a narrow-gauge railroad. Endless patience will have gone into the making of this foothold, also craft, and strength of will beyond my sedentary man's comprehending. A tracker's wage kept body and soul together, nothing extra. But inching along the side of the mountain, he looked up into a purple immensity, as close as nature has ever come to the mysterious order of art.

Look again, and Tiger Leaping Gorge will be gone. China's rulers, acting out of some deep personal compulsion, are going to force a snaffle through the teeth of the river god. Like that Daedalus who made wings for himself and his son, they aim to transcend nature, within an engineer's compass. But the new social engineers are more ambitious even than this. Anticipating an end to the age-old struggle with the river, they see the chance for replacing man's intractable will with more feminine virtues, niceness, cunning, cajolery, better suiting the era to come. With luck they can annul the potential for tragedy, predicable of all of us who try and fail, necessarily as we are human.

Failure seemed of the essence of things, when General Stilwell commanded in China. But reading about him, I feel how elation was part of his story, even in the dark days, maybe then most of all. He had a plan to save the Chinese Republic, and some believe it could have succeeded. At his death, however, defeat was just around the corner. He didn't claim to see light at the end of the tunnel. He said, "I claim we took a hell of a beating." An odd way to put it, as if the idea gave him pleasure.

One of my T'ang poets has an image that sets him before me. In the poem the weary traveler has still got a long way to go. Night closing fast, his horse, stung with gadflies, can hardly take another step. Ahead, uphill, he hears the tiger roar. Times like these, says the poet, his heart is a flag a hundred feet high in the wind.

Flying Horses on the Silk Road

London after the war was like a beautiful woman, sadly mauled by the years. Mile upon mile of redbrick tenements, a legacy of the previous age, turned the edges of the city to a wasteland. Craters around St. Paul's, still waiting to be filled, told of German bombing. Meat was rationed; coal, in a hard winter, justified its old name, black diamonds. Elegant women at the opera stuffed newspaper in their Italian leather boots. My then-wife developed chill blains.

I lived on the second floor of a semidetached "villa" in NW3, northwest London, the shabbier part. The man in the flat above us, decidedly Blimpish, thanked his stars for the "moat defensive" separating him from French, Irish, and "Gypos." He nearly took to his bed when they rampaged through Cairo, burning down Shepheard's Hotel. London had its homegrown toughs, and you didn't venture into the city's East End or along the Thames in the gloomier precincts of Southwark, not unless you saw a bobby walking his beat. Of old, a billy club had been his only weapon; now he carried a handgun.

Since then London has undergone a metamorphosis. The East End, upscale and priced to suit, mimics Chelsea, and in the newly gentrified South Bank, a friend of mine owns a pied-à-terre across the river from the Tower. This transformation of the old deserves kudos and gets them. So two cheers for modern London. I ration the cheers, doubting as I do that this city has changed for the better. The dead days—dear dead days— were a great time to be living in a great place that won't come again.

My jingo neighbor upstairs had us in for drinks, and from him I learned about London burning. As an air raid warden during the war, he had stood on Hampstead Heath, a little to the north of us, watching the Germans come over. He and his mates in Belsize Park, our venue, stayed up half the night more nights than not to put out the fires. Tears filled his eyes as he re-created the scene. He had never been so alive.

One of the mates was the butcher on the corner. When we went to him each week for our ration, he looked at us sadly over an ounce or two of sinewy gristle. That was what there was. At Thanksgiving, however, "knowing how you Americans like to celebrate the day," he found us a genuine turkey. It was small, off-ration, and costing a bundle, but he found it. Part of the net that sustained us was the milkman, known as the milk. You had to be up early to see him and his horse-drawn wagon stopping before each house on the street. Since we had a new baby he left us two bottles, making sure that the cream had risen to the top. Nobody had a fridge, but he told us to keep the milk, also butter and eggs, in a pitcher of cool water on a window ledge facing north.

When we wanted a drink, we drank warm English beer or Devon cider at a few pence a half pint. The public house on the Heath, called the Castle, became our poor man's club. Years later I was put up for the Cosmos Club in Washington, but after Jack Strand's Castle it seemed a bit ho-hum. No darts! At least once a week we went to a playhouse like the Old Vic or to concerts at the Stoll Theatre on the Kingsway. If it looked like a rush on tickets, we queued up at the box office the day before. London's queues, civility raised to the nth power, are worth more than the cursory glance they get here.

We meant to be cultured, and our resolve was put to the test. The day of the Oxford-Cambridge boat race, a blustery day in March, we took the Underground to St. Mary's Cathedral in Southwark. Shakespeare's brother is buried in a side chapel. They were doing one of Bach's passions, and as hour followed hour I thought of the Oxbridge boys in their skivvies, sculling on the near-frozen Thames.

At last it was over, and we stood outside, clapping our mittened hands to get the blood going. Suddenly a burst of song broke over us, birdsong from the trees in the cathedral porch. Their branches were lifeless sticks clicking in the icy wind, but a glowing in the sky told us of the end of day, and I thought of the line from Shakespeare: "bare ruined choirs, where late the sweet birds sang." That sounds melancholy and partly it was, but I haven't often been so happy as on that long-ago day in London.

The warriors of Xi'an stood in darkness for two thousand years, watching over their dead emperor. He was Qin, pronounced *Chin,* whose successors built the Great Wall and gave a name to China. The warriors are ranked in battalions, archers, cavalry with their horses, charioteers, and infantry wielding lances and swords. Though unmistakably Chinese, each has different features. Their hairstyles are different, close-cropped or luxuriating like their mustaches and beards. The baked earth they are made of is easily broken, and thousands have gone back to dust. But thousands remain, lifesize and still at the ready.

In 1974 farmers digging a well outside town brought them up to the light, catapulting a provincial backwater into the modern world. Tourism is big business in today's megacity, and Xi'an's hotels are as upscale as any. In the Golden Flower a string quartet, three young men and a woman, plays Haydn and Mozart in the lounge after dinner. A huge building like an airport hangar, erected over a deep pit, houses the terra-cotta army. Souvenir shops cater to the tour groups that bus out to see it. Though the yuan is China's currency, the shops don't mind taking your dollars.

The horse's head in my living room comes from one of these shops. Mounted on a wooden platform, it looks across the room and out the window to China. The ears stand straight up, listening for the trumpets, and the nostrils are flaring, as if it smells the battle to come. Give it wings like Pegasus, the horse of the Muses, and it would be off in a shot.

"You can hardly believe it's not real," I tell my seatmate, a middle-aged Japanese from Hokkaido.

He nods politely. "An interesting souvenir. Not a work of art, of course. But then the artistic side rarely matters in China."

I have crossed an ocean and two continents to pay my respects to this country's art, and hearing it belittled doesn't please me. What about the glazed pottery of the High T'ang, their calligraphy, their landscape scrolls, the cave paintings of Dunhuang?

"The cave painters were Buddhist," he says. "Their eye was on eternity. Chinese as a rule are materialistic." Emphasizing the obiter dicta, he wags a finger under my nose.

Thick glasses like the bottom of a fruit jar magnify his watery eyes. Sun glints on the glasses, setting them afire, and his outsize cranium hints at a CD-ROM's worth of facts. "Who are you?" I ask him, less nettled than amused.

"Dr. Yamaguchi!" he says. "Textiles engineering, Sapporo University." Though Japanese, he studied in Europe, including a stint at New College, Oxford. The rep tie is Oxford, "from the Burlington Arcade," and his English accent is modeled on the BBC's *Third Programme*. Was I aware that New College is actually one of the oldest?

Dr. Yamaguchi loves the past, much of it filtered through American Westerns. John Wayne is his favorite, and he would like to lead a cattle drive across the wide Missouri. At the university he teaches in, he gives a course in sericulture, the life cycle of the silkworm. Romans doted on the see-through look of their "glass togas," fruit of the loom in faraway Xi'an, and he would barter all he has to climb the steps of the Capitol with a toga draped over his shoulders. As it is, he wears a silk jacket, its pocket handkerchief matching the old-school tie.

Following the silkworm "from the mulberry leaf to the market," he has traveled to Xi'an, step one on a journey halfway around the world. He plans to take the Silk Road from its jumping-off point in China all the way to Italy, "where the Adriatic meets the Grand Canal." Like Marco Polo eight hundred years before him, he hopes to cross the desert on the back of a camel. "A Bactrian camel," he specifies, the two-humped kind favored by the great Venetian.

In the local silk factory, an obligatory stop on every tourist's itinerary, the showroom is crammed with shifts and camisoles, mandarin dresses, and shimmering toques, some studded with synthetic gems. Color photos brighten the walls, telling us all we want to know about silk. Peasants in cone-shaped hats are setting out rattan trays heaped with mulberry leaves, and a silkworm is eating its way to the surface. Dr. Yamaguchi, translating the caption, says this worm will multiply its weight ten thousand times in a month. Spinning its cocoon, all it needs is a single thread, but the thread is half a mile long.

The souvenir shop in a corner of the showroom features cheap reproductions from Banpo Village, a Neolithic dig east of Xi'an. Displayed on the countertop, the pottery bowl is seven thousand years old, says the sales clerk. The painted horse below the rim, satiny black, its eye rolling wickedly, had to be drawn from the life. Except for its enormous wings.

Sprouting from the horse's withers, they flap like the sails of an oceango-ing junk.

"The Heavenly Horse of the ancients," says Dr. Yamaguchi. "Ages since, it lived on the western slope of the Pamirs." Eyes blazing, he says, "I think it still does."

"I've read about horses like that one," I say. "Weren't they supposed to sweat blood?"

"Color of red resin," he says. "A lake dragon begot them on a wild mare. Mix the dried penis with honey and wine, and your sexual prowess will grow with the years."

The emperor Wudi, wanting such horses for China, sent an army over the Pamirs. They brought back three thousand horses to his capital city, Chang'an. "Imagine!" says Dr. Yamaguchi. "It stood where we're standing today."

"I never heard of that city," I say.

"A poet said its walls were like iron," he says. "The moat that sur-rounded it was like an abyss. But nothing lasts forever."

In the parking lot another tour bus disgorges its passengers, bringing the expert on sericulture down to earth with a thud. "The course of em-pire has moved westward," he says. "Now the eyes of the world are on your Magic Kingdom."

"Not mine!" I tell him.

"But will they make silk in Disneyland?" he says. "More likely polyester."

Just inside the shop door, a train of two-humped camels is winding across the wall, heading for the exit. Changing the subject, I point to the photograph. "Where are they going?"

"That settles it!" he says, adding as an afterthought: "To Lanzhou. We'll take the Northern Silk Road and leave the desert on our left."

"Will we?" I ask him.

"It's the same route Marco Polo took," he says. "And I know you want to see the cave paintings at Dunhuang."

I nod feebly.

"There's a plane out of here in the morning. We'll be on it."

Lanzhou is China's Heart City. Draw a line from the Yellow Sea, passing through Dunhuang to the mountains of Central Asia, and you will find it in the mathematical center. A million and a third people live there, at least as many in its suburbs. But coming in for a landing, we see nothing below us, no streetlights or car lights, not even that pale telltale spreading over the sky, like a TV screen when the channels shut down for the night. Where have all the people gone?

The Heavenly Mountains hem the city in, and the coal that powers its industry turns into greasy smoke without any outlet. Settling over Lanzhou, it resembles a cloud of cigarette smoke bouncing off the low ceiling of a restaurant you don't want to eat in. Freezing rain drives in our faces as we climb down the steps to the tarmac. My throat is rasping, even though a gauze face mask covers both nose and mouth. I feel self-conscious wearing the mask but have a lot of company, and the streets of the city look like the contagious ward. Health-care providers are mostly women, however. Chinese men, like Italian men who don't bother with seat belts, have their macho image to think of.

On the long drive into town, blackest night shrouds the highway. We come near ramming a huge hayrick, but in the nick of time its darker shape against the darkness warns us to slam on the brakes. Glimpsed from the roof of the Berlin Hilton forty years ago, the night sky was like Lanzhou's. Below us the Kudamm, West Berlin's major thoroughfare, sparkled like the Milky Way, but a black hole to the east sucked in the light, letting none of it out again. The hole was the DDR, East Germany's Socialist Republic, known as "the Zone." Next door in East Berlin ("the Sector"), Socialists had unscrewed all the lightbulbs.

Light never did come to that part of the world, not until the Wall went down, and whether it will shine on China is for the future to tell us. My Japanese friend points to the napkins on the restaurant table. "There is the future!" Each napkin is a sampler, embroidered with the legend "Home Sweet Home." I think of the little card on the night table in my hotel room, inviting guests to "Have a Good Dream." When it comes to Tibet or Taiwan, however, they cut out the bullshit.

Pale green tea arrives at the table, meager portions the size of a thimble. But fresh fruit tumbles from a horn of plenty, pulpy watermelon, slices of apple still in the skin, ripe tomatoes, fuzzy peaches, and a platter of grapes. Every foreigner with his head in order knows he mustn't touch it, though, sanitation in China existing largely in the abstract. Water isn't potable, and in every hotel room they leave a thermos of boiled water, *kaishui*. But downstairs in the restaurant, the supply of fruit is inexhaustible. In the land of a billion hands it costs almost nothing, and its bright color pleases the eye.

Tobacco smoke eddies over the tables, drifting our way. Big, shouldering men are vociferating while they chomp on cigars. "Would you mind?" I want to ask them, but decide not to. At the table next to ours the smart young women wear silk chiffon dropwaists, the men wear pinstripes, like American bankers before bankers began putting their feet up. Cupping their hands, they light each other's cigarettes, reprising an old Hollywood movie.

Summoning a waiter, I ask for the toilet. Filthy toilets are the rule in China, and people fail to see the point of a clean one. What you are used to is the way things should be. This hotel caters to commercial travelers, however, and the toilet gleams like a Roman sudarium. The dados are finished in black-and-white tile, and a gold handle flushes the water closet, raised up like a throne on a dais. But beside the Western-style toilet is a hole in the floor, flanked by two foot-shaped depressions.

Sooner or later, the modern world will ring out the old one. Change is in the air, electricity, flush toilets, and "No Smoking" signs heading up the parade. But when spick-and-span wins the day, what will happen to China under the skin? Will the soul dilate its being, making people feel more nearly human? Or will cleanliness outrank godliness in the scrubbed and affluent society to come?

In the morning we visit the museum in Lanzhou. Soviet engineers, everywhere in China when Mao and Stalin were having their lovefest, faced it with a staircase fit for a palazzo. The first floor has clay jugs and old mastodon bones, while ethnic costumes take up much of the second. At the head of the stairs is the museum's pièce de résistance, the Flying Horse of Gansu. Bronze and dating from the Han Dynasty two thousand years ago, it strains like an airship against invisible wires, wanting to soar into the heavens. One hoof rests on a swallow, the other three treading air. Farmers came upon it in a field in the Hexi Corridor, running through Gansu Province north and west from Lanzhou. In the corridor, arid but livable unlike the frying pan above it and the fire below, civilization got a jump start.

On the south are mountains, more of them on the north, and the endless desert going by different names. Han soldiers, the same who brought back the Heavenly Horses, patrolled the corridor on horseback, securing the eastern Silk Road against the forerunners of Attila the Hun. Creating his masterpiece, the anonymous sculptor sided with civilization. But the

Flying Horse, though an object of art, draws strength from the earth it spurns with its hooves.

Fog thickened with rain makes life hard on our cabbie as we drive along the Yellow River, heading back to the airport. The river isn't yellow but viscous gray, and the many who drown in it every year in flood time give it a nickname, "China's Sorrow." What kind of fish live in the water? I ask the cabbie. Grinning at me, he bares his teeth and says nothing. Locust trees line the embankment, however, taut with life like the horse in the museum. Buds are metamorphosing into white flowers, promising a brighter future, if not tomorrow, any day now.

Outside town a Muslim graveyard, dug into the hill, is decked with plastic flowers. Leaning crazily or fallen over on the earth, the gravestones look like the end of the line. Pylons like giant stupas stand on top of the hills, tunneled with caves where farmers store tools and potatoes. Sheep skitter across the highway. The herdsman with his switch wants them to go faster, but when they reach the far side of the road they put their heads down and graze.

Coming over the hill is a single plowman, hands gripping the wooden shafts of his horse-drawn colter. He is breaking up the clayey soil, but it doesn't part easily. A poem I like gets the scene: "Only a man harrowing clods," his old horse nodding beside him. Back in Beijing they are talking automation, and hope to get rid of this man and his horse. I can see how that might be a plus. The poet is skeptical. "Though dynasties pass," he says this scene isn't going to change much.

The pickup truck is like a water glass whose contents rise above the rim but don't overflow it. Mattresses lie on top of bedsprings, and I see an ancient console beneath a table veneered with formica. Having come to a halt, the truck blocks the road between Dunhuang's airport and town. Our limousine, a new Red Flag owned by China Travel Service, showcases the People's Republic. It has air bags, automatic windows, leather seats, and an instrument panel like a DC-7's. But it isn't going anywhere until the truck does. Sighing, Dr. Yamaguchi takes out his preposterous calabash, the only one I've ever seen other than Sherlock Holmes's. Not lighting up, he sucks on the stem, and I hear the dottle gurgling in the bowl.

Beside the narrow ribbon of road, a blur of faint green breaks the monotony. The ground has been irrigated, and in flooded patches that look like rice paddies, wheat has begun to germinate. Rainbow-shaped huts covered with plastic or straw sit on balks of turf between the paddies. These signs of intention look wistful, however, and beyond them stretch "the lone and level sands."

A wooden refrigerator balances on top of the pickup. Straddling the door, a dark-skinned, dark-haired boy offers moral support to a pair of men lashing the fridge to the truck bed. "Okay," he says in his best American, and they climb back in the cab, setting off firecrackers as the truck begins to roll. They keep the firecrackers going all the way to Dunhuang. Our driver, related to one of them—everybody in the desert is somebody's cousin—says this is moving day, and the firecrackers salute the occasion.

In the center of Dunhuang a tenement lies in ruins, and a man is attacking slabs of concrete with a maul. Fire smokes in the rubble, above it a battered tin pot holding water for tea. The man, setting down his maul, lifts the pot between thumb and forefinger, tears the flap from a paper packet with his teeth, and pours the grains of tea in the kettle. Lines from Hardy's poem are still moving in my head: "Only thin smoke without flame / From the heaps of couch-grass; / Yet this will go onward the same / Though Dynasties pass."

Whitewashed cottages line the main street, presenting an unbroken front to the world. The wall that ties them together, pierced by little doors, otherwise blank, has a message for strangers: "Keep Out." Each cottage is like its neighbor's, reminding me bizarrely of those semidetached "villas," color of a slow burn, that go on forever in London. The people in the cottages must like living in them, telling each other that "a Chinaman's home is his castle."

Dunhuang marks the terminus of the Great Wall, but the Silk Road, driving for the unknown world, kept going. Leaving Gansu Province, it passed through the Jade Gate, where the known world came to an end. Beyond lay the Taklamakan, no desert on earth more ferocious. Man hasn't let its hegemony go uncontested, however. Dunhuang means "Blazing Beacon," and two thousand years ago it shone a light across Gobi land. The caves from which it comes are cut into the Mingsha Hills sixteen miles to the south, a maze of zigzagging staircases, ladders, and ramps like a parking structure's. Work on the walls and ceilings went on for many centuries, while dynasties rose and fell. Only historians remember their names.

The master motive of the painters is love for the fact. My senses instruct me that this motive inspired the builders of Angkor Wat and Chartres Cathedral, both dating from the twelfth century when Dunhuang was still a going concern. One of the East, the other of the West, they have their different take on things. But both celebrate the inquisitive and affectionate side of our nature. The artists of Dunhuang weren't entirely disinterested. Some, at the begining of a journey, propitiated the powers above. Or they said thanks when the journey was over. Well-to-do travelers paid for the work out of their cargo of gems, precious metals, ivory, coral, and textiles. Sometimes the donor is part of the "canvas," and you see him kneeling in prayer, like Masaccio's patrons in the Carmine church in Florence. His prayers have been answered in ways he couldn't have dreamed. Dunhuang's survival depends on its paintings, and tourism is the only game in town.

Prepping for the hegira to come, Dr. Yamaguchi wants to try out his seat on a camel. The concierge at our hotel—he is also the doorman, desk clerk, and bellhop—sends us by taxi to the dunes outside town. They go up like a roller coaster, then fall away, seeking their angle of repose. Some curve gracefully, others making a triangle with its apex off to one side. The falling-away part is always in shadow. After the blinding light is the absence of light, no chiaroscuro leading from one to another.

At the foot of the dunes we find the Rent-a-Camel office. The owner is Han Chinese, but his assistant, a raggedy boy, is Caucasian. Kim, I call him, after the young hero in Kipling. From a hook beside the entrance he lifts a metal token with a number on it, finds the camel that matches, and points. Startled, I realize that he is pointing at me.

Putting on my best sangfroid face, I size up the opposition. Legs tucked under him on the desert floor, he looks negotiable, no taller than I am. His wooden saddle is roomier than a horse's, and padded helpfully with thick carpet. The metal bar across the front must be for hanging on to. Throwing a leg over this saddle, I mount.

"Cheese!" Kim calls out to me, holding up an Instamatic. As if on cue, the camel lurches to its feet, the hindmost part first, and I come near pitching over its head. The head is enormous, crowned with a ratty mop of camel's hair like an ill-fitting toupee. I grab for a fistful, but the camel rises on its front legs, shooting me backward. Tying a rope to its tail, Kim passes it through the nose ring of the camel behind me. Across the sands we go, camel bells tinkling. We are laden with bolts of silk, furs,

ceramics, bronze weapons, and panniers of cinnamon and rhubarb. Our
destination lies on the other side of nowhere, but we laugh at dangers to
come. "Take 'em to Missouri!" says Dr. Yamaguchi, the sun doing a dance
on his glasses.

Mingsha's great dune, 250 meters high, looks like meringue baked to
dark amber. Marco Polo said its "rumbling sands" gave off a sound like a
drumroll. On the lee side of the dune the sound is muffled, but I hear the
faint soughing of wind. At a fork in the camel track, a many-tiered pagoda
looks across the sands and down on a mouse-colored spring, Crescent
Moon. Fragments of ice litter the water line. High up on the dune, car-
toon figures are gesticulating. How do they get down again? Kim, bending over, pats his bottom.

Guileless, the eyes in his dark face are palest blue, like dungarees
soaked in Clorox. Two and a half millenia ago, Alexander the Great was
here. When I look at the painted figures in Dunhuang's Mogao Caves,
Greek faces look back at me. Though Greece is only a genetic memory in
the heart of Asia, a muscled torso is Greek, and the Buddha, like Antaeus,
is renewed by the earth as he touches it with his right hand. A celestial
musician has a Thai dancer's tapering fingers, but the big nose tells of some
Western antecedent, and in the Cave of the Palace of Devas the flautist's
burning eye is a satyr's.

Apsaras is their word for the elegant young women. Lissome in body,
these flying angels keep moving. In spirit, however, the murals strive
toward nirvana, a contradiction. Why such a to-do, if all is illusion? Dart-
ing at us like swimmers in an aquatic ballet, the *apsaras* hold out their
hands, their legs curving up in a fishtail. The water parting before them is
stylized, an Eastern version of the River Jordan in early Christian mosaics.
But like everything in nature, it flows. Streaming rearward as if on fire, the
skirts of the women are scalloped. Selvage is closure, and the ragged scal-
loping doesn't want it. Deer flee across the rock face, pursued by a man
on horseback. Bending his bow, he releases the arrow. He means to bring
them down, but not yet.

Though lit only by dim electric light and the electric torch in my hand,
the caves take light from their paintings. Against the neutral taupe of the
sandstone, the greens and whites, color of Lop Nor's sand flats, blacks,
pinks, and blues seem more nearly themselves. The technique is tempura,
and I wonder if the artist, when he made his emulsion, mixed his egg with
the water that trickles down the sides of the cliff. His work says he was

meticulous, spreading a special mix known only to him over his clay under-coat. He liked the way it hardened to the texture of polished cement. The background color he chose depended on how he felt getting up in the morning, pale red on a good day, dark gray when his woman had crossed him. Centuries later the colors still glow. In the Cave of the Sacred Mountain I feel like St. Paul, struck down on the road to Damascus.

Not all the paintings and sculptures gladden my eye. In the Cave of the Thousand Buddhas, one of the statues, not the largest one, stands a hundred feet tall. The iconoclasts in Afghanistan demolished statues like it but weren't appealing to taste. Mogao painters participate in this iconoclastic psychology and like to represent the overthrow of our carnal being. Mara, illusion personified, tempts the Buddha with desire, the way the devil solicits Christ. Eventually the good triumphs in this contest, though their good looks like inanition to me.

But Dunhuang's heroes aren't naysayers. Compassionate men and women who help others on the road to nirvana while postponing this goal for themselves, they are the Bodhisatvas, saints of the Buddhist pantheon. The ascetic life, practiced by that Simeon Stylites who sat on top of a pillar watching the world go by, isn't for them. Immersed in our destructive element, they seek to better the lot of their fellows. Let us praise the Bodhisatvas.

The misanthropes we have always with us, and little by little they gained the upper hand. Cave painting ended with the ascendancy of Islam, another psychology that rejected the world. But this one brought with it a sword. Revolted by our "human face divine," Muslims cleansed the land of statues and paintings. But Dunhuang's art, hidden in the desert, escaped them. A thousand years later, "foreign devils" gave it back to the world.

They were Swedes, Russians, French, an American, and a mysterious Japanese, Count Otani, who lends his name to hotels in Tokyo and Honolulu. Von Le Coq, the German, chiseled entire murals from the rock face, transporting them to the Museum of Indian Art in Berlin. Preserved in the arid air of the desert for more than fifteen centuries, they were lost to Allied bombing in World War II. The Soviet Army scooped up what was left, and where it is now, no one knows.

Nothing easier than to stigmatize the foreign devils, but if I were given to votive candles, I would light one every night to Langdon Warner, the American. In 1923 he trekked into Dunhuang, where he spent ten days looking at the paintings. "The Holy Men of fourteen centuries ago had left their gods in splendor on those walls. Tens of thousands of them, walking in slow procession, seated calm on flowering lotus blossoms, with hands raised to bless mankind, or wrapt in meditation or deeper still sunk in thoughtless Nirvana." But outside the sacred precincts, barbarians were on the prowl. Three of them, Mongols, slouched in to have a look. "One placed his greasy open palm on a ninth-century wall-painting and leaned his whole weight there as he chatted. Another strolled to the pictured wall and, in idle curiosity, picked at the scaling paint with his finger-nails. As they crowded out through the narrow entrance their vile sheepskins scrubbed a row of saintly figures by the doorway," scrubbing their middle clean of paint. "This was enough."

Guilt-tripping moderns will fasten on the "vile sheepskins," a transferred epithet, to highlight Warner's insensitivity. But he himself felt pangs of remorse at what he contemplated doing. He conquered his remorse when he saw the paintings he'd removed securely packed and ready for the eighteen weeks' trip by cart, train, and ship to the Fogg Museum at Harvard.

Sir Aurel Stein, the Silk Road's greatest explorer, wanted to distinguish the different links in its chain. But like Lord Elgin at the Parthenon, he lingered over ancient treasures, saving them for the British Museum. In a sealed cave in Dunhuang he found fifty thousand manuscripts and read them by the light of a candle. With his translator at his elbow, he read in Chinese, Uighur, Sogdian, Tibetan, Sanskrit, old Turkic, other tongues, some unknown. Among his trophies was the ninth-century Diamond Sutra, the world's oldest printed book. It said the phenomenal world was illusion, but Stein, an equivocal hero, both terms applying, knew better. He died in Kabul at eighty-two, seeking permission to explore Afghanistan, the last link in the chain he was forging.

Between Dunhuang and Liuyuan, the eye doesn't pause on man, beast, or dwelling. This is a dead land, unredeemed by the life-giving presence of art. Night falls, but no one turns on the lights. We follow the dirt road through the center of Liuyuan, flanked by shops and a filling station. The shops are putting up their shutters, and anyway have little to sell. The radiator in our touring car needs water, but we learn that every drop is trucked in from outside. Liuyuan is a hub, though. The railroad stops here on its run from Beijing to Turfan.

Near midnight the ticket taker, a woman soldier in olive drab, jerks a thumb at us. Time to be on our way. Hurrying over the tracks in darkness, we slip on the ice between ties. Wheels begin turning as we hoist up our bags. Like the train in *Bad Day at Black Rock* that stops just long enough for Spencer Tracy to jump off, this one can't wait to be gone.

A sign in the corridor says smoking is forbidden, but the air is blue with smoke. Two drunks are talking themselves into a fistfight. The plank-like beds in our compartment don't have sheets, only a soiled blanket, and you wouldn't care to lay your head on the bolster. I cover it with my raincoat, close my eyes, and in an instant am sleeping.

Like the drunken porter in Shakespeare, I wake to pounding on the castle door. The conductor is rousting us out of our compartment. Sitting up in bed, Dr. Yamaguchi has his shoes on and is polishing his glasses. "Turfan," he announces. "Except for the Dead Sea, the lowest place on earth."

The clock in the corridor says it is 7 A.M., but the sun hasn't risen yet and the compartment is dark. Whatever the clock's idea, nature isn't persuaded. All over China, though, across time zones and thousands of miles, natural time defers to Beijing time. This is the modern China of edict: only so many children per family, and the family's dog to weigh no more than prescribed. Far to the east of us, early risers have had breakfast and are doing tai chi in the park. Here in western China we could use a good night's sleep. But if it's morning in the capital, it has to be morning in Turfan.

Aboard the local bus for town, I look from the window as the Flaming Mountains, not really mountains but red sandstone hills, emerge out of darkness. Carved by wind and weather in vertical lines, they are like the raddled face of a very old woman. I think, looking at them later after the sun has climbed up the sky, they are ready to burst into flame. In the well-known Chinese novel, Monkey the hero tries to cross the Flaming Mountains. His tail catches fire, though, and that is why monkeys have red bottoms.

Shedding a baleful light, the fireball of a sun isn't beautiful but sinister, like a disk of plutonium leaking carcinogens as it runs down. The last pages of Wells's *Time Machine* come into my head. Shot millions of years into the future, I am alone on a shingled beach in a dying world. But beside the road, plastic bags and wrappers are caught in the dessicated stubble. This modern disarray makes me feel right at home, and gloom and doom go back to their kennel.

In the irrigation ditches that slice up the fields, women are scrubbing what look like pajamas. Ducks paddle in the water, and willows on the banks lean toward it, growing in rows three deep. Ahead of us a funeral procession, many men but no women, bumps along jerkily, like a Chinese dragon. Following the hearse is an old car, a tractor and backhoe, and a motorcycle, its engine popping softly. Honoring the dead, Turfan people are putting their best foot forward.

The sidecar hitched to the motorcycle has an orange awning, and men hunch together beneath it. Knife handles, inlaid with silver and mother-of-pearl, stick out from the backs of their belts. Most wear the yarmulka, except for an older man in a white turban. He is the imam, a Muslim priest. The others, Uighur, not Han Chinese, look like Romantic heroes in a poem by Lord Byron.

Channels on either side of the road move the water downhill from the mountains. In front of mudbrick shanties chickens and roosters peck in the dirt, a donkey grazes a bale of hay. Across a freestanding mud wall I see a scribble of graffiti, like clothes hanging from a clothesline. Dr. Yamaguchi, all eyes, leans out the window. "Tokharian," he says. "The old language of Turkestan. Before Islam, another people lived and died here."

The ruins begin not far from the road, and a donkey cart, waiting beside the entrance, takes us out to what is left of Jiaohe. On the flat plain the cyclinders and oblongs of sun-dried brick resemble loaves of bread on the breadboard. Once the high adobe walls enclosed a private dwelling, and looking up I see the outline of a bake oven and somebody's washtub. The big rotunda-like hall, hollowed out into apses around the periphery, was where they met to talk over state business. My companion wants me to notice the *dagoba,* a dome-shaped stone sacred to Buddhists. Inside it are relics, a hank of hair, a carious tooth. Subdued, I think of the things that sustained them.

Vanished cities dot the desert, and perhaps the souls of the dead haunt about them. I remember that first book of Sir Aurel Stein's, *Sand-Buried Ruins of Khotan.* Digging in the sand near this long-defunct oasis, Stein found mummies, recognizably Caucasian after three thousand years. "A strange sensation," he wrote, "to look down on figures which but for the parched skin seemed like those of men asleep." Everything hereabouts belonged to the king of Gaochang. Dr. Yamaguchi, spreading his hands, takes in the four points of the compass. Twelve hundred years ago the royal capital, adorned with paintings, was home to fifty thousand people. All this is gone.

"Mother Nature?" I ask him.

"Men are part of the story," he answers. Unluckily for the painters, their pigment made good fertilizer, and the farmers who lived here took note. They were Muslim, and thought painted men and animals came down from the walls at night, doing mischief. The way to prevent it was to slash the mouths and pick out the eyes.

Some ancient painting, undetected by the pious, survives in tombs below ground. Like Orpheus descending, I follow the stone-flagged steps into darkness. Dr. Yamaguchi clicks on his torch, and in front of me a mummy, wrapped round with bandages, springs into the light. The painting on the tomb wall looks as fresh as the morning. Men in the lotus position are praying, birds circling their heads, around them green growing things. They came from far away, some verdant country cleansed by running water, and in death they remember their homeland.

I think of the dead perhaps too often these days, some of them dear to me, others I never knew, gone hundreds of years. The poet Li Po died in 762. China, almost as old as time and indifferent to its passing, puts this gloomy habit in perspective. Aware of my labored breathing, a little Uighur boy takes me by the elbow, and we ascend the stairs together. Looking back at the ruined city, I forget, like Orpheus, that this is verboten. In a wink of the eye the metropolis that used to be resolves to blocks and cubes, like a view from above of the Badlands.

Sooner or later even these fragments will go back to the earth, and nothing will be left of Jiaohe. That won't matter to the scorpions, as big as a pigeon's egg, nor will the cockroaches register a difference. Before Muslims, Christians, and Buddhists, they called this place home. Some are two inches long, with red eyes and inquisitive feelers.

Banners festoon Turfan's main street, like a street in provincial Russia when the Party still ran things. "Glory to the Soviet Union!" But this isn't Russia, and our CTS driver says the banners are announcing a sale on washing machines. People in the street don't walk under a cloud. Unlike Han Chinese, they aren't throwing their weight around. The government, playing demographer, has relocated thousands of Chinese to Turfan and points west, but Hui and Uighur still predominate, each doggedly Muslim. The white pillboxes belong to the Hui, while the hats of the Uighur are gaudy with rickrack.

The mosque is a letdown. Like much religious building in modern Islam, it tells of a slackening temper. This isn't peculiar to Muslims. Present-day Catholic churches, sentimental in their core, come from a different universe than churches in the older time. Between then and now, somebody switched gods on all those unsuspecting Catholics. Some such imposition has befallen Islam.

But an austerely elegant spirit, very different from today's, imagined the minaret of Emin. Part of a Muslim school complex a mile east of town, its pale brown facade, in muted contrast to the eggshell white of the madrasa, acknowledges its surroundings but doesn't capitulate to them. Tapering as it goes up, the circular column pulses with stylized flowers and geometric designs. Some in Islam, Christianity too, prefer the naked truth. But against the desert, the minaret sets the work of hands.

School is getting out, and the children rush toward us, greeting the stranger. Their native Uighur dress, emphasizing pinks and reds, honors the feast of Korban, when Muslims celebrate the new year. Alert and happy, they want to try out their English. One of them looks up at me. "My name is Alya," she says. "What is your name?" I warm to a culture that nourishes such children. But this child will grow to womanhood hidden behind the burka, and her schoolmates, boys no longer, will look on her sexuality with fear.

If you are taking the Northern Silk Road, you must go through Urumchi. The temptation is to get through it fast. Once, doing ninety in the Panhandle, I was stunned when another car passed me. Both of us, of course, were breaking the law, not a problem in Texas or China. As we approach a tollbooth on the new highway, our driver, seeing the cop in the booth, fastens his seat belt. Back on the road, he unclips it.

Gas tanks, topped with plumes of orange flame, squat on the stony sand. Dust in the air is like a Seurat painting, but ahead of us the Heavenly Mountains grow ever sharper. Water from melted snow snakes down their sides, feeding a frozen stream that keeps the road company. Just when we are sure we have run out of mountains, "Hills peep o'er hills, and Alps on Alps arise." Heaps of rubble, a broken wall, and concrete blockhouses loom up like an apparition. The locals, says our driver, call this place "Salt Lake City." Against the horizon a long freight train, retracing our journey, is going all the way back to Lanzhou. Of all the doleful sights I've seen, none is sadder than this one.

On the outskirts of Urumchi, the pollution comes on us like the descent of night. Black puddles stand in the potholes, and the grainy air smells of coal. If you kick at the snow, you see things you don't want to. I remember how Dylan Thomas found a nose in the gutter. Walking through the market, I try not to look at the stripped animal carcasses and the heaps of knobby produce, an obscene cornucopia. A young Chinese, smiling like a villain, thrusts a packet of powdered Snow Lotus in my hand. "Good for you know what," he assures me.

I am too finicky, no doubt about it. But the temperature is falling, fast oh fast. I badly need a cup of coffee and a bed with sheets on it in the Holiday Inn. Mirabile dictu, it turns out there is one. Not a mirage, it rises foursquare in the center of town, and I push through the doors to the lobby.

The gladhander behind the counter is a take-charge American. I don't have to know him to know what he's like. Rung by rung, he has been climbing the ladder of success in the Holiday Inn Corporation. But his boss, the VP for overseas development, has begun to feel threatened. At the next meeting in the boardroom, he smiles his Ivan the Terrible smile. "Prendergast," he says, "you're getting promoted. We're posting you to Urumchi."

Kashgar is different, the cordial that warms the heart of Sinjiang. Three times bigger than France, this Chinese province borders Tibet on the south, Mongolia on the north, also Kazahkstan, Kyrghyzstan, Uzbekistan, Tajikistan, Afghanistan, Pakistan, and India. Some of these 'stans I don't want to go to. Between Kashgar and Urumchi is the Taklamakan Desert, compared to which, said Sir Aurel Stein, the Sahara is a cupcake. Skipping the scenic route, we decide to fly.

Sinjiang Air brings us in over the desert, and as the last of the sun is going I look down on crevasses and tossing peaks, like the petrified sea that washes the Antarctic landmass. Some dunes, resembling icebergs, shift while I stare at them, driven by the pitiless wind. Though the land is amber-colored, shading to dun, it appears denuded of color, like death. The scene is unearthly, bordered by mountains far on the horizon. The highest mountains on earth, they are literally out of this world.

For more than two thousand years, travelers on the Silk Road have hated and feared the Taklamakan. In Turki it means: "Go in and you will not come out." Confronted with this alien place, I find myself thinking of former colleagues of mine, back home in American City. Spring term is approaching, and they are working up a syllabus for the cultural diversity course. I wonder what they would make of China's Wild West and the exotic characters who struggled across it, Parthians, Indians, Jews, Syrians, Iranians, Greeks.

Not all were friendlies, and it behooves me to distinguish among them. Some, bad in the grain, smelled to high heaven, first of all morally, though physically too. Others, done in by their culture, are to be pitied, at the same time condemned. (Cultures, like men, don't weigh equally in the scale—if one were as good as another, none would merit attention.) A few wanted "to know the causes of things," and they are the saving remnant. The bodies of many, dead thousands of years, have turned up in the sand, still intact. Cherchen Man, from south of the desert, has the high-bridged nose characteristic of Caucasians, and auburn hair still frames the face of the Beauty of Loulan, buried four thousand years ago near the lake of Lop Nor. Guessing at their ethnic background, archaeologists give them names and a local habitation.

In American City ethnicity is in, but particularity is a term of reproach. Outside the classroom a greater world that runs the gamut is asking the colleagues to notice, but they don't consult the eye or ear. Talking up one big happy family, they have little to say on behalf of him and her, special in and for their idiosyncrasy. Getting involved up to the elbows makes generalizing tricky, so they construct models or theories of "the other." That way, they needn't go to Sinjiang.

Horse- and donkey-drawn carts clop through the streets of Kashgar, alive with the jingling of bells. No one on the streets is speaking Chinese, but a sixty-foot Mao-Tse-tung overlooks the People's Plaza, his arm out-flung as always in statues. Korban is going full blast, and everybody is out of doors, the men promenading arm in arm like Italians. Those who aren't wearing pillboxes wear cloth caps or Abe Lincoln hats, the flat brim edged with fur. Song shrills from the loudspeaker on the wall of our restaurant, belted out in Uighur by a woman whose voice could shatter a wineglass. Sidemen, backing her up, lay down a barrage on stringed instruments, a sax, and steel drums. Soothed by this white noise, the customers tuck into their dinner.

Every time the door swings open, smoke from the little brazier on the sidewalk floods the room. A large pot holding a goat's head sits on the brazier, beneath the head a coil of simmering intestines. Unlike the weak green tea ubiquitous in China, the tea they serve us is black and cut in rough bricks like pressed wood. You break off a piece and crumble it in the teapot. The shish kebab is gristly, and mutton fat swims in the vegetable soup. But John's Café advertises itself as "A Little Bit of Home on the Silk Road," and we are grateful.

Walking off dinner, we walk through the Old Town to the Aidkah Mosque at its heart. China's largest, it went up half a century before Columbus discovered the New World. Slender minarets flank the yellow and white facade, and a muezzin on top is calling the people to prayer. There must be ten thousand men crowding the courtyard and spilling into the plaza in front of the mosque. Many are dancing, men with men, whirling, taking hands, stamping the earth with leather boots that come up to their knees. More men, perched on the roof above the tall, rectangular doorway, are banging drums and tooting on horns.

Rows of felt-covered tables, as many as fifty, take up the far end of the square. Men and boys, caps pushed back on their heads like the Dead End Kids, are playing billiards. In Kashgar profane and sacred coexist without fuss. Children, clots of brightness in a gray woolen sea, mill about the square, looking for a handout, coins or candy. When they get what they want, they aren't demonstrative but accept their due. The old men with forked white beards have come down from the mountains or in from the desert to buy and sell at the bazaar. They scowl without meaning to, their faces screwed up from staring at the sun, and might be Old Testament prophets.

The bazaar, Sinjiang's biggest, held every Sunday, sells sheep, horses, ponies, and goats. The ponies descend from that breed Mongol soldiers rode bareback over the plains of Asia. I imagine myself, one hand gripping the mane, the other holding aloft the great Khan's banner, a yak's tail. "Posh! posh!" says a voice in my ear, "Out of the way!" and a man with a camel leads it past me, yanking the rope tied to its wooden nose peg.

Over the market hangs the smell of dung and blood, and cutting through it a subtler smell of spices, kumin, coriander, and saffron. Piles of Karakul lambskin lie under foot. I can buy a hunting falcon, a felt carpet, a slab of red meat. The lambskin isn't cured and after a while will smell. The carpets, colored with vegetable dye, are less uniform in color than chemically dyed carpets at home. Many are garish, and though the product of great painstaking, look like Sears, Roebuck.

At breakfast in the morning, our CTS driver finds us in the coffee shop. He is Ibrahim, early twenties, smallish, black-mustached, his voice high-pitched, his smile an index for once of who he really is. Without a hat, he looks out of place in a land of hatted men. But he hopes to be a modern man, and this means going hatless. Having our interest at heart, Ibrahim wants us to visit the holiest place in Sinjiang.

Called a *mazur*, the tomb is named for one of their rulers, famed for piety and dead a long time. His descendants, lying around him, stretch to the crack of doom. Green glazed tile, the Prophet's color, covers the dome of the tomb hall, and the tombs below it blaze with the idea of a flower. Among the descendants is the Fragrant Concubine, mistress of the emperor. When she died in the Forbidden City, 120 people spent three years carrying her coffin back to Kashgar. They still have the palanquin it lay on.

Unlike Americans, people in Muslim lands don't take the stranger to their bosom, not after five minutes, and the invitation to lunch at Ibrahim's is special. The house, built around an interior court, looks inward, its second-story balcony looking away from the street to the courtyard. Carpets hang on the walls, and the outsize tablecloth we eat off is laid on the living room floor. I lose track of the number of courses. There is wonton soup, mutton soup, mutton-and-onion dumplings, hot noodles like spaghetti, almond nuts, pistaccio nuts, melons, yogurt, crusty bread, and a carcass of boiled lamb on a platter. Having pulled the lamb to pieces, we eat the platter, flat bread like a large slice of pizza. Did Marco Polo introduce them to spaghetti and pizza, or was it the other way round?

When my teacup is empty, Mrs. Ibrahim pours. Doing as the others do, I make a stab at sitting cross-legged, but she offers a leather stool. She is almost as tall as I am, big-breasted with wide hips. Her unwaisted dress is silk, the colors blending like tie-dye, and she wears her hair plaited under an embroidered square cap. Her lips are painted, the necklace at her throat matches her earrings. Speaking no English, she is in her own house and at ease.

While we are eating, a pair of beards appear at the door, dropping by unannounced to visit with the neighbors. "Peace be with you," the old men say in one voice, "*Es salaam aleikum*." Stroking their gray beards, they bless the house and the people in it. "*Wa aleikum es salaam*," Ibrahim answers, passing his hands over his face.

At the airport we exchange addresses, though it is near certain I will never see him again. My flight is already boarding, stage one on the long journey back to Beijing and home. Overloaded with culture, I am glad to be going. Dr. Yamaguchi wishes I'd stay. With Ibrahim at the wheel of our rented limousine, he is heading the other way, over the Pamirs through the Torugart Pass. On the far side of the mountains, in the ancient kingdom of Fergana, the Heavenly Horses are waiting. Will he find them in some hidden fastness, high above the tree line? He thinks so.

"When I come back," I say to Ibrahim, shaking his hand, "I want to ride a Mongol pony."

"That you ride a Mongol pony is my heartfelt desire," he tells me.

1 2

Antarctic Convergence

I joined the navy the day I turned seventeen—seventeen plus a day, the recruiting office being closed on the Sunday. The words of a popular song evoked the girl I left behind. "I threw a kiss in the ocean, I threw a kiss in the sea." The bosun's mate, hollering obscenities when he woke us in the morning, didn't sound like Peggy Lee, though, and I didn't have a girl-friend. But the navy, after prep school, was a picnic.

No sadistic headmaster smacked us with a wooden paddle, no fire-breathing padre sermonized on the evils of sex. True, there was that lecture with slides on elephantiasis, featuring a testicle bigger than the globe in Rockefeller Center. That could happen to you if you didn't take precautions, said the chancre mechanic, a.k.a. medical corpsman. He didn't say we were going to hell. An Englishman I got to know, interned by the Japanese during the war, suffered from nightmares—dreaming, I guessed, of what they'd done to him in prison camp. No, he said, it was his prep school he was dreaming about.

Much of life is like this Englishman's prep school, and traveling is a way to evade it. Rocketed out of the everyday world on jet-propelled wings, you pack up your troubles in your old kit bag and leave them to their own devices. Back at the ranch your hostages to fortune need taking care of, the doctor must be paid, not to mention the lawyer, if your luck runs you foul of the law. With only a carry-on in hand, you go with a lighter tread. Leaping over boundaries, you murmur ironically, "Something there is that doesn't love a wall." It took me a while before I saw that walls have their uses.

Wide open space appeals to sheep ranchers, also to mystics who want to escape our muddy vesture of decay. I've discovered that I don't want to do that, despite my gloomy sense of the ills our flesh is heir to. Jet travel gets me places in a hurry, all to the good, but I count on it returning me home at journey's end. The point is to bounding lines, which don't imprison but define us. Over the years my house has filled up with pictures, one willed me by a friend, old carpets, a Shaker rocker I got for a song at a garage sale, a pig-sticking bench that doubles as a coffee table. Not to be denied, they have a life of their own. If Troy were burning, I'd bring them away on my back.

An early hero of mine, St. Francis of Assisi, despised our temporal habitation, a version of the coffin that awaits us. Alone with his God in the Umbrian hills, he stripped off the body's paraphernalia. When I traveled among the Bedu of Arabia, those Franciscans of Islam, I wondered why we cluttered our lives with what I called "fripperies." The world has had its revenge on me, and my present wife knows me as "the Grand Acquisitor."

Much reason to acquire things. If there is a void beneath us, a prudent man will want to paper it over. I mean to deny the void with my last breath, even if, like Dr. Johnson, I am only kicking the stone. But coming to terms with the world and its draperies—not fripperies, a distinction with a difference—isn't simply expedient. Who can love a skeleton, only bare bone? Like the old poet who raised the question before me, I want "a nakedness with her clothes on." Simplifiers like St. Francis think the reason for clothing is to keep the body warm. I am a reason-not-the-need man myself, and my wardrobe is its own justification.

Most men in my family have gone into business, but my great-great grandfather sailed round Cape Horn. He had skippered a merchantman in the Malay Archipelago and off the coast of China. A sense of something yet to do nagged at him, though, and in 1848 he left his Washington desk job, meaning to make landfall on the last of earth before you got to ground zero. Along the way he lent a hand to other travelers "in peril on the sea." The job he signed on bade him to do this. He was Alexander Fraser, first commander of the Coast Guard, and a saying of his gave a motto to the service he founded. "You have to go out," he told them, "but you don't have to come back."

Having crossed the Equator many times over, he was a "shellback" but younger than I am when he stood out for the Horn. He sailed on the brig *Lawrence,* among the last of the clipper ships in an age already yielding to steam. Built of white and live oak, cedar and mahogany, she crowded on a lot of canvas, both fore and aft. The captain barely found his footing on her maiden voyage, jumping aboard as she slid down the ways. Before they got home again, she tested him hard. In heavy seas north of Rio the cranes went over the side, after them the chain slings on the lower yards and the bobstays securing the bowsprit. Lightning struck the masts, and evil-looking vegetation sprouted in the sodden foresail. By early May, winter below the line, provisions ran short. Rationing water, the captain kept going.

The Coast Guard Academy has a painting that gives his likeness: heavy-lidded eyes, not sleepy but considering, touched with a fractional smile. The dark, full head of hair, thickest at the temples, crowns a high forehead, and the thick dark moustache falls away in a half circle above the sensuous lips. His jaw, though it doesn't jut, says he had a sticking point. Twice he clapped a man in irons for insolent behavior, and on the Pacific Station flogged a sailor for shirking his duty. But he bore down harder on himself than his men. Squally weather off the Falklands found his junior officers snug in the fo'c'sle while he walked the quarterdeck, keeping an eye to windward. "I will cheerfully relieve any officer who from indisposition cannot do the same," he said. Not easily shamed, they took him at his word, and he stood all the watches alone. His face in the painting, leaping over generations, is the face of my son, Alexander.

For both of us the glass is running, but mine hovers on empty, and much of my life is like a ship's wake on the water. For years I taught famous authors, most fallen out of favor. I still quote them at the drop of a hat, disconcerting younger friends of mine who think the dead should bury their dead. Sitting in the ashes of the world I grew up in, I do a good imitation of Job. My body as it used to be, legs like tree trunks and a heart of oak, has gone with the Andrews Sisters. Not enduring, it isn't likely even to prevail.

But I have been reading Captain Alex. His ship's log, still there in the National Archives, makes a good prophylactic, and getting out of the doldrums, I follow him down to the bottom of the world. Flying most of the way, I keep going at land's end, finishing the journey in a Russian icebreaker. The *Admiral Bellingshausen,* out of Murmansk and dispensing with frills, lets you know where it comes from. A broken VCR takes up half its library, and the tiny gym below the waterline has a pair of barbells and a stationary bike. Working with the barbells when I poke my head in, the Russian sailor has given up baths and shaving. Our tour director, not Russian but American, wants us to restrict ourselves to a single set of sheets and towels, an "act of generosity" toward Mother Earth. I learn that he comes from Colorado. The first meal aboard, served by one of those grannies who swept the streets and ran the cloakrooms in the Soviet Union, is borscht.

Most of my fellow passengers are high on the inner self. I like to get dolled up, and they think me affected, perhaps a Republican. When you meet them, they look through you to the underlying reality, so have a hard time remembering names. Many teach school or used to. In the classroom they favor sweatshirts, lumberjackets, and corduroy pants. Their sneakers, though expensive, are apt to be scuffed, but their hearts, if you could see them, are pure.

The Romance languages instructor from the state university at Madison, Wisconsin, an exception to the rule, wears stick-on lashes and blood-red polish over long nails. This seems promising. The legend on her T-shirt tells us, however, that "Fur Coats Are Worn by Beautiful Animals and Ugly People." "Junior" Hotchkiss, who shares the same table at dinner, likes the sentiment but not the "Dragon Lady" or her black leather trousers. An instructor in phys ed—kinesiology, he calls it—at John C. Calhoun College, a feeder for the Citadel, he hails from the Bible Belt. Though the best Russian food is Argentine beef, Junior is death on animal products and sticks to the veggies and fruit juice.

Travel in Antarctica isn't for the underprivileged. Most passengers are oldsters with money in the money market. Youngsters, pre-yuppy, bunk together in a cabin without a porthole, share a "head" in the corridor, and carry all they need in a backpack. The one who teaches English at Miss Roper's Country Day near San Francisco carries a laptop, pecking at it after dinner in the lounge. Active in the Sierra Club, she chose our tour because it advertised on recycled paper. The rape of the planet dismays her, and she pins her hopes to Antarctica, still an "unravished bride." Seniors on the tour, having been to the Galapagos and Isles of Greece, and so on, look forward to more of the same.

"Terra Australis Incognita" old mapmakers called the unknown southern land. Something was down there, marked *P.D.,* Position Doubtful, on their maps. Legends of Polynesia spoke of a "frozen ocean," but not until Captain Alex's young manhood did a Yankee seal hunter set foot on its shores. Caught in the pack ice almost in sight of land, Captain Cook turned back and never saw it. He had a vision of "the horrible and savage aspect" of Antarctica, however. "Here be dragons," his sailors said, giving it plenty of sea room. It turned out that you brought the dragons with you, though it took me a long time to learn this. Real enough, they lived in the mind, like the Hell the poet tells of. "Why, this is Hell, nor am I out of it."

As the *Lawrence* drove south, dolphins hugged the bow, farther off whales sounded, and the ship sliced through kelp, tons of it torn from beds in deep water. On April 3 the log records the first albatross, then, at latitude 54°, longitude 56°, macaroni penguins. The ship is east of Cape Horn, and in the night the captain says he has "heard" them. Raised in the East Indies trade, no tougher finishing school, he knows about hurricanes, the Horse Latitudes, and Zulu pirates, but nothing prepares him for the terrors of Cape Horn. There are even pirates lurking north in the Straits —Patagones, or "Big Feet," Magellan called them, Indians shod in enormous boots of fur. Navigating the great pass three hundred years before, he saw their campfires, never extinguished, and called the shore to the south Tierra del Fuego.

High above it and above the straits that separate island and mainland, sailors look for twin galaxies, beacons to sail by. Light, traveling from these Magellanic Clouds, left the heavens when Magellan left his strait to cross the Pacific. Still traveling, it won't come to earth for another 795 centuries. The flames Magellan reported are still visible from shipboard. No longer warming the natives, they burn off waste gas in the oil fields. To reach the continent of ice, you have to pass the land of fire, a ritual testing like the one Mozart's hero undergoes in *The Magic Flute*. At the end he wins the girl, but more important he comes to terms with himself.

Tierra del Fuego's seaport, Ushuaia, lies inland on an arm of the sea. Named for a tribe of Indians wiped out long ago, it can't have changed much from their day to this. The naval base is new, flying the blue, white, and gold flag of Argentina, but the glacier was there before Captain Alex passed it to starboard, and the mountain it covers is the same Darwin saw from the observation deck of the *Beagle*. Melting snow on the mountain collects in freshwater ponds, still a habitat for Alpine geese and grebe. The box-leafed barberry that grows beside the ponds bears fruit, dark blue berries, at the end of summer. Mirrored in the water, the beech trees have shiny, buttonlike leaves, and some of these "lenga" trees, the bigger ones, are evergreen.

Scott of the Antarctic knew them at first hand. He had a yen for classifying, and his passion for the look of things played a part in his terrible death. Avid for knowledge more than glory, he and the others paused to gather plant fossils on their journey back from the Pole. At the top of the Beardmore Glacier, embedded in a coal seam, they saw the clear impression of layered leaves and thick stems with the telltale cellular structure. A little after this they died, but beside the frozen bodies, the fossils, packed on sledges, waited until the search party found them. Identified as specimens of the southern beech tree, the same that grows in Patagonia today, they were two to three million years old.

The yellow earth movers are strictly twentieth century, like the plastic litter, mixed in with garbage in Ushuaia's town dump. Scavengers, blue-eyed shags, sort out the garbage, and across the road is the "World's Southernmost Golf Course." Houses in town huddle close together, though they have all the room in the world to spread out in. Many are Quonset huts, gray and white metal with corrugated roofs, but others, concrete block or board and batten, imitate Swiss chalets. The land of ice, even its fringes, does a number on man's spirit, and locals seem indifferent to the look of things. Like most of my travel mates on the *Admiral Bellingshausen,* they think that what's up front is superficial.

But settlers who mean to survive in Ushuaia invoke the superficial world against nature. Civilizing the inhospitable place, they distinguish between things as they are and things as they might be. Improving on nature, things in this second class aren't accidental but tell of the hand that made them. As you approach the Horn you see a lighthouse on the bluff, flashing a warning to ships out at sea. Behind it are ranches where men have tamed the earth, making it fruitful. In Ushuaia down by the water, a natty brown bungalow tries for a flower bed, and under the windows red lupin poppies are growing.

A decade or so before Captain Alex, Darwin sailed past Tierra del Fuego, gathering data on the descent of man. Horrified by the native Fuegians, he thought about the difference between civilized and savage. Human nature, left to itself, seemed amorphous to him. It needed licking into shape, the way a potter shapes his clay, until the lump beneath his hand turns into an artifact. In *The Voyage of the Beagle* he said, "The more civilized always have the most artificial governments." He wasn't a bully who meant to keep the natives down, and his "artificial" regime meant to free them.

Captain Alex bypassed the Beagle Channel, but our Russian icebreaker takes it to the sea, through the last of Argentina and Chile. Mountains on the port bow dwindle to hills, and at last there are no more of either. Long shouldering rollers hoist the ship, then let it fall. Standing upright is an act of will, shaving an act of courtesy, strained, however, and I dab the blood from my chin. The open sea calls to us hoarsely, and dropping the pilot, we begin to "make our Easting down" from Cape Horn. First, though, we have to get 'round it.

Cape Stiff is an old name for the Horn, not an easy-to-negotiate headland. A last peak of the Andes, it sits apart on its island at latitude 55°59' south, longitude 67°12' west. Offshore, the continental shelf falls away to abyssal plains sixteen thousand feet deep. Ragged teeth, left over from ancient volcanoes, churn the water, known to Darwin as the Milky Way of the Sea. Contemplating it, he dreamed at night of death. High on the flying bridge, I see a petrified wave looming over the world. Dutch sailors almost four hundred years ago saw a crouching lion. Captain Alex is laconic and notes his ship's position in the log.

Between the tip of South America and the Antarctic islands six hundred miles below is a roller-coaster drop, the Drake Passage. Sir Francis Drake sailed through it the "wrong" way, from east to west, Atlantic to Pacific, and it took him fifty-two days. Crystal mountains in Antarctica rise to a dome shape, almost the "dome of many colored glass" Shelley dreamed of. From the rounded top, winds sweep down and outward, gusting at one hundred miles an hour. Westerlies blow at twice that rate, and between them they blow up a storm.

A big sea is running, abetted by "williwaws," short-lived squalls but violent. In a rare burst of hyperbole, Captain Alex calls them "tremendous." On May Day, the haunch of winter, he orders his men to haul down the foretopmast sail. When the summer sun sets, a long night begins, and prudent sailors furl their wings, like the petrels. A giant sump pump, the Drake Passage sucks up gale-force winds funneled south by the Andes, then, exhaling, turns them loose on the sea. In the Roaring Forties and Screaming Fifties, between latitudes 40° and 60°, it moves against itself, forcing up Cape Horn Rollers. Some of these "graybeards," a mile from crest to crest, reach heights of fifty feet. Behind a double thickness of

glass, I watch while the ship's bow cuffs one of them, shudders, and prepares for another. We have two days of this before we reach the Antarctic.

Captain Alex, beating about near the Horn between its parallel and the
meridian of Cape Pillar, had more than a month. Recording the blow-by-
blow in the log, his entries are matter-of-fact. Sometimes, however, a man
shows through them. "With a commander or his subordinates," he wrote,
"relaxation from duty is to be considered a privilege, not a right." The
time I live in looks askance at duty, a four-letter word. But for him it
meant more than spit-and-polish or shaping up when you heard the
bosun's pipe. Devoted to duty, he preserved the forms that kept life
intact, and he ran a trim ship in its interest.

The *Bellingshausen*'s happy hour is like a revival meeting whose patrons,
their tongues loosened, come forward to testify. Our second day out, the
English teacher from Miss Roper's School—her name is Cassandra, shortened to Cassie—testifies for the Adélie penguin. Inquisitive and full of
fun, plus a model of decorum in its black tie and tails, it could give all of
us a lesson in behavior. Adélie chicks group together in "crèches," protecting the weakest among them from cold. Mothers will lay down their life
for their young, and she has seen males and females in San Francisco's
Steinhart Aquarium encouraging a timid neighbor to jump off the simu-
lated ice floe. Whirring their flippers, they seem to say: "You know you
can do it!"

Rudi Windt, "the Professor," smiles at this and polishes his glasses.
Instinct drives mother penguins, he assures her, and it's a wise one who
knows her own child. What "you, my friend," witnessed was self-preser-
vation larded with animal cunning. Under the water a sea leopard might
be lurking, and one way to find out was to push an unwilling comrade in
first. Cassie's word *crèche,* suggesting a nursery school, pleases the Professor. "Whereas," he says, "lesson one in the penguin school is survival."
Only the fittest get to be grown-ups, the stronger forcing the weaker to
the edge of the group. There the skua waits, "his beak like the nose of an
Arab."

Windt isn't the professor people take him for, but owns and runs a
wine bar on the Kudamm in Berlin. "Windt's Vins," he calls it, pronounc-
ing both words with a *V.* When he opens his mouth, Latin proverbs tum-
ble out. *In vino veritas* is his favorite. A silk foulard is tucked into his shirt,
setting him apart from the others. Though he can remember way back

when, he has just begun to gray at the temples. Wincing at Cassie's verbal
slings and arrows—*racist* is one of them, *chauvinist* another—he is plead-
ing no contest when the intercom stutters, signaling the end of round
three. "We have a humpback," it tells us, "two points off the port bow."
Tree huggers and litterbugs rush for the exits, ideology forgotten.

I make out the distinctive profile, black knobby head and the dorsal
hump that gives it its name, in the lee of Nelson Island. One of the South
Shetlands, pips from the sorb apple that was once a single landmass, it sat
unnoticed in the freezer until Captain William Smith opened the door. In
1821, landing to the east of us, he raised the Union Jack while his men
cheered three times. "Hip hip, hooray!" they cheered, and the hills echoed
"Hip hip, hooray!" Penguin bones, picked clean, and broken birds' eggs
litter the stony beaches. In the distance the Antarctic Peninsula leans away
from the wind. Look at the map and you see it do that. Together with the
offshore islands and the rest of the Southern Hemisphere, Antarctica
included, it was "Gondwanaland," but a jealous god wedged the pieces
apart. The southernmost piece is bigger than Europe and the United
States, higher than the Alps, drier and emptier than the Sahara. Forty
years ago explorers, uncovering the stone igloo Scott used for a bivouac,
found a packet of salt left inside. It ran through their fingers like water
from the tap.

The dry place is cold. Wearing longies will keep the cold off your
bones in the "Banana Belt," the Professor's witty phrase for the islands and
peninsula. Further south, however, temperatures go down to −126° F,
and life reduces to simplified forms. Germs don't make the cut, good
news for me, but my dinged-up lung wheezes in protest. For half the year
darkness covers the earth. Mountains like Erebus, thirteen thousand feet
high, reach for the sun but don't find it. At their base is the ice shelf,
scored with bottomless pits out of nightmare. They might have dropped
Scott's Terra Nova into one and not filled it, said Cherry-Garrard. In "the
Worst Journey in the World," Scott's second and last, he looked back
across a lifetime, recalling the best of it, the time he spent in Antarctica.
His account of the expedition makes an epic like Xenophon's. But the
price was an overdraft on his vital capital, one he could never pay off.

Below the Horn and above the Antarctic Circle, the Atlantic and
Pacific mingle their waters, and polar water, coming north, slides underneath them. This is the Antarctic Convergence, marked by mist like dancing bedsheets. At sea in the *Lawrence,* Captain Alex felt the temperature

drop. Battened down against the wind, he couldn't sail west and wouldn't sail east, but weather permitting kept his men at their stations. Davey Jones's locker waited to claim the unkempt and unwary, and they caulked every surface, painting the lifeboats and scraping and slushing the masts. One entry in the log has them packing seams with oakum, the sailor's definition of make-work. The captain wasn't a martinet, but knew how free-and-easy put his survival at risk.

South of the Horn, day and night lose definition, the sky empties except for "mare's tails," a scattering of cirrus clouds, and earth sinks to the bottom of a thermometer. Not steamed up by life, the air is clearer than it ever is where people refract it, and the uncanny light, like a halogen lamp's, fools the senses. Things look bigger than they are, or look close when far off. Promenading on the distant hills, penguins dwarf the men beside me. The summer sun, dropping only briefly beneath the horizon, never shuts its eye, hard on peccant mortals. Dawn follows dusk like spring that begins again as soon as the harvest is over. Standing on deck at 10 P.M., I read the ship's daily bulletin, sans electric power, then turn in for the night. But night is a convention, and sleep doesn't come. "Sleep after toil," the old poet says, "port after stormy seas." Not in the Antarctic.

Aristotle, guessing at a southern continent, thought it went by contraries. The constellation Arktos, Greek for "Bear," identifies the Arctic, but Ant-arktokos, a negative, is only the place that isn't. Older than religions, it stays when we go, absorbing the Decalogue and the Sermon on the Mount. Demarcation is nil in the crystal desert, oppressing Scott with "the terrible sameness of gray." Ice, melting, turns into water, and water, sublimated, into air. In 1898 Belgian explorers, trapped in the ice, wintered over, driving two of their party insane. Captain Stokes of the Beagle shot himself in winter quarters. Fitzroy, who succeeded him, cut his throat with a razor. Some of this rubbed off on Darwin. In training for the ministry when he agreed to go south, he found his belief dropping away.

Plants, men, and animals, it seems to make no difference. On the islands off Antarctica, vegetation withers, and "the hungry sheep look up and are not fed." Herds of them scrape a living in the Falkland Islands, above the Antarctic Convergence. On South Georgia, in the same latitude but below the bounding line, they die.

Crossing into Admiralty Bay between Nelson and Roberts islands, we slow from our sea speed of 35 knots. Out of the fog floats an iceberg, shadows at the waterline hinting at more than meets the eye. Terns swoop around it, patrolling the heaving sea, and in the middle stands a macaroni penguin, his yellow plume, a dandy's, blowing in the wind. Beak open wide, head in the clouds like Lenny Bernstein, he is conducting a Romantic concerto. Some bergs are cathedrals, splendid with pinnacles, some are ships of the line, and a few have been recorded up to sixty miles long. Sooner or later, time melts them all, says the Professor, "Sic transit gloria mundi." This one, tabular shaped, not jagged, resembles a loaf of bread dusted with confectioner's sugar. Though harrows indent its white "biscuit" of ice, the wind that creates them is like the Invisible Man. Nobody sees him when he moves through the drawing room, but the china cups smash on the floor.

Antarctic wind, such an efficient snow-blower, always blows from the south. Facing into it, the windward shore doesn't look like a Christmas card, no drifts of white powder banked against the family homestead. But in low-lying swales, snow lies deep enough to entomb both the old clapboard house and the barn. Rocky tors above the shore, unlovely in their nakedness, seem put there on purpose, so many stones in a dolmen. "Seem" is the operative word, though. Some are glamorized with mineral outcrops, red and rusty orange, or carpeted with greenish-gray lichen. In these upper shelves of the icebox, life still puts out feelers. Look long enough and heathenish faces look back from the rock, like heads on Easter Island. British explorers, roaming the planet, came home with one of the heads, and when I worked in the British Museum I used to see it, occupying a niche in the stairwell. Ages ago a native carver set his chisel to the rock, but in the Antarctic no hand has touched it.

When the wind drops, fog builds, thick enough to stand on. Then it parts again, and we see Half-Moon Island, coming into focus like the fabulous island that rises from the sea in *King Kong.* On the foreshore lies the broken hulk of a whaling boat, behind it a range of mountains as stupefying as the Andes. Volcanic dust in the air and pumice sand on the shore say what will happen to them. Blue carbuncles bump out the snowy surface of the mountains, like those plastic bubbles that cover a basement window well, keeping out the leaves. Air is trapped in the bubbles, turning them blue, and Captain Smith may have breathed it the day he raised the flag for King George.

"Bergy bits" and "growlers," fragments of the glacier, bob in the bay, and giant petrels called "stinkers" follow our wake, eyes peeled for garbage. A black seal swims with us, and a covey of penguins arcs over the water, like stones skimming the pond's surface in back of the family cottage in Maine. Homey images like this one come naturally to most of us, eager to put the best face on the business. Seen from far out, the Horn is a cowboy's ten-gallon hat, its crown the island in the middle. Smaller islands left and right fall away like the brim. Icebergs don't split from the glacier, they "calve," and Ross the explorer, whose name is remembered by an island, a sea, and an ice shelf, thought when he saw the ice of the White Cliffs of Dover.

I think of my mother, and the poem she recited when I was a boy. It began with an if clause: "If I were drowned in the deepest sea," she knew whose love would come down to me. "If I were hanged on the highest hill, a mother's love would follow me still." One way or another, she wasn't about to let go her hold. But no mother's love comes down to me here.

Wanting to get back in one piece, I take defensive measures. I choose a scrap of verse to say to the winds, or burst into song if sure that no one can hear me. Sometimes I do *The Magic Flute,* seeing myself, a younger version, in the heroic tenor's part. He isn't fledged yet but will be, as soon as his trials are behind him. My favorite text is *Figaro.* When the Countess puts a question to her skirt-chasing husband, I come in with apologies but try to maintain perfect pitch.

Scott and his "band of brothers" give me my cue. "Brothers" was how they saw themselves, often quoting Shakespeare, chief among my dead authors. But they lived at close quarters in a savage environment, so kept the natural man at a distance. This didn't mean wearing hair shirts, it meant reordering priorities, "me second, you first." Calling themselves to order, they set themselves free. For meals they cleared their work surface, sweeping charts, books, and instruments into the corner. "Table, please," said Hooper, who had the housekeeper's job and covered the surface with a blue linen cloth or white oilcloth. Before dinner at night they drank formal toasts. Saturday nights they toasted "sweethearts and wives," drinking to "absent friends" every Sunday.

Some find their pieties childish. In our alfresco time, if you are on best behavior you are likely repressed, and there is even a recent novel, highly praised in the Sunday papers, that zeroes in on the formal way they kept birthdays. "Lost boys," the author calls them, remembering the childhood classic by Scott's friend J. M. Barrie. "Get hold of 'Peter Pan,'" she says, the clue to Scott and his "merry men." My fellow passenger Samantha Castro, the linguist from Madison, Wisconsin, takes a savvier view of the "band of brothers." Love of family obsessed them, a dead giveaway, according to her, and she notes especially the affection each felt for his mother. As to their male bonding, what was it but "the love that dared not speak its name"? Living in a puritanical age, they never owned up to this. Dr. Castro, the title she prefers, is glad to do that for them.

It is Christmas Eve on the *Bellingshausen* but almost no one takes notice. Sprays of plastic misteltoe hang on a few doors, and old Professor Windt tries to strike up a chorus of "Heilige Nacht." Response is halfhearted, even disapproving. Why Christmas if not Chanukah, Ramadan, etc.? As the holiday drew near, Scott and the others began to talk about it, celebrating with a feast of pony meat on the day itself. Captain Alex celebrated red-letter days too, pouring "from his own stores" a tot of whiskey to each of the men. The ship's doctor shook his head at this spendthrift behavior. He would have sold the ointment that washed the feet of Jesus and given the money to the poor.

Struggling into my Robert Bly suit, ordered from the he-man pages of the Eddie Bauer catalog, I am a heavy breather making an anonymous phone call. In the queue by the gangway I practice sangfroid. Ste.-Mère Église coming up fast. Little problems drive out big ones, and I have all I can do to cope with the smell of diesel oil or the guano smell from Paulet Island. Its rookery, they say, is world class, and I believe it. Rubber bunkers, keeping us off the hull, cushion the smack of the Zodiac boats. Dropping into the boats, we use "the sailor's handshake," right hand gripping an extended forearm, left arm held out behind us for the next man. The flyboy at the tiller pulls out the throttle, and we hydroplane across Hope Bay, just at the turning point between water and ice. Spray from the water, ropey like shaved ice, catches me full in the face.

Sending up green spouts that threaten to capsize us, the glacier is easing its load. Snow on the hills is streaky with grime, but when we circle closer the streaks turn into thousands of penguins. Waddling on pink webbed feet, pear-shaped, pointy-headed, they go back and forth, up and down, skaters on the rink at Rockefeller Center. The gentoos have red bills, monkish cowls, and beaver's tails sticking out like a flag. Chinstrap penguins wear First World War helmets. The strap under the chin holds the helmet in place. Atop a raised circle of pebbles, female penguins brood eggs or offspring. Males tote that barge, seeking to build up the levee. In their beaks they carry pebbles, part of the ritual of courtship. "Hooligan" penguins steal the pebbles the courtly lover deposits, however. Though the levee gets no higher, he fails to notice.

The lime-green hull of the *Bellingshausen* rides at anchor behind us, and getting down from the Zodiac into a foot of water, I head for Captain Larsen's stone hut. In 1902, hunting seals in the Weddell Sea, he and his men wintered on Paulet Island when their ship sank in the pack ice. The hut they built, roofed with canvas and caulked with guano, was only three feet high, but tent poles pushed the canvas higher and in the center a man could stand up. Outside they killed and stacked 1,100 penguins, much of a muchness, but it got them through the winter. Spring brought a rescue party. By then, however, the damage was done.

In his captivity Larsen saw the future: "vary big vales and I seen dem in houndreds and tousends." In no time at all whale hunters came down like the wolf on the fold. First to go was the right whale, hunted to extinction, next the humpback and the great rorquals. Larsen lived a long time, enjoying the fruits of the harvest. At age sixty he killed the largest whale ever known, a blue more than one hundred feet long. Laxity in faith and morals nettled him on his religious side, and out of his own pocket he built a church on South Georgia with a high steeple and white wooden walls. The church didn't last, but his stone hut, a magnet for tourists, still stands.

Around Larsen's hut the going is tricky, cumbered with "brash" ice, chips off the old block, that is, the pack ice, and stones left behind by volcanoes. Some are lemon-size, some grapefruit-size, and some as big as VWs. Penguin droppings, hardened like concrete, make pathways in the snow. Over this surface hop the gentoos and chinstraps, athletes in a race run by one-legged men. The tidal pool they drink from is awash with slime, but they appear not to mind this. Drinking deep, they excrete the salty bit into the bloodstream, sneezing it out through the nose. Oily feathers hang on them like fur, and they ruffle their feathers when they want to cool off. "Ruffled" as in angry is another matter. Taking aim at the offending party, they eject their feces with velocity and skill. Under the black tuxedos their white shirts are stained reddish green.

Assessing the penguin scene, Cassie has her camera out but keeps a respectful distance, not wanting to upset "the balance of nature." Her half glasses straddle the tip of her nose, and squinting through them, she captures a brooding female on film. "Tuned into nurturing," as she puts it, it pays her no notice. Offshore a sea leopard, its long neck and reptilian head propped on an ice floe, considers us, thinking of dinner. From a pouch in the penguin's gut like a kangaroo's pouch, a ball of light gray fluff pokes up toward the light, its beak already open. The female's beak envelops it, emitting a stream of white krill. Satisfied, the chick wriggles free of the nest and explores the ground beneath it. Bigger birds claim this turf, though, and squawking like grumpy oldsters, push the latecomer aside.

For the cruising skuas, opportunity beckons. On a one-to-one basis, an adult penguin is a match for a single skua. Two-on-one is a mismatch, and this pair has worked together before. The first, peeling off, divebombs the nesting female, driving it in panic away from the nest. The other, in sync, takes the chick in its bill. Now you see them, now you don't. Aware that something has happened, the Professor hurries up on the double. "Was gebt?" he asks, lapsing in German. Cassie doesn't answer, but behind the glasses her eyes are enormous.

Showing the flag, Argentina has a toehold on the Antarctic Peninsula: Esperanza Base, Spanish for hope. Soldiers and scientists, including some women, rotate in and out all year round. Kelp, called "holdfast," tangles the foreshore, holding on to the rocks for dear life. From the Zodiac boats you can pick out the mountains in the interior, ridged like a brontosaurus in the Natural History museum. The capilla or chapel overlooking the water follows the Catholic communion. A plaster statue of the Virgin guards the front door, paired with it a monkish saint with a tonsure. Identifying St. Francis of Assisi, the inscription calls him a fool for Christ's sake. "Estamos de acuerdo!" says Samantha Castro ironically. "We are in agreement."

Pushing in past me, she cocks her head sideways, looking with disbelief at the statue of St. Theresa, familiar to Catholics as the "Little Flower." A painted scroll in Latin has the saint saying, "Deus Est Nostra Spes"— "God Is Our Hope," if we can believe the Professor. The wax flowers at her feet are more vivid than nature's, and votive candles flare and gutter in a tray by the altar rail. The wafers you light them with cost fifty centavos. Over the altar, little more than a table covered with cloth, the painting of St. Francis shows his stigmata. Like Didymus, called Thomas, the doubting apostle, Samantha wants to probe the wounds with her finger.

"Better not, missy!" says Junior Hotchkiss. His voice, surprising in a big man, is high-pitched, almost girlish. Junior doesn't hold with graven images himself, but when in trouble dials a prayer to the Big Guy Upstairs.

At JCCC they have a saying: "No atheists in foxholes." The church of your choice doesn't matter to him. Siamese cats or alley cats, who cares what you call them if they catch mice? All of us are children of the one God, he says, "Catholic, Protestant, even Jewish."

Batting her long eyelashes, Samantha lets him have it. "Children" is right, lining up behind the Pied Piper, and she tootles scornfully on an imaginary flute. An atheist who had coffee once with Madelyn O'Hare, Samantha bows her knee to no one. As for prayer, she saves her breath to cool her porridge. Junior is sorry to hear this. Smiling his Jimmy Carter smile, he promises to remember her name in his prayers.

Behind the chapel warring winds fight to a standstill. *Nunataks,* like buttes in an old John Ford Western, poke up through the glacier, and a cluster of prefabs accommodates the mess hall, sleeping quarters, and workshops, also a gift shop for tourists. Low, warehouselike buildings, buttressed by iron girders and yellow pine "4 bys," they won't discredit your travels if you don't get to see them. But somebody built Esperanza Base, and it cheers me. "Man begins where Nature ends," says one of my dead poets.

Scott's people read poetry, some of it mnemonic like nursery rhymes, easy to keep in their heads. On the cross in his memory they inscribed a poet's line, "To strive, to seek, to find, and not to yield." This was their choice, said Cherry-Garrard, the women preferring something religious. Scott himself went faithfully to church, not caring to distress his mother. But he wasn't devout, and the journal he left records no turning to God at the end. Like most who are young and all who went south with him, he had youth's assurance and prided himself on his physical toughness. Of course, his body betrayed him. But in place of muscle he summoned strength of will, and toning down assurance, learned to bend the knee. In Antarctica he wrote, "the 'gods' dwindle and the humble supplant them."

Weak by nature and subject to depression, he might have been a petty tyrant. He cried more easily than any man Cherry-Garrard had ever known. I used to think that womanish, and still think the habit bears watching. What got him through was character, and his conquest of the Pole impresses you less than the victory he won over himself. It meant living with fear and transcending ambition. When two men ride a horse, one must ride behind, and Amundsen won the race to the Pole. But though it is folly to talk of prevailing, you can make up your mind not to yield.

"You've got it in the neck," they said to themselves, and had no choice but to "stick it." (You have to go out, but you don't have to come back.) Stick it they did, cracking jokes, some poor but they pretended to smile; singing songs off the gramophone; finding words for others' troubles; remembering the please and thank you. They had a grace about them, not made in heaven but earned. They kept their tempers, even with God.

"For what?" says Samantha. "And why go to the Pole in the first place?" The Professor considers this, then lays a donnish finger next to his nose. Before Scott, he tells us, there was that Frenchman, but the name escapes him. Exploring Antarctica, he called the ship he sailed in *Pourquoi Pas?* Wit, Gallic or otherwise, wins no points with Dr. Castro, and the Professor fits another string to his bow. In 1903 Scott, en route to the Pole, found a seal carcass five thousand feet up. Seals are aquatic, living in the sea or near it, and why was this one all that distance from home? The Professor is willing to tell us. A "rogue male," old and cantankerous, it had left the herd, he thinks, traveling on alone into darkness. Before death took it, it wanted to know what was out there.

Up on his podium the old man looks inward, addressing himself. Something about the dark side of the moon and our need to map it and bring it into the light. "Is there not a kind of fitness," he asks, "in doing what hasn't ever been done? Are we not men in wanting to arrive at the answers?" Darwin, winding up his travel book, believed this. Though he had satisfied "every corporeal sense," a craving still possessed him to discover the truth. Man, he said, was the thinking creature. "Homo sapiens," the Professor says, putting this in Latin for us.

Truth is a word that doesn't roll off my tongue, and I leave its sonorities to others. But I like living at full tilt, and some I know remember the war as the happiest time of their life. "Why not?" seems to me a question worth asking. Considering what we might do, line our pockets or be nice to the neighbors, it strikes the right disinterested note. Why not ask how effects relate to their causes? Most never raise the question, said Cherry-Garrard, asking instead, "What is the use?" Contemptuous of his nation of shopkeepers, he went away on his own to sledge the Antarctic. However, he said, "those with whom you sledge will not be shopkeepers."

North of the Bransfield Strait, a big storm takes our measure as we journey homeward, snow pelting the sea and shredding the sky outside the portholes. For a day and night we hold our ship's head into the wind, then an albatross alights on a stanchion up forward, and the sea that meant to destroy us turns friendly. A type of survivor, killed by a poet's crossbow but returning to life, the great bird flies the oceans for years at a time, finding what it needs in the destructive element, fish and squid for food, water from their bodily fluids. Murderous but innocent, it slides down the wind, dipping gracefully when it marks out its prey. A pod of killer whales, hunting the same waters, swims alongside us. Their black and yellow torsos are the color of fever, but ice is the element they live in. With their massive heads they ram it from below, catching the sleeping seal unawares.

Hereabouts mist rises, and Captain Alex, making for calmer seas, swung the wheel over hard. In California where the gold was, men were killing to get it, and when he reached San Francisco, his job was keeping the peace. The *Lawrence,* ready to do this, bristled with armament, twin thirty-two-pounders, carbines, pistols, and pikes. But as with Darwin's *Beagle,* she sailed to discover "the causes of things." The captain heaved the lead, monitored water temperature, currents, and trades. Bureaucrats back home said this data showed tax dollars spent for a purpose, but he gathered it up for its own sake.

Though "complete" in navigation and nautical astronomy, the way his file in the archives puts it, he liked doing without instruments, and determined latitude by looking at the moon. Sailors who sailed by the book got the scornful edge of his tongue. He had a tongue that needed bridling, and more than once it ran him afoul of politicians. When the Civil War began, this wrecked his hopes of a naval command. The web of his life mixes sad and happy, and in his last years the man my son looks back to looks forward to me, old enough, though not an old salt, and ready to go down with the ship. He didn't end that way himself, dying disappointed, away from the sea. But while others eyed the bottom line, he rounded Cape Horn in winter, battling westerly winds all the way.